GONE, BUT NOT FORGOTTEN

Willye B. White, the First 5-Time U.S. Track Olympian Event(s): Sprint, long jump
"A dream without a plan is just a wish."
(December 31, 1939–February 6, 2007)

Wilma Rudolph was an American sprinter and the first American woman to win three gold medals in one Olympics at the 1960 Rome Olympics. Wilma became a world-record-holding Olympic champion and international sports icon in track and field. Her performance also earned her the title of "the fastest woman in the world."
(June 23, 1940–November 12, 1994)

Josh's memorable words about Willye and Wilma—"I was like their big brother in '56, and I was like a protectory of them. They were 16 years old; and to tell a joke, which we shared until both of them died, was I told them—"that they always look at me as their big brother"; and then when they became (*whoa!*) 20 some years of age, they became just absolutely gorgeous; and so, I told them, "I don't want to be your big brother anymore" *LOL!!*

Josh's words about his childhood friend—"…and boy I tell ya his name will live forever in baseball and that was Tommy LaSorda" (September 22, 1927–January 7, 2021)

FOREVER BESTIES
IN LOVING MEMORY OF OLYMPIC
CHAMPION GLENN DAVIS
September 12, 1934 (Wellsburg, West
Virginia) – January 28, 2009

Glenn Ashby "Jeep" Davis was an American Olympic hurdler and sprinter who won a total of three gold medals in the 1956 and 1960 Olympic games. Davis later played professional American football with the Detroit Lions and was a teacher and coach in his adopted hometown of Barberton, Ohio, for thirty-three years.

1956 Melbourne, Australia USA Olympic Champions and teammates Glenn Davis (1) and Cousin Josh (3) 400m hurdles

Coach Payton Jordan, Josh, Glenn Davis, Glenn's beautiful wife, Delores, and Roger Kingdom two-time Olympic Gold Medalist in the 110-meter hurdles in 1984 and 1988. He spent the 2018 season as the interim director of track and field/cross-country at UCF. Prior to that, Kingdom worked as an assistant strength and conditioning coach for the Arizona Cardinals for four seasons (2014–2017).

1956 OLYMPIC MEMORIES – FOREVER BESTIES

1956 Melbourne, Australia USA Olympic Champions Eddie
Southern (2), Glenn Davis (1) and Josh Culbreath (3)

The OLYMPIAN LEAP
The Life and Legacy of Josh Culbreath

For sixty-six years, I am presenting you to a local resident, a man who became an international, world-class Olympian and world traveler. Someone important who brought admirable attention to this town called Norristown, Pennsylvania. He made his town well, with significant contributions to track and field and this country. It's a beautiful thing. I took that leap of faith, writing a story during my downtime after the devastating fall of the pandemic crisis that gripped the world at a complete standstill. It's a celebration for me to tell his story and share his history with you. It is also about maintaining someone in my family who's distinguished to keep his legacy alive. This book is so dear to our family because we would like you to learn about this man that you don't know about him already. The Olympian gods have instructed me to complete the assignment and resurrect him back to life through the written story in a book on his life and legacy. Announcing **JOSH CULBREATH!**

By
Cynthia Culbreath

THE WORLD OF CULBREATH

On Your Marks, Set, Go!

på dina märken uppsättning gå
(Swedish)

auf deine marken setzen geh
(German)

em suas marcas, vá
(Portuguese)

en tus marcas, listo
(Spanish)

à vos marques, partez
(French)

अपने मार्क्स सेट पर जाएं
apane maarks set par jaen
(Hindi)

在您的标记集上
Zài nín de biāojì jí shàng
(Chinese Simplified)

あなたのマークセットに行く
Anata no mākusetto ni iku
(Japanese)

당신의 마크 세트에
dangsin-ui makeu seteue
(Korean)

về điểm của bạn đặt đi
(VIETNAMESE)

téigh ar do
mharcanna
(IRISH)

sui tuoi segni lasciati
andare
(ITALIAN)

στα σημάδια σας
πήγαινε
sta simádia sas pígaine
(GREEK)

pe marcajele setate
du-te
(ROMANIAN)

علی علاماتك مجموعة الذهاب
ealaa ealamatik majmueat aldhahab
(ARABIC)

ձեր նշանների վրա
դրված գնացեք
dzer nshanneri vra drvats gnats'ek'
(ARMENIAN)

kwenye alama zako
weka
(SWAHILI)

siap berangkat
(Indonesian)

na tvé známky jít
(CZECH)

op uw plaatsen gaan
(DUTCH)

บนเครื่องหมายของคุณตั้ง
ไป
Bn kherụ̄xngh̄māy k̄hxng khuṇ tậng pị
(THAI)

işaretlerinizle yola çıkın
(TURKISH)

на ваші позначки йти
na vashi poznachky yty
(UKRAINIAN)

Таны тэмдгүүд дээр тавь
Tany temdgüüd deer tavi
(MONGOLIAN)

Contents

Foreword by Edwin Moses

An American former track and field athlete who won gold medals in the 400 m hurdles at the 1976 and 1984 Olympics. Between 1977 and 1987, Moses won 107 consecutive finals and set the world record in the event four times.

I first met Josh Culbreath in 1976 and I was introduced to him by Dr. Herb Douglas 1948 bronze medalist in the long jump in London. Being a student of the 400-meter hurdles, I, of course, had gone back into the history books and looked at every Olympic champion, and every Olympic competitor, every medalist to see exactly what their times, and what the times they had run and also their progression. So, I started in the 1936 Games of course there was none in 1940. But then I came to 1948 and 1952 and 1956. The first time I met Josh I was in awe to meet him because he was the first 400-meter Olympic Champion that I have ever met, thanks to Herb Douglas. Josh was very much like my father in the black men of that era. They grew up under extreme oppression, Jim Crow, and they grew up under segregation very similar to what we are experiencing today.

In 1948 Herb Douglas reminded me that he and his African American colleagues had to ride on the bottom of the boat thanks to Avery Brundage who was the President of the United States Olympic Committee for many, many years. He remained in place even up until 1986 where he harshly dealt with John Carlos and Tommy Smith. Josh was a great guy, very much like my father who was in the military; and that reminds me of the men, the African American

1

men, the great African American men of that time. They came out of the military and really suffered the indignities of what America has to offer. As my father, Josh was a disciplinarian, and he was a straight talker. He didn't mince words, and he was very aware of the experiences that he had and the differences between what I would face as an African American young man. Those men, I ride on their shoulders because they experienced things that I did not have to because the times have changed. But one of the things that was common with that generation of African American men was that they were very disciplined. They were very tough. Whether they were doctors, lawyers, professors, businessmen, teachers, whatever their profession was, they were full of discipline and always wore suits and ties. I remember my father being an elementary school teacher there was never a day when he didn't walk out of the house with a suit and tie and shoes shined.

This was fantastic. It's a fantastic legacy to remember, and one that has followed me throughout my whole life. Even today, my son has grown up under very disciplined fatherly experience. Hard work, doing chores, academics—were the number one on the list. Without that, there was no hope for him.

So, my hat is off to guys like Josh Culbreath, Mal Whitfield, Herb Douglas, Harrison Dillard, Lee Calhoun, Fred Thompson from the Brooklyn Atoms—all of these gentlemen were true heroes to me and true mentors. They guided me and gave me a start on how to deal with my fame and championship running. Dave Albritton is a sweet reminder of my childhood upbringing of character. He was a friend of my father, my brother's high school teacher, and we went to the same church. 2005 Hall of Fame Inductee—Miami University RedHawks Mr. Amsden Oliver was a Gym Teacher, a friend of Dave Albritton, and my father. Mr. Oliver encouraged me to join the Utopian Track Club and run during the summer. They all were teachers at the elementary and high schools in the neighborhood. Not to mention the great late one Jesse Owens. My hat is forever off to them and God Bless Josh Culbreath.

Josh also served with distinction at Central State University as track coach, and also at my alma mater Morehouse College where we selected him as the Athletic Director where he served for many years. Our hats are off to him forever at Morehouse for guiding and leading young men to the best of their ability. These are the attributes and aspects of African American men born in the early 20th century that survived and thrived throughout the mid-20th century like none other.

I would challenge the young men of today to be able to stand up to that level of achievement, dignity, honesty, and integrity.

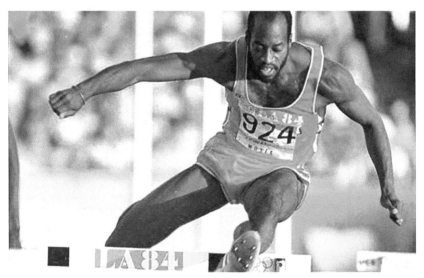

Edwin C. Moses, Sc.D h.c

Edwin Moses jumps a hurdle on his way to winning the gold medal in the 400-meter hurdles in Los Angeles, August 5, 1984. (AP)
Edwin Moses was one of the best ever at clearing hurdles on the track.

EDWIN MOSES
AWARDS AND ACCOMPLISHMENTS

1976 At U.S. Olympic Trials, sets new American record in 400-meter hurdles

1976 Wins Olympic gold medal and sets world record of 47.63 in 400-meter hurdles

1977 Sets new world record of 47.45 in the 400-meter hurdles

1977 Wins world championship in 400-meter hurdles

1980 Sets new world record to 47.13 in 400-meter hurdles

1983 Sets new world record of 47.02 in 400-meter hurdles

1983 Receives Sullivan Award for best U.S. amateur athlete

1984 Named *Sports Illustrated* Sportsman of the Year

1984 Wins second Olympic gold medal

1987 Wins second world title in Rome

1988 Wins Olympic bronze medal in 400-meter hurdles

1994 Inducted into National Track and Field Hall of Fame

Preface

A *Who Do You Think You Are?* moment—as a young girl, I always wondered about the history of my family. Where did they come from? Who are they? I heard stories they were from the South. How did they end up in Norristown, Pennsylvania? I overheard conversations listening to family members in the household talking about "Olympian Cousin Josh Culbreath" who ran in the 1956 Olympics in Melbourne, Australia. As a young girl, and through my teenage years, I always wondered, *Who is this man?* As I got older and I will be out and about, people will ask me, "Are you related to Josh Culbreath the Olympian?"

I would say, "Yes, on my grandfather's side of the family." I knew he was family from the talks I heard in the house growing up.

As a teenager, I signed up to run for The Greater Norristown Area Track Club headed by the late track coach Theodore "Ted" Ellis. Ironically, you will read soon how Mr. Ellis happened to transition into my life during my track days trained by him after discovering later who he was close to in athletics during his high school years. We held our track practices at the Roosevelt Track Field in Norristown. People will tell me, "I see it's in your blood," or "in your DNA, running track like your Cousin Josh Culbreath." Even then, I never personally met Cousin Josh. But I sure heard a whole lot about him! Great stories by people who really admired him—people said wonderful things about Cousin Josh, and he made a name for Norristown, Pennsylvania. His name put Norristown on the map! I always said to myself through the years, "One day I'm going to meet him in person." I was told he was a busy man, always traveling on the road and hard to catch up with. But deep down in my heart, I knew one day, I will meet him. Finally, I did in 2018.

It all started in 2013 when I started looking into researching my family history. I wanted to compose a book documenting the Culbreath Family history on my grandfather's side. It was a lot of hard work trying to pull questions and answers from family members, accessing Ancestry.com, locating family obituaries, and lots of Google searching. It was so much work that I put an end to my research because of my busy work schedule and busy life. Until 2016, I started again. This time, I was very much determined to "do this." I had completed and finalized the Culbreath Family history book as of May 28, 2018, titled: *The Ancient Arms of Culbreath—The Culbreath Family History 1833–2018*. During my findings, I had researched the Culbreath Family History starting from 1833. At first, I did not share my accomplishment with my entire family members. Only a few. The reason is because there were a whole lot of taboo secrets revealed that family members did not want to talk about. Explanation of that story begins the year 2013 when Culbreath Family members wanted to start back up again the family reunion we have not had in ten plus years. We formed a family committee and held our meetings at Cousin Ken-Do's Barbershop in Norristown. Cousin Yvonne and Cousin Evelyn (nicknamed "Weenie") insisted Cousin Josh should be aware of the family reunion plans and to attend the meeting if he was able. Because of his age and health, he needed commute assistance. I was very excited because, with all due anticipation and years of waiting, I was finally going to meet my Olympian cousin!

Sure enough, Cousin Josh was able to attend one of our meetings. He was very happy to see his family members, and especially seeing Cousin Evelyn. They are first cousins. They have a very special connection together because they grew up in a tight-knit family unit. They will always talk about their memorable stories of their childhood.

When he arrived at the barbershop, we were all excited to see him! Everybody gathered around to welcome him and talk with him. After the hype died down, he sat down at our meeting, and I finally introduced myself to him. I told him, "I heard so much about you and I am so excited to finally meet you!"

He smiled and told me it is a pleasure to meet you too. So I went on to tell him my name and who my parents and grandparents are. He knew who they were, and he told me to let them know he asked about them. I sat next to him during the entire time of our meeting to make sure he was comfortable in case he needed anything such as a beverage, etc. When our meeting was over, he did not stay for dinner but was happy to be in the presence around the family. We all were very happy and excited by his presence at our family reunion meeting. Due to his health, we understood he had to leave and return home. That was the best moment of my life. It was like a universal déjà vu, an out-of-body experience manifested by my thoughts through the years for this moment to finally become a reality.

"Our Roots Run Deep, from Saluda, South Carolina to Norristown" Family Reunion was held at Mermaid Lake in Blue Bell, Pennsylvania on Saturday, August 16, 2014. A very, hot sunny day, it was a great time seeing family who traveled the distance from deep South Carolina and neighboring friends and family enjoying lots of BBQ food cooked by Norristown's Willis Brothers World Famous BBQ, serenaded by a DJ and live music, fun games for the kids, swimming, mingling, and socializing good 'ole Southern hospitality! We had a "back down memory lane" moment of our introducing Cousin Josh to speak about his life, his Olympian days, and our family history of Scottish and Southern settlers. It was very emotional and something to hear.

Rewinding back to the conversation of our family reunion meeting gatherings at Ken-Do's as we sat around discussing the history of past family members, everyone would try to figure out who was married to who, what year someone died, who married who, who was related to who, and of course, the highlight of our heart-to-heart would be talking about our beloved Olympian Cousin Josh. We made sure he was informed by his dearest and close cousin "Weenie" (Evelyn) about our family reunion event for him to attend the festivities. As I sat in my chair at the barbershop, listening to my family trying to figure out the name and history of our past family members, it really intrigued me to start finding out the truth and start researching. The hysterical humorous part of our family reunion gatherings is when family members started reminiscing satirical remarks by our deceased loved ones. Someone commented and said Aunt Docia "Docie" used to say, "Yaw leave them old dead folks alone before they come back from the grave to haunt ya!"

Cousin Kenny would say, "You better leave them trees alone." We all fell out cracking up laughing imitating them in mockery how they used to say it with their memorable cocky attitude and Southern drawl talk!

Back in the day, as a young girl, whenever I tried to ask my grandfather (also named Josh) questions about his past living down South, he would look at me with a sharp piercing "don't ask me" look and not say a mumbling word. I knew to leave that alone. Understandably, the South was a conversation he never talked about. Nevertheless, I was able to find answers and give those inquiring minds who want to know answers piecing those puzzles together. I notified a close family friend, who is very close to dear Cousin Josh, about the completion of the Culbreath Family book. She told Cousin Josh about the book, and he wanted to meet with me! How surreal is that?! Very unexpected? My prayers were answered! A dream come true—finally, I was going to meet my Olympian again! Cousin Josh wanted to personally view the book to see how accurate I was with my findings of our family history. In the end, Cousin Josh told me I was very accurate, on point, precise, and I did a great job. That was a wonderful great moment of my life to finally meet with my Olympian Cousin personally at his house in Lower Gwynedd. I am meeting history in the flesh. Cousin Josh was very happy with the book and meeting me again. He said, as well as other family members who knew what I did, no one in our family ever bothered to make time pursuing the research and writing of our family history like I did. I was told, "I am the chosen one."

A labor of love, it was in my blood to always tell the story about my family history. Given all the above, I became very intrigued to know more about my Cousin Josh's Olympian history and his past life. Pulling the trigger, I grew motivated researching by online Google searches; making visits to the Norristown Historical Society, Norristown Public Library, The Upper Merion Public Library in

King of Prussia, Pennsylvania, The Free Library of Philadelphia, inquiries by other outside resources; and by a family friend who provided me tons of correspondence given to her by Josh himself. An OMG moment with my mouth wide open and eyes stretched, I could not believe my discoveries with the wealth of information I was reading about Cousin Josh—all the places he traveled around the world, the track competitions he participated in setting world records, winning bronze and gold medals, running against the best of the best and Who's Who in track and field, celebrities he has encountered as lifelong friends; he even ran against USSR Russians and he is inducted into countless Halls of Fame. Like a time capsule, this man is history—he is a trailblazer, he is a pioneer, he is Olympic Royalty—this man is a legend. Writing Josh's biography was challenging and emotional. There were tears shed as I had researched and discovered other private trials and tribulations about Josh I never knew about. It was not easy. I spent many long days and nights into the morning hours researching and writing. Most definitely, I lost some sleep; at times, it interfered with my personal to-do schedule. I was determined and passionate to have his story completed. In his honor, I am called to duty to write his legacy. As a tribute, I am very much elated and proud to revitalize and be the voice to share a memorable sports biography story reliving the life and legacy of my beloved Olympian champion Cousin Joshua "Josh" Culbreath. My heart to you is for you to enjoy the reading and be inspired by a great American Olympic athlete, coach, and friend—Joshua "Josh" Culbreath. Let us all stand at attention and salute this notable man.

*****

Acknowledgments

First, I want to thank God for blessing me, keeping me strong, giving me strength, giving me wisdom, guiding me all the way, and changing my life for who I am today.

I would like to graciously express many thanks to the epitome of a wonderful, great life and the oldest-living Black Olympian legend medalist, Mr. Herb P. Douglas, Jr., for keeping your dear friend Josh's name alive, for talking about the many loving memories both of you had together during your Olympian running days. Thank you for all your advice and words of praise for Josh to make his sports biography possible. It was an honor to meet you in person to wish you an incredible ninety-ninth birthday on your day of March 9, 2021. Jokingly, you were telling everybody during your many phone calls, "No, I'm sixty-six! Ninety-nine upsides down!" I enjoyed your sharp, quick-witted sense of humor. God bless you, Mr. Douglas. You are an amazing, incredible man, and you most definitely lived a monumental life.

I would like to extend my deepest appreciation and gratitude to Steering Committee Chairman for the National Track and Field Hall of Fame, an internationally recognized historian, and Penn Relays Director Dave Johnson, for your valuable support and encouragement. Your fact-checking on Josh's career was invaluable. Thank you.

Thank You, God, for having Miss Barbara Eunice cross my path. She saw something in me at our first meeting when celebrating Cousin Weenie's birthday party at her daughter Brazay's house in Willow Grove, Pennsylvania. Miss Barbara sensed right away I was the chosen one to write Cousin Josh's sports biography. You told me, "I need you." She believed in me and knew I could do this.

I would like to express my deepest appreciation and gratitude to young talent artist Hagar Eldeeb for her illustration gifts, designing Cousin Josh's book cover. You are an amazing young lady with a beautiful loving heart, soul, and spirit. You are a shining light through the opened windows and doors of immeasurable opportunities in all you do. The world is waiting to see you shine and make a difference.

Thank You, God, for my mom, Jeanette Culbreath. Thanks, mom, for your immense unconditional love, your strong strength, encouragement, praying for me, and your loving support in everything I do.

I would like to express my deepest appreciation and say thank you to Barry Rauhauser and Karen Ploch with The Norristown Historical Society for assisting me during my research on Cousin Josh.

I would like to express my deepest appreciation and say thank you to Norristown Area School District Athletic Director Anthony Palladino to reactivate the online link on the article about Cousin Josh's ceremony celebration recognition at Penn State University State College, Pennsylvania held during the PTFCA Indoor State Championship 2020.

Thank you, Mr. Ron Lopresti with Plymouth Whitemarsh High School, for putting me in touch with Mr. Gerry Stemplewicz.

I would like to express my deepest appreciation and say thank you to Chairman of Hall of Fame Gerry Stemplewicz with L&G Stemp for honoring and inducting our beloved Cousin Josh into the Pennsylvania Track and Field Coaches Association (PTFCA) Hall of Fame Class of 2020 during the meet festivities at Penn State University's State College, Pennsylvania, in March 2020.

Thank you, Montgomery County—Norristown Public Library, for providing me the needed book resources during my research.

Thank you, Upper Merion Township Library, for providing me the needed book resources during my research.

I would like to extend my deepest appreciation and gratitude to Cousin Naomi Satterwhite for sharing her memorable stories about her husband Robert and Cousin Josh.

Thank you, Ernie Hadrick, for your expressions as a lifelong dear friend, your valued support, and your much love for Cousin Josh. It is greatly appreciated.

I would like to acknowledge and express many thanks to Owners Amy and John George with Norristown's Five Saints Distilling for their thoughtful dedication, to naming a cocktail drink the Culbreath Smash in remembrance by paying homage to Josh Culbreath as Norristown's Olympian Champion.

To the joy and love in my life, my little three-year-old cousin Joshua Allen Michael Bell. You are carrying the family generational first name "Joshua" since 1833. As I watch you grow, I pray the plans for your future life are filled with hope, wonderful success, and a righteous path.

To my cousin Erik Michael Stead Jr., you have the adrenaline of sports in you just like your Olympian cousin Josh. A spoken word to you by Cousin Josh "There's a thing called education. You never want to get away from there." I wish you all the best for your future goals in life.

Thank you, cousin Alexis Bell, for commenting your tribute about cousin Josh in Facebook as one of Norristown's GREATEST legends, a precious diamond in our family's history.

Thank you, Yvonne Livers Massie, for using her beautiful artistic gifts and talents in designing my memorial page on our dear, beloved cousin Josh, the tribute pages by Quantico Marines, Morgan State, Central State University, and the well-renowned Olympic athletes' foreword page by Edwin Moses. Thank you, Yvonne Livers Massie, for being a blessing and contributing to a job well done.

I would like to express the incredible surreal experiences I never knew would happen to me in my lifetime. Out of the book pages jumping at me were historic, amazing, incredible men I personally got to speak with and meet in person were Olympian legends Herb Douglas, Morgan State's Flying Four Jimmy Rogers, Otis "Jet" Johnson and Herman Wade, Charlie Jenkins, and Al Cantello. I have no words to express but only wow. These men are giants! They are the unforgettable originals who have paved the way of the Olympic Games in their track and field competitive events to what it is today. These were serious warriors on the playing field. They were trained athletes, and they certainly trained hard. They are the winged shoe-laces of greatness in track and field history. The new Olympian generation of track and field, and the world need to know about these greats. They need to be recognized for their sacrifices, their endurance, and all their obstacles they had to encounter to become who they are today. Full circle, they have accomplished and achieved so much in their lives. They have traveled around the world and seen it all through their prominence as Olympians. During my conversations with them, the candid smiles on their faces and the excitement in their tone over the phone were priceless. They enjoyed reflecting on talking about memorable stories during their running days. To this day, all of them remain in contact with one another. That explains their energy and their will for life is why they are here with us today. Once again, that is the power of kismet given by Josh's belief. We need to continue remembering these celebrated Olympian pathfinders. Applause, applause to all of you gentlemen and Cousin Josh. All of you are the epitome icons of the Olympic victory stand.

To all young athletes and future Olympians: the baton bestowed by past Olympian legends like Josh Culbreath is now passed on to your predestined journey to the road of victory onto the track and field. It is your time now to carry the torch for your event in competition to begin and for you to win the race across the finished line. You are the continuation of the next Olympic generation. May the halo of the Olympic rings shadow upon you to Olympic Gold!

Καλή επιτυχία!

*****

Brief History and Facts of the Melbourne 1956 Olympic Games

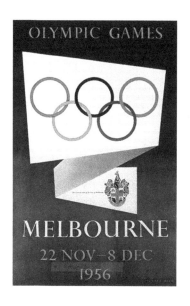

Melbourne 1956 Olympic Games, athletic festival held in Melbourne that took place Nov. 22–Dec. 8, 1956. The Melbourne Games were the 13th occurrence of the modern Olympic Games.

1956 Melbourne Olympics: First Games in the southern hemisphere

The 1956 Olympics were the first held in the Southern Hemisphere. Because of the reversal of seasons, the Games were celebrated in November and December.

1956 Summer Olympics
Facts

Competition type	Olympic Games
Host city	Melbourne, Australia (Venues)
Opening ceremony	22 November
Closing ceremony	8 December
Competition dates	22 November–8 December
OCOG	Organizing Committee for the Games of the XVI Olympiad Melbourne 1956
Participants	3190 from 67 countries
Medal events	145 in 20 disciplines
Other events	2 in 2 disciplines

A Brief History of the Melbourne 1956 Olympic Games

Melbourne was selected as the host city for the 1956 Summer Olympics at the 43rd International Olympic Committee Session in Rome, Italy in 1949. These Games would be the first time the Olympics would be held in the Southern Hemisphere and Oceania, and it also marked the first occasion that the Games were played outside of Europe and North America. However, in the lead up to the Games, there were a series of boycotts, political problems, and controversy that threatened to overshadow what would come to be known as the "Friendly Games."

*****

From the words of Olympian Champion Josh Culbreath:

All of you better be Champions someday, or
I'll have to take this picture back!
(Schools—January 10, 1957,
Quantico, Virginia)

Sound Advice

If you ever want to be a Champion, you must train very hard and sincere, and make great sacrifices by disciplining your mind and body!

Remember this little poem and you will be a champion, have your mother and father explain to you what it means:

To often do we blame ourselves for failure and defeat;

When we ourselves for merits lack, our missions can't complete;

And yet in shifting blame; do we find strength to go on endlessly!

Spoken Word by Josh

"They called us 'The Flying Four,' and we kicked everyone's butt," Culbreath said. "We won every championship from Madison Square Garden to the Boston Garden."

"People used to laugh: 'You're Culbreath?' I'd say, "This is all of me," and then I'd run their tails off."

"…it takes three things to succeed in track and in life—focus, hard work and sacrifice." (Josh Culbreath)

"You don't earn recognition by stepping on people," Culbreath said.

Josh Culbreath

Josh Culbreath won the Bronze medal in the 400 meter hurdles at the 1956 Olympic games in Melbourne, Austraila. His 300 yard oval grass track time in that same year set a world record. One year later, Culbreath set another world record in the 440 yard hurdles in Oslo, Norway.

Culbreath participated in the first USA vs. USSR track meet in 1958, taking second in the 400 meter hurdles in Moscow, Russia. In 1959 he took second in the same competition held in Philadelphia, Pa.

A graduate of Morgan State University, Culbreath was inducted into MSU's Hall of Fame in 1975. He is also a member of halls of fame with Black Athlete in New York, Norristown, Penn. (hometown) and the United States Marine Corps Sports Hall of Fame.

In 1993 Culbreath became the first USA head coach of men's and women's track and field to win both indoor and outdoor National (NAIA) Titles. He currently serves as a consultant to institutions of higher education.

"As I pursued things, I had good people, good teachers with me."

*****

Teammate Shout Out!
Olympian Dr. Charlie Jenkins

JOSH CULBREATH

During the 1950s Josh Culbreath was an outstanding student athlete while attending Morgan State College. He was trained by the late Edward P. Hurt, a leader and educator. Morgan State had one of the best track and field teams in the country. For example, two of his teammates were Art Bragg and George V. Rhoden. Art was a member of the 1952 United States Olympic Team, held in Helsinki Finland and George Rhoden represented Jamaica at the same Olympics. George won two Olympic Gold Medals, in the 400 meters, and as a participant on the winning 1600-meter relay team.

From the time Josh was a freshman he quickly followed the tradition of these great athletes that preceded him. He participated and won championships in the 400–600-yard runs as well as the 110 high hurdles. However, his strong event was the 400-meter hurdles.

Josh and his teammates competed in the best track and field meets in the country. For Josh, the season began with the indoor track circuit, two months of competition throughout the eastern part of the United States. The competition in each of these meets was the best in the world at the time. Josh and his teammates won individual races and relay championships during the indoor season.

Following the indoor season was the outdoor season. The competition was equally as challenging. The first large outdoor track meet for east coast competition was the famous Penn Relays, held at the University of Pennsylvania Franklin Field. Josh and his team competed and won many of the various relay events. For four years Josh won the 400-meter hurdles at the Penn Relays.

The last track and field meet of the season was the AAU National Championships. Placing in the various events qualified an athlete to compete in various countries in Europe. Josh never failed to qualify and represent the United States each summer in Europe. He was the winner of many European competitions.

At the 1956 Olympic Trials, Josh made the United States Olympic Team in the 400-meter hurdles. At the 1956 Olympics held in Melbourne Australia, Josh won an Olympic Bronze Medal.

It should be mentioned that during the time that Josh competed at the Olympics he was in the U.S. military a member of the United States Marine Corps. A large number of people were proud of Josh. Morgan State College, his family, his friends and the United States of America.

Josh was liked and admired by people that knew him. He always reached out to people and people liked and respected him.

Yes, Josh is a dear friend. END

All the Best,
Dr. Charles L. Jenkins

*****

Jamaica Shout Out!
Geneive Brown Metzger

My dear friend Josh Culbreath
—Dr. The Hon. Geneive Brown Metzger

George Bernard Shaw said, "A gentleman is one who puts more into the world than he takes out." Where Josh is concerned, that's a whole lot of goodness all the way round. A gentleman, Josh gave, gave, and gave some more. He has enjoyed tremendous athletic success and is loved and respected by scores of athletes and friends around the world. His legacy can be measured in many ways, but the most lasting will be his impact on the lives of young athletes. I met Josh on the infield at the Penn Relays in 2009 as I was there representing Jamaica as Consul General. It was a crisp Friday afternoon at the end of April; the 4X400 was about to kick off; the infield was packed with athletes, VIPs and dignitaries; and the buzz emanating from the bleachers was downright palpable. As my husband and I pulled up close to the line for a better view of the race, there was Josh wearing a broad, warm smile, excited as if he were about to take off down the track himself. I introduced myself and we became fast friends.

Josh was 16 years old when Herb McKenley, the Jamaican runner, won at the Olympics in

1948. Josh shared stories about McKenley and how McKenley inspired him as a young athlete. After Josh stopped competing, he became involved with Jamaican athletes—traveling to the island to coach them. He was there for them when they competed in U.S. meets, and guided those who would later as US college athletes. He knew all of them—from McKenley to Bolt, and no doubt had an impact on their lives. The Penn Relays was Josh's athletic home and over the years, I had the privilege of serving with him on the Penn Relays Carnival Committee where it was clear how loved and revered he was. I learned so much from Josh about track and Jamaica's rich history in the sport. The Penn Relays was for me an opportunity to wave the Jamaica flag as a proud diplomat and revel in the prowess displayed by Jamaican athletes year after year; but it was also about seeing, learning from, and spending three amazing days every April with my dear, dear friend Josh Culbreath.

*****

Morgan State Shout Out Dear Friend Larry Wilson's Remembrance of Josh

In 1956, Josh returned to the campus of Morgan State University from the Pan American games held in Mexico City. Josh had won the gold medal in the 400-meter hurdles. I can recall the night that he entered his room with congo drums and other Mexican items draped over his shoulder... Much to his surprise, he had a new roommate. Josh's success in track was due mainly to his dedication, work ethics, and mental toughness. For all his accomplishments in track, he was inducted into the PA track and field hall of fame.

*****

Dear Friend Al Cantello's Remembrance of Josh

My dear friend Josh Culbreath
—Al Cantello

Josh Culbreath was the male counterpart of Meghan Markle. He was acceptable. The male counterpart of his time. He was nonthreatening. He was handsome. If you were going to accept him, he was the guy. I went to high school with him. Josh was your guy in high school. I didn't go to college after high school. I worked in a factory. Josh went to college at Morgan State. In college there was an event called the 440-yard hurdles which opened the door for him since he was only 5'7.5". In the intermediate, hurdles were only 36 inches high. When that door opened, he had a guardian angel.

Plus, there was a legendary coach at Morgan State named Eddie Hurt. It was a miracle born in heaven. That guardian angel stayed with Josh a long, long time. So, he wins the intermediate hurdles at the Penn Relays three consecutive years.

Josh saw the opportunity and became an absolute specialist in the 440-intermediate hurdles. To this day, several dozen high school conferences only run the 330-intermediate hurdles. So, based on Josh's size, somebody opened the door for him. A divine force. Subsequently, he set the world record while touring as an athlete in Norway at 50.6. So, now we have Josh pinpointed at that point in history.

After Morgan, he went to the Marine Corp in 1956, and I went in 1956. Both of us were stationed in Quantico. Virginia. There was a Lieutenant who was able to convince the Commanding General Quantico Marine of the base that it would be a great idea to compose a track team to compete against colleges. This would help the Marine Corp. recruiting. They already had football teams to play against Army bases and some colleges. They started in the early 1950s. We travelled to Michigan, Ohio State, and Penn State for dual meets—Quantico vs. Ohio State Buckeyes.

We had a lot of stars. They were competing as Marines mostly on the east coast. We made the Olympic Team while we were Quantico Marines. That same guardian angel showed up at Melbourne. I can't divulge how these things happened. An angel opened the door and Josh hurdled through.

The Olympic Trials—I was at LA Coliseum competing but did not make the team. But Josh did and he won third and received the bronze medal; and that same guardian angel travelled with him 2000 miles all the way to Melbourne,

*****

1

Josh's Early Childhood Years From Saluda, South Carolina, to Norristown, Pennsylvania

Josh Culbreath, what a man, what a man. In his early years, his family was from Saluda, South Carolina. As he became a younger fella (maybe around eight, ten, twelve years old), his mother would send him down to Saluda, South Carolina by train to visit his relatives and his grandmother Clarisa "Classy" Satterwhite. Also, his grandfather Josh who he was named after was there. The street name Joshua was named after them (see photo inset). Josh loved the country. He loved going walking all around. It was an open area where he can just be free. He enjoyed visiting a lot of his cousins. What was good about it, Josh was able to help his grandfather at the two cemeteries: Branch Hill Cemetery and Mount Zion Methodist in Saluda which they took care of the two churches of our Black people. Josh would go and help sweep up, clean up, and do whatever was necessary.

On this trip, Josh was a grown man and the first place he wanted to go see were the two undertakers in Saluda. After he left there, he wanted to go to the two churches and to the Culbreath Family cemetery at Branch Hill Cemetery. He would go walk around and look at the tombstones, point out to the different family members that he remembered, take pictures of them, and for some strange reason, he got very quiet. I looked over and Josh was either praying or he was in a trance. Later, when he did talk to me about it, he said something came over him, and he felt his grandfather's presence. Just being in the cemetery all that time away from Saluda and back to Saluda as a grown man, the spirit of his grandfather and other family members just came over him. It just goes to show you that no matter where we come from, and no matter where we go, these things happen. Especially when you're deeply rooted into your family, and you love your family and your friends.

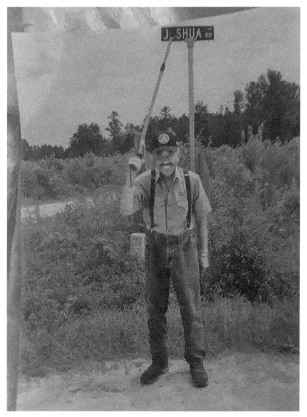

Joshua Road street sign named after Joshua's grandfather and Cousin Josh in Saluda, SC. Courtesy: Culbreath Family photo

As Josh was down in Saluda with his grandmother, he had cousins down there. One of them was Robert Satterwhite. He and Robert were cousins and best friends for life. Robert then moved up to Norristown and that just continued the friendship. But the reason Robert was crazy about Josh, 'cause Josh would help him help his mother. They had chickens down in Saluda, and Robert was supposed to go and get the fresh eggs that the chickens had just laid. But his mother did not know Robert was afraid of snakes. So what did Robert do? He recruited his cousin Josh Culbreath 'cause Josh could do everything! Joshua was fearless. So Josh went and look to see what he had to do. He went and checked the chickens, and he figured how they could take the eggs away from the chickens without the chicken hawks coming after them. This is what he did most of the summer for Robert's mother as well as for Cousin Robert. Robert's mother would reward Josh when she made freshly baked cakes or pies or whatever she did with the chicken's eggs. What an experience that was for them when they still talk about those moments as men way into their eighties! That is how much fun they had in Saluda.

When Robert moved up to Norristown, and Josh was in high school—as well as when he went into the military—he came home a lot. But when it was time to go back down to the area where he was stationed who did he take with him? Robert. Robert would love to take Josh back to where they were stationed when he was in the Marines. Josh being in the Marines, and Robert knowing how to drive, Josh said, "Can you take me?" and Robert said, "Of course, I can." So can you imagine a friendship going that long?

This is what happens in the town of Norristown. Norristown is known as the seat of Montgomery County, and Josh has lived there all his life. Robert and other people from high school knew Josh as well. What was great about it, each person in Norristown was either a cousin or a relative in some way. One of his relatives, when Josh wanted to get his haircut, he called Ken-Do. Ken-Do would pick Josh up and take him to get his haircut. While he was in the barbershop, all the young boys and girls who heard about Josh would come in there and said, "Oh my God, we can't believe we're meeting THE JOSH CULBREATH!" and Josh would be so humble he said, "How would they know anything about me?" Not realizing that people were in the audience and stands or at school or had parents and grandparents who would talk about the Norristown Josh Culbreath.

So now, he had a chance to talk to the young fellas, and he enjoyed doing that. Especially when he was an educator himself. He went to college and one of his specialties was Special Ed. Josh was in school with the children that nobody thought they can do anything with. What did Josh do? He showed them. He taught the children how to sing "Silent Night" in German. Nobody could believe it when they had the Christmas Pageant; those children got up there and sang the song in German. Josh loved learning other languages. He would learn how to say any language as far as *thank you, no, yes*, or pronouncing somebody's name because he thought that was respectful. That's how he did when he traveled the world, he could always be polite and be respectful; and that is why a lot of people would respect you. You don't have to speak their language, but it's how you try to by calling them by their proper name. Josh Culbreath, what a man. He wasn't a big guy, but he had a big heart and he did big things.

Robert and Josh. Photo was taken at Culbreath Family Reunion on August 16, 2014, at Mermaid Lake, Blue Bell, Pennsylvania. Courtesy: Cynthia Culbreath Family photo

Having silly fun at Culbreath Family Reunion!
Courtesy: Cynthia Culbreath Family photo

*****

As he got older he went to different places. He did know how to cook and make different things. But his specialty was—and you won't believe this, but this is what he said he invented. A lot of us know what chitterlings are. Josh knew what chitterlings are being from the South and coming up North. A lot of people would eat them and do different things with them. But that is not what Josh did. Josh Culbreath told me he invented the "deep-fried chitterlings;" and when the people found out that they were chitterlings that they were eating, they loved them, and they just couldn't believe that they would ever eat chitterlings. But the way he fixed them, I guess it must have looked like a French fry or maybe a chicken finger! But he said they would just devour those chitterlings not knowing that they were eating chitterlings that most people saw and said, "Oh, I love them," or "No, I don't want them." That's the way he was. He would come up with anything to please people and make them feel good.

Josh had a lot of friends from high school that are in the Norristown area, and he would go visit different ones when he came into Philadelphia. He also lived in Las Vegas. He also lived all over the place. This man loved to travel. We call him the "International Renaissance Man from Norristown." The name is Josh Culbreath and he would always talk about Frog Hollow. Does anybody know where Frog Hollow is? Well, they don't know now, just keep reading. Some of you will know because some of you did live there, and you know exactly where Frog Hollow is. Josh loved the streets of Norristown. That is where Josh would spend a lot of his young years all around Frog Hollow playing with his friends. Frog Hollow, was this a premonition of Josh's leaping abilities like a frog to become a hurdler in track and field? Josh loved to tell many stories about his young days growing up in the streets of Norristown, and one of them was about, "I would go to Arch Street because the houses had front yards with hedges. Each yard was a different height. I would run and jump over the hedges no matter how high the hedges got."

This was the beginning of his jumping ability, maybe, or maybe not?

"There was one house I really loved to get to, because it had a very large dog that was to protect the yard. That was my challenge."

He loved getting ready to run, jump, and beat that big dog from catching him. He would jump over that hedge and never look back. As years went by, again, Josh Culbreath would always run and not look back. Do you think maybe because he knew that dog would have bit him?

"Hearing the dog behind me, as I look back now, knowing this was a lesson or training I was doing. When I ran in all my tracks events, I never looked back. I want to thank that Big Large Dog for his help in making my confidence in my career choices. Also, thanks to the house owners on Arch Street. I never looked back."

Food for thought: An inspiration to anybody—do not look back; just leap forward.

*****

He also played with Tommy LaSorda. He also played with Charles Blockson, Jimmy Smith; he had various friends from high school he would be with. But some of the fellas wouldn't go over to the quarry. But Josh said, "I'll go over there." He would go into the quarry, and if they jumped off, he jumped off. The water in the quarry wasn't the cleanest, but Josh knew that "I could do anything anybody else can do, and I might be able to do it better." So all in all, that is what he did, and he had friends for life because that is all the things he was capable of doing. Nothing could stop him. He was able to do a lot of things. He had a nephew named Kenny Smith—his sister had five children—and he would be called on to help with the children. Kenny became a Morgan student. Josh helped him get into college. Kenny was very good with track and field, and he would get him on different track events after he came out of school. They all would call Josh, "Can you get me on?" What would Josh do? Make a phone call and got them on. So when you go to look back at what have I done in this life, I can say I never did as much as this man has done and is still doing. So if you are interested in reading or hearing anything you will be able to find it in this magnificent fun-filled book about the greatest legend from Norristown who came out of Frog Hollow—Josh Culbreath, the International United States Marine Olympian who won the bronze medal.

As a young boy, Joshua Culbreath's family joined Mt. Zion AME Church in Norristown. His Sunday School teacher was Mrs. Lillian Bright of Willow Street, Norristown. Mrs. Bright encouraged Josh to be in the church program plays. He was a small boy for his age at that time, but he was a very good speaker and he can remember his lines.

A few years went by, and Josh was much older he said to Mrs. Bright, "Why do you always want me to be in the same plays doing the same thing? I'm older now."

Mrs. Bright said to him, "Josh, you do such a good job, and because you speak so well, you make people stop, look, and listen to you, and everybody cannot do that." A foretelling sign of his embodiment of the Greek god Hermes who is also the inventor of speech… more about this twist later in the reading. So at that early age at Mt. Zion AME Church in Norristown, Mrs. Lillian Bright recognized some of the talent—besides the sports and other things—that Joshua Culbreath was a very good speaker, and he could get attention from people just by talking.

As time went by, he would go by Mrs. Bright's house on Willow Street, after he had practice from either football or maybe a track meet and stop and just talk to her. He said he just enjoyed her so much because she would listen, and he also knew by going by her house it would keep him out of trouble, because sometimes boys do get into trouble. But Josh kept on going back, and as years went by, he really became a good speaker, and all of this is because, again, sometimes our neighbors and friends recognize talents that others may not, and that might have been what helped Josh do the things that he did.

Later in adult life, you will read stories in Josh's sports biography his invitations to numerous speaking engagements as guest speaker.

*****

2

Josh's Memorable Years
at Norristown High School
Days in the *Hi-Eye News!*

NORRISTOWN HIGH SCHOOL CLASS OF 1951

Hall of Champions

James Randloph
1986

Clarence Smith
1987

William Werkiser
1983

Donald W. Shank
2001

Hall of Fame

Joshua Culbreth
1980

Peter T. Standbridge
1994

William A. Steinbach
1998

William H. Markley
2000

Hi-Eye News, March 10, 1949

As a young boy Josh was a gifted athlete in high school. The eagle eye of NHS Track Coach Pete Lewis noticed his talent. From then on, the whiff of the beginnings of an Olympian champion began to surge. Josh also had exciting, good 'ole fun times during his three years at Norristown High School. Let us leap through memory lane and relive the beginning memories of Josh's high school days leading up to his life and legacy:

1949–1950 Josh's Junior Years in the *Hi-Eye News*, November 4, 1949

STRICTLY CONFIDENTIAL—CLUB PENNY GAVE A DANCE OCTOBER 22, SATURDAY NIGHT

It was party time in "Conshy" (Conshohocken, Pennsylvania)! and those present was Marian Abney, Fred Waldrop, Delores Maiston, Lemuel Rogers, Lillian Wells, John Spearman, Polly Williams, Richard Rogers, Claire Marston, Charles Mason, Dorothy Allen, Jimmy Brown, Vivian Lindsay, Billy Johnson, Theora Lindsey, Jimmy Glaston, and Josh Culbreath.

SIDE BAR NEWS—a close family friend who knows Josh told me the following story about Josh's laughable dance moves:

> In high school, I do not believe Josh went to any proms because he was too busy practicing track. He played basketball. He also was on the football team in various years in the Norristown School District. One of the other reasons was is because his legs were meant for track. They were not meant for dancing. When he showed me one of his dance moves I thought it was Willy The Worm on the string! His legs just went from one side to the other real fast. So, I still say his legs were meant for the track and not for dancing. But all in all, Josh like to do that because it made just people have fun and laugh!

Josh made not had the moves on the dance floor, but he sure knew how to burn cinder tracks on fire and fly like an Eagle as an athlete on the Eagle Cinder Squad Track Team. Josh's track talent already was receiving spotlight in the NHS *Hi-Eye* news headlines boasting: EAGLE NINE BATTLING FOR TOP POSITION IN SUBURBAN ONE LOOP: WIN OVER UPPER DARBY, CHELTENHAM, HAVERFORD, AND ABINGTON. COMPETITION KEEN. Here are a few brief excerpts surrounding Josh's winning high school track days.

Hi-Eye News reported, EAGLE CINDER SQUAD SHOWS PROMISE IN WINNING FIRST FOUR, headlined on Friday, May 12, 1950, and announced on April 6 the track team opened its regular season at home against Reading. Showing lots of potentialities, John Spearman led the attack with three first places. After winning the hundred-yard dash and the 440 run, Spearman also won the 220-yard dash. Charlie Blockson, sophomore, Clarence Smith, and Josh Culbreath each won two events as Norristown beat Reading by the score of 91–26. The next interscholastic event took place once again at Roosevelt Stadium. In the first triangular meet of the season, Chester and Lower Merion, two of the most highly rated track teams in Suburban District One, competed with the Eagle Cinder Squad Track Team. In a surprising upset, the Eagle Squad once again came out on top.

Under the same news date, in another track competition event, *Hi-Eye* school news headliner reports, DISTRICT ONE TITLE WON BY EAGLES under the direction of "Pete" Lewis. Such was the success of the Norristown High School track team in 1950, the boys went through the season undefeated, and won the Suburban I championship and the District I championship. Besides this, they took the Norristown Interscholastics, two dual meets, and two triangular meets, placed well to the Lower Merion and Venzk relays, and ran in the Penn Relays.

Norristown took eight first places. This reserved strength is just what Coach Lewis needed to win the District Championship at Upper Darby. The winners scored 20 points, while the reserves captured 31 points to win the meet with 51 points for Norristown and 28 1/2 points for closest competitor, Lower Merion.

Of the Norristown team, eight members qualified to go to the meet at Penn State. They are Sebastian Bufo, Joshua Culbreath,

Clarence Smith, John Spearman, Andrew Livingston, Joseph Hadrick, Ted Ellis, and Charles Blockson.

*****

1950–1951 Josh's Senior Years in *The Hi-Eye News*

SEPTEMBER 22, 1950—WORKING HARD ON THE GRIDIRON

Well, what do you know? It's time for football because *Hi-Eye News* reported Jim Randolph, John Spearman, Josh Culbreath, Charlie Blockson, and Bill Johnson have been working hard on the *gridiron* these days. Here are a series of standout football events by Josh and his Eaglemen posse.

October 13, 1950, *Hi-Eye* reported Josh Culbreath has been quite popular since football season has opened.

October 1950, Josh made his moves carrying the football to about the ten-yard line with a thrown pass by Jim Randolph during an Eagles Upset by Phoenixville, 19–13.

EAGLES COME FROM BEHIND TO KNOCK OVER ABINGTON, 13–7, defeating them with a win on November 11, 1950. The Eagles were slow in getting "on the warpath" to chalk up two touchdowns. Both of these TDs were made in the last quarter of the game. Guess by who? Josh Culbreath made both TDs. *Hi-Eye News* reported one of the main reasons that Josh was so successful is "due to the fact that he is very fast as a runner on the track team." Jim Randolph was one of the key men who made the first TD possible; he threw a twenty-six-yard pass to Culbreath who had just run about forty-three yards down field. The second TD was made by Culbreath on an end run.

An aha moment, that explains why Josh's bio mentions his "Christmas Pageant" participation under High School Activities. Not only was Josh a sports star, but did you know he was a creative artist too? A prophecy in the making with his involvement entering his school's float, which was entered in a Christmas parade December 1950. Later, you will read about Josh's parade and Chamber of

Commerce foretelling. More than 25,000 looked on as Norristown's entry in the Christmas parade tied for third place honors in the non-professional division, sponsored by the local Chamber of Commerce, which included thirty-one floats and eight bands, among them in the Blue and White musicians of NHS. The high school float was one of several manger scenes. It was planned and constructed by instructors and students of the Vocational Department under the direction of William E. Butler. Miss Emma E. Christian, principal, sponsored the float in response to an invitation by the Chamber of Commerce. Guess who? Students in the stable were Cherry Fair, Barbara Butera, Joseph Ginther, Janet Foulke, Joshua Culbreath, and William Meyers. The following boys in the Vocational Department helped build the float: Donald Kehr, Gordon Armstrong, David Heebner, Bill Yocum. These people did the artwork: Edward Guzzardo, John Spearman, Nancy Campbell, Josh Culbreath, Walter Smith. Later, in January 1951, the Christmas Parade Committee received two awards from the Chamber of Commerce for their part in the Christmas parade. They got $50 for the high school band and $15 for the float, which tied for third place in its division. Both checks were deposited in the band uniform fund.

The end of the road, and it's December 1950. THE EAGLE'S END FOOTBALL SEASON WITH 8 WON, 2 LOST. Norristown closed its books on one of the most successful football seasons that old-time residents have seen. They defeated Olney, Radnor, Overbrook, Pottstown, Chester, Haverford, Abington, and arch-rival Bridgeport, losing only to Phoenixville and Lower Merion. They rolled up a total of 179 points to only 98 for the opponents. Norristown almost doubled their scores. Leading the scoring parade was big Charlie Blockson with an impressive total of 69. Congratulations to all the seniors for the fine spirit and great play: Rail Sylvester, Jim Randolph, Josh Culbreath, Ted Ellis, Don Shank, Dick Keyser, Vince Pizzico, Len Pisano, Al Stead, John Lock, Sal Gailo, Joe Hadrick, Glenn Martin, Jim Dannehower, and Lou Valerio.

What's up with Josh and the 411? The social given by Club Boomers reported in the *Hi-Eye News* Josh Culbreath really stays broke, making all the phone calls at lunch time that he does. That explains why he likes to tell stories and he's a good speaker.

Love seems to be in the air during his senior year 1951 for Cousin Josh and Dot Allan.

Setting a record and making great plays constitutes Josh's talents in basketball under the direction of Coach Art Herr. It's February 1951, and SUBURBAN WINNER WILL BE DECIDED AS EAGLES MEET HAVERFORD as last game to decide who journeys to Penn Palestra. By beating Abington, Lower Merion, Upper Darby, and Cheltenham, Norristown tied Haverford for the league lead with a record of 10–1. Although hampered in the latter games by the loss of such stellar performers as Lee Huber, whose 39 points in two games enabled Norristown to defeat Abington and Lower Merion; Phil Bugg, whose play lately has dazzled spectators; and Chet Green, who turned in brilliant plays in all of them; Norristown was able to call on Jim Randolph, Josh Culbreath, and Earl Schrack—all able players who turned in great plays when the occasion called for it. In defeating Abington, Norristown broke a record set by the famous Buzz Boys on February 11, 1947, by scoring 86 points to top the previous high of 84. Josh Culbreath stole the ball away from Abington, and dribbling the length of the floor, put the ball in, and also a new record on the books.

It's March 1951, and with the end of winter comes the end of one of the favorite sports in NHS Basketball—BASKETBALL TEAM WINS 19, LOSES 3. Although the basketball team nosed out for the chance for the Suburban Section One title, they did have a very successful season. With that being said, they had a strong leader as captain of the varsity team by the name of Bill Werkeiser, encouraging the boys on. The other members of the team were recognized because they backed up the starting five and were the ones who put them through their paces during the practice scrimmages. The rest of the team was as follows: Joseph Hadrick, Philip Bugg, James Randolph, Earl Schrack, Pierce Ostrander, George Ortlip, James Bealer, Francis Sylvester, and yours truly, Joshua Culbreath.

Well, fellow readers, Josh's high school Sports Chatter during his impressive three-year NHS performance in sports finally comes to a close. It is May 1951, Josh's senior year. Although Josh was a standout in football and basketball under his tutelage by Track Coach

"Pete" Lewis, new records were broken at each meet. Mr. Lewis had a spectacular track team doing itself up proud consisting of Charles Blockson, Josh Culbreath, John Spearman, Bill Werkeiser, Johnny Bosler, Jimmy Dannehower, and many other members of the team. On Monday, June 4, 1951, Josh was one of 350 seniors to receive his high school diploma, which was presented on stage in the school auditorium.

So on an ending note, a local Norristown boy is about to emerge as one of the greatest Olympians in the world. Fellow readers get ready, take your mark, GO!

*****

3

Straight Outta Norristown, Pennsylvania

"The Flying Four" and "The Speed Merchants." No, these are not titles of Billboard record chart songs or The Sound of Motown by a singing group. You are about to read about a man who dominated the blazing trails of track and field with leaps and bounds, setting the corral of hurdles on fire! He was a "Tailwind Turner," blowing like the wind in swift directions, blasting his competitors in the dust. The dust has not settled yet because the resurgence of this Olympian great has risen back to life as a monumental memory to be known by all who broke records and won bronze and gold medals in past Olympic and Pan American Games. A true Olympian athlete who had pride for his country, and at the same time, was an honorable veteran who had served his country in the US Marines. His tireless life was full of acclaim and achievements. Encouraging, empowering, and coaching others had absorbed much of this Olympian muse's "post-competition" years. He was a celebrated track-and-field coach for many collegiate, United States, and international teams representing countries around the world. He had coached many Olympic athletes and has been described as the "Martin Luther King of athletics." He sent four Olympians to the 1996 Olympics held in Atlanta, Georgia. Down to the wire, the stopwatch never stopped ticking because he trained young talented track athletes, honing their skills such as Olympians: Deon Hemmings, Catherine Scott Pomales, Neil de Silva and Sayon Cooper. He was "known as 'Pop' to his athletes." Twice, he was honored face to face by presidents of the United States of America: (34) Dwight D. Eisenhower and (42) Bill Clinton. He rose all the way to the White House Rose Garden invited by the forty-second president of the United States, Bill Clinton, in June 1993 to be honored for leading his track-and-field team to ten NAIA championships within eight years. His biography is an opportunity for you to learn more about the past history of this sports legend and develop an appreciation for those that have influenced our generation of athletes. Are you ready to celebrate the life and legacy of this remarkable Olympian champion and run the race to cross the finish line with him? On your mark, set, GO!

Dr. Joshua "Josh" Culbreath was the first great Black intermediate hurdler. Unstoppable and *undefeated* define Joshua "Josh" Culbreath, who is among the ranks of famous inspirational track-and-field TOP OLYMPIAN GREATS, and comparable to celebrated athletes like Jesse Owens, Harrison "Bones" Dillard, Arthur "Art" Bragg, John Youie "Long John" Woodruff, Eugene Beatty, and Charlie Moore. They broke the barrier before Josh's time, but Josh followed pursuit in their footsteps along with Willye B. White and Wilma Rudolph. Josh does credit Jesse Owens in one of his candid interviews with CBS National Sports Radio Network host Rich Perez at the M Resort Hotel in Las Vegas, Nevada, quoting, "Had it not been for Jesse setting the precedent in which he did, we wouldn't have what has come about now." These Camelots of track and field passed the baton and paved the way for Florence "Flo-Jo" Griffith-Joyner, Jackie Joyner-Kersee, Edwin Moses, and Carl Lewis to name a few. All the makings of an Olympian, Josh Culbreath came into the world as a born athlete and as a fierce competitor, residing along with these track greats who all seared the burning track fields on fire!

Culbreath gained worldwide fame during the 1950s for his ability to run and leap hurdles faster than anyone else in the world. His primary competition, the 400-meter hurdles, is regarded as the most difficult track event. The challenges of running hurdles are the most difficult and the most technically challenging form of running. It involves both the athletic ability to generate muscle power and the science of integrating the speed of maximum forward movement with the efficient grace necessary to clear the hurdles. Despite Josh's height, he had many physical factors that contribute to a hurdler's success, the primary ones being speed, power, physical, mental, endurance, flexibility, size, and quickness. At the time of his retirement as an athlete, Josh had scored more *Track and Field News* world ranking points in the 400-meter hurdles than any American in history, trailing only the Soviet Union's Yuriy Lituyev, the hurdler Josh beat for the bronze medal at the 1956 Olympics. Josh earned *Track and Field News* world rankings in eight successive years from 1953 through 1960. Only in 1960 was he ranked below third in the world. He may stand at five feet, seven inches, but Mr. Culbreath is a giant among giants. He had a dominant stallion stature, with controlled timing of his calculated movements leaping over hurdles, striding to the finish line. He is regarded as the shortest hurdler to accomplish so much. As a youth, coincidental a neighborhood section where he resided called Frog Hollow could ironically signify his leaping abilities. A predestined aura, was he visioning for bigger things?

Josh also grew up in the Norristown surrounding neighborhood with other neighbors who excelled in sports such as Tommy LaSorda, Al Cantello, Clarence Smith, Charles "Charlie" Blockson, James "Jimmy" Randolph, and Ted Ellis. The athletic journey of Joshua "Josh" Culbreath has led his life of running, serving, leadership, and commitment. Josh travelled all over the world throughout his career (not only as an Olympian), but he was also a coach recognized for his leadership, training, and preparing young athletes for many track events including the Philadelphia, PA Penn Relays, and the Olympics. He was an educator educating students at schools and colleges. He was very committed to teaching kids. Josh was accomplished speaking many languages. He knew greetings and would learn from each country he went, even Russia and India, he wanted to be polite. Josh was a man of many stories. He always had so many stories to tell about where he came from growing up in Norristown, Pennsylvania, living in the same neighborhood with former Los Angeles Dodgers Manager Tommy LaSorda. Josh enjoyed telling stories about his family; his Olympic days; his college relay days with "The Flying

Four"—one, two, three, four buddies comprised of Herman "Bitsy" Wade, Otis "Jet" Johnson, Jimmy Rogers, and Josh was number 4; his service in the US Marines; and his travels around the world. While delving in nearly every sport as a youth, Culbreath had track and field to thank for taking him around the world as a world traveler. Early on from his childhood years, growing up in the neighborhood with Tommy LaSorda, Jimmy Smith, and Charles Blockson, who knew, in his future life, Josh would be surrounded by top-shelf wealth of athletes and celebrities. The spirit of kismet in the midst? More explanation on that later in the reading of this biography. His energy was surrounded by many achievers of all walks of life by those who closely know him dearly including athletes and celebrities such as good friend Phylicia Rashad; former Miss America Suzette Charles; "The Greatest" Boxer, Muhammad Ali; Mike Tyson; The A-Team's actor, Mr. T; comedians/actors Chris Rock, Adam Sandler, Eddie Griffin, Cuba Gooding, Jr., and Anthony Quinn; NBA Basketball Greats Julius "Dr. J" Erving and Joe "Jellybean" Bryant; football greats Randall Cunningham and Terrell Owens; CBS Sportscaster Rich Perez; and many more… He had met Sammy Davis Jr., Dizzy Gillespie, and Miles Davis. Josh met all kinds of people. This man of short stature was an unassuming man. Josh got along with everyone. I've been told by everybody that Josh "was always polite."

Did you know Josh had a small church scene appearance with hat in the 2001 movie *Boycott*?

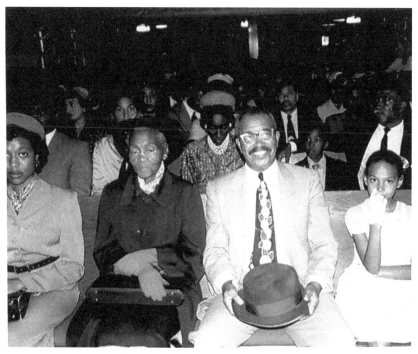

Josh Culbreath church scene with hat in Boycott
movie. Photo courtesy: Cynthia Culbreath

*****

We need to start somewhere, so here we are how it all started at the beginning of it all with Josh telling his story.

"I was born and reared in Norristown."

Joshua "Josh" Culbreath was born and raised in Norristown, Pennsylvania, to parents Jesse and Annabelle (neé Satterwhite) Culbreath on September 14, 1932. He arrived in the world chosen as an Olympian champion. He was conceived by fate. The halo of the Olympic rings begins to shadow his future journeys around the world. Who would have ever thought on that day an Olympian legend born *Straight Outta* of Norristown, Pennsylvania, was about to set history at the Melbourne, Australia Olympic Games of 1956 and at the Pan American Games? The chronological events of his predetermined life and future are amazing. Makes you wonder if he mystically voyaged from the times of Mt. Olympus, casting as the embodiment of mythical Greek god Hermes, known as the fastest of all gods and wears winged shoes.

"Norristown was a city with an international flair," was the way track icon Josh Culbreath describes the town when he recalls his youth. Growing up, Josh had many memories way back in the day. The Borough of Norristown was a beautiful little town and a thriving place. He always acknowledges, "This was my place of birth, and this is a place that I love to talk about and let people know where I'm from all over the world."

In his early childhood years, Josh reflects on his school days as a young boy growing up in Norristown. Due to overcrowding, Josh attended three different elementary schools. Josh grew up in the East End of Norristown. His address was 725 Walnut Street, and a few doors down, at 713, was legendary Los Angeles Dodgers manager Tommy LaSorda. That is unbelievable! A surreal encounter of two superstar greatness growing up as neighbors in the same neighborhood; what are the chances of that? Josh used to eat at LaSorda's house. Tommy LaSorda spent his youth running the streets of the East End with the likes of Josh and Jimmy Smith. While he was known for his years in baseball and taking Team USA to a gold medal in the 2000 Olympic Games in Sydney, Australia—beating a Cuban team that had won gold at the previous Olympic Games—LaSorda also has spent a lifetime giving back to communities throughout the nation and the world.

Josh went to Washington Elementary School in his first grade located up the hill between Oak and Marshall Streets. Later, Josh and his family moved to 822 Smith Street. Down the street from Josh was another great athlete by the name of Clarence Smith. His brother was the number one progressive jazz organist in the world, Jimmy Smith, whose boss playing skills on the Hammond B-3 organ with the companion sound of the Leslie speaker rocked the popular 1958 album *The Sermon!*, 1960s wicked rendition "A Night in Tunisia" on album *Crazy! Baby*, and 1962's biggest hit, "Walk on the Wild Side" on album *Bashin'*. Later, Jimmy influenced bands and musical artists. Jimmy also recorded and can be heard on Michael Jackson's title track the *Bad* album, as well as the Beastie Boys famously sampling funky beats of Jimmy's classic song hit "Root Down"—and saluted Smith in the lyrics—on their track of the same name, dropped in 1994 from the *Ill Communication* album. A head-nodder, that fierce drum beat and instrumentals on "Root Down" is wicked! The incredible Jimmy Smith, a master of the Hammond B-3, was Adam "MCA" Yauch's "man," and he wanted to "give 'em a pound," for simple enough reasons.

"There was this Jimmy Smith record lying around," Adam Yauch explains in the excellent liner notes to Beasties anthology, *The Sounds of Science.* "We used to listen to it all the time while we played basketball. The title track, 'Root Down,' was ridiculous. I remember thinking, 'How can a groove be this nice?' It was the type of music that you hear, and it immediately improves your game... Someone came up with the idea of looping up big parts of it and making a song over his groove. Basically, just rhyming over his song without any other beats. And that's what we did."

Yes, Josh even grew up in the neighborhood with this accomplished great jazz-funk musical genius!

Other than track and field, Josh played other sports he enjoyed besides just running the races he was known for. Josh and Clarence played basketball together at Rittenhouse Junior High School under Coach Jim Couglin. Their basketball team was undefeated in 1948. A neighbor and longtime friend of Culbreath was Charlie Blockson. Josh and Charlie played high school football together. "Some people think I was a better football player than I was a runner," Culbreath said.

Charlie was a fullback and track star at Penn State in the 1950s. Charlie played football with Lenny Moore and Rosie Greer. Like Culbreath, Blockson was a multisport athlete. Blockson ran the lead leg in the mile relay, Joseph Hadrick was second, Culbreath ran third, and John Willie Spearman ran the anchor. "We won it two years in a row, and we had a shot putter leading off," Culbreath said of Blockson.

A member of the Penn State football Hall of Fame, Blockson went on to become a prominent author and nationally renowned historian specializing in Afro-American history and is a world-renowned expert on the Civil War Era Underground Railroad. "He was collecting artifacts when he was eight and nine years old," Culbreath said. "People thought that he was crazy back then, but I had faith in him." The Temple University Library has a special section housing his enormous collection of Afro-American books, literature, and artifacts.

Josh was also an active member in other high school activities such as baseball, football, Sports Club, and Christmas Pageant. "So, in that neighborhood there were quite a few people that we felt was quite a thing to have Tommy LaSorda made it in athletics, and I running, along with Jimmy Smith as a number one jazz organist in the world." Culbreath said that he learned a lot from the guys he hung out with as a child, including Tommy LaSorda, Charles Blockson, and Jimmy Smith. Josh goes on to say he had attended Hancock Elementary School until the sixth grade, which was near the Carver Community Center and historical Ebenezer Church. After Hancock, Josh went on to attend Rittenhouse. He mentioned there were two junior high schools, Rittenhouse and Stewart. At Rittenhouse, Josh spent his time there and that is where he started doing his interest in sports—from playing basketball, to football, and finally his fame in track and field.

Culbreath (bottom right) on the JV Basketball team,
Spice Yearbook 1949, HSMC Collection

Culbreath (top left) on the JV Football team, Spice
Yearbook 1949, HSMC Collection

*****

Whether you are an athlete, a person who follows sports, a person from different parts of the state or world, or a neighboring Norristown resident, when you hear Culbreath, everyone mentions "living legend" Olympian Josh Culbreath. Everybody has heard about and has followed Josh's journey and all his accomplishments. Everybody knows he was an athlete who ran in the Olympics of 1956. People still ask about him and speak about him with passion. Through his years, Josh was in the media spotlight and countless times when asked to explain his thoughts on entering the Olympics and the things what he did there. Josh replied,

> "Well, first of all, it's about how you got there. Because I was like any other kid growing up. I was interested in sports. I grew up on Walnut Street, between Oak and Marshall in an interracial neighborhood. We had so many different nationalities on our block. It was a wonderful environment in which we grew. We knew who the people were in our neighborhood. At Chestnut and Arch, they called it Frog Hollow. Across the street from my home, at the corner of Marshall and Chestnut, was Holy Savior School. We learned our skills there. We had "no ickling" about who was going to be whom? We just had a lot of fun. If we got a baseball, we beat it to death until it became like a golf ball. The cover was gone and what you had was a golf ball. We taped it up and beat it to death some more with a stick if we didn't have a bat. We played marbles on the sidewalk because there was no pavement next to the school. Therefore, we had skills about many things. They don't do those things anything more. They don't shoot marbles, and they don't have other things we used to do. Kids today do not know how to improvise with pretty much anything to play sports such as "hanging up the

wire on a phone pole." Children in Norristown need to learn how to be more involved in organizations such as East Norriton Girls Athletic Association (ENGAA) and Norristown Little League. These are things which are destiny for people because kids don't know what they want to do until they are exposed to things. If you have the sports that are there, you have a choice, and you having the choice to do what you want providing you can do it well enough; and you took those skills that you had and you can make them work for you by going to college free. Therefore, you find out you go to camps now that you have that we didn't have when we were children, and they are specialized in sports and it's an investment. Well, we invested in ourselves. I didn't want to see my mother and father work like that, being the youngest, to pay for me to go to college. So, I said, "I have to do something" and I did. I said, "If I can run that fast, I can get a free education," and therefore, I took it upon myself to run, train and to become focused on learning.

We used to form a group Tommy LaSorda and his youngest brother Joey we called "Smokey;" there were five brothers including Eddie, Harry, Morris and I had one, Ernest ("Ernie"). We go down to Main Street and DeKalb, and they had supermarkets. There was Marshall and DeKalb Streets there was a fish market, and the Acme was next to it. So we go and ask people, now Tommy and my brother would be like the overseer's and we would have to ask people "would you like to take your order" that meant that they came out with their bags and we would carry their bags or we made a wagon that we put together and the brothers were like supervisors and tell us to carry them. Smokey and myself and Tommy and my brother were the guys that would follow behind us, and then tell us how much it costs; and then if they were 10 cents or a nickel or a quarter to carry their groceries—you know, to their homes. We never knew what kind of money we made. But that was what they were about "big brothers" in those days. But you had to do something constructive if you couldn't find something to do that was worthwhile. In the meantime, we were having a lot of sports. We were doing baseball. We took that stick (not a bat, a stick) and we had a basket that we used to put on a telephone pole and we used a little tennis ball and we developed skills this way. We were doing something constantly outside of school or we tried to find something to keep us occupied. Growing up in Norristown there were a lot of things. At Chestnut and Arch they called it Frog Hollow. We had a field called Blue Mill Field. It was an area that was a dead end at High Street and did not have any homes during those times. Blue Mill Field was on the corner of Violet and Basin Streets. There we played baseball. It was wonderful growing up. We had imagination. East End was a bunch of proud people. LaSorda used to say, "Our fathers never had to come to City Hall for us."

If you were to ask who Josh's biggest inspiration throughout his career as an athlete, Josh would say,

There were a lot of them. Just like any other child growing up, we watched sports, and we always wanted to emulate people. We had a hero like in any sport because when I was growing

up, we used the word *colored*. Colored guys, you
know, if they were selected for something it was a
big thing because we being a minority. But it was
a way with Tommy like their father and so forth
were born in Sicily, and they came to America,
and it was a new thing for him as well. We knew
what it was like and so forth being a part of being
said a minority. But we made a difference because
of the way we grew up, because we only knew
what we had a thing that in the neighborhood,
you didn't come there into our territory and
act like a fool. Therefore, we didn't get into any
fights like that. We had a club called LAM. It was
down on Main and Arch Street. We learned the
skills for boxing. I was a boxer, my brother was a
boxer, Tommy tried to box. We only had in elementary school a Field Day and that was once a
year. We always go to Roosevelt Field which was
"a big thing for the elementary schools because
we had quite a few of them in Norristown at that
time." Roosevelt Field had been used in the past
by district athletic teams and home field to The
Norristown Area School District Eagles football
team. So as we ventured at the Field Day, we
didn't know what we were doing, and we just ran
a relay and that was the size of it until we got in
to junior high school.

What encouraged Josh to run track was "because most of the
time if we got into any kind of trouble in doing something that we
shouldn't be doing, we ran! We ran away from the problem, not to it.
But the thing is we were very most mischievous like most of the kids.
It was growing up. We didn't have any organized sports. We had a
lot of fun. Harking back on our early lives playing ball in the street

Tommy and I will always say, 'But we never forgot where we came from. We share an expression, 'We were so poor that we didn't even know we were poor.'"

*****

4

Barefoot on the Cinder Track

Josh's running days all started at Rittenhouse School before his notable track career took off in college. The Field Day was the only time he was exposed to running during that one day at Roosevelt Field. Normally, it was a relay and that's where everything had begun because it was organized sports. There were two junior high schools, Stewart and Rittenhouse. It was just wonderful because those schools played a major role in the development for a lot of the neighborhood kids and for Josh who were interested in playing sports; and because it put Josh in a situation that he would learn about more people and then have a greater interest to go to college. Culbreath began running the hurdles in high school, and in 1951, during his senior year, he won the PIAA state championship in the 200-yard hurdles. By the end of the year, he was the nation's tenth fastest high school runner for the event.

Josh went to college and attended Morgan State in Baltimore. At Morgan, he majored in political science and received his bachelor of arts degree and has a master of arts and education from Temple University. Josh also attended University of Colorado Law School from 1955–1956. It was strange how Josh got to college because he did not want to see his father—who worked at Alan Wood Steel Company for thirty-eight years—working. Josh was the youngest of five children—three sisters and one brother. He did not want his mother to be working like she did or his father. So Josh said if he didn't get a scholarship, he wasn't going to be going to school. But Josh found out that he had a talent. Then, it was running. Josh found out that you can go to school for free if his grades were there. So he happened to be an honor student which helped a great deal. But Rittenhouse is where it had begun with a great man by the name of Mr. Vincent Farina.

Culbreath was always undersized, acknowledging that he was not bestowed with the height of his six-foot father. But under the tutelage of Vince Farina, history teacher and track coach at the Rittenhouse Junior High School, the five-foot-seven Culbreath learned of his talent in track and field. Although he played football and basketball at Norristown (Pennsylvania) High School, Josh says he "wanted to excel at something, and I was too small for the major sports. So, I looked around for a sport that nobody wanted to do—the hurdles in track and field. Hurdling is complicated, requiring precision, concentration, and fortitude. You have to get your steps perfect. If you clip a hurdle you lose six inches from your stride. When you try to compensate, 'rigor mortis' sets in."

After WW2, Mr. Farina watched Josh. Josh was a very mischievous individual, but Mr. Farina saw something in him that a lot of people didn't see. Josh had some type of ability, and Mr. Farina tried to encourage Josh and he did. Mr. Farina was Josh's track coach for a while. Mr. Abraham Burger who taught geography who lived across the street from Rittenhouse also was a track coach, being Josh's first track coach in junior high school. As he began to recall his days growing up in Norristown, Culbreath remembered:

> Norristown is where it all began to get to Melbourne. Rittenhouse Junior High School is where it actually started. We're talking about the '40s now. I was on the track team when I was in seventh grade. I couldn't buy a race. I was on the eighty-five-pound team. I was the fifth guy on the wheel. They wanted to win, but they didn't think they could win with me. Mr. Burger said they were going to use Inky Wagner. His name was Robert, but his nickname was Inky. Inky wanted to give me the medal he won the year

before. I told him I didn't want his, I wanted my own.

But Mr. Farina was the one that inspired Josh to continue to run and to study; and Josh was very fortunate. "I learned an awful lot from him, and it stuck with me," Culbreath said. Josh was a good student, and "I taught myself how to run hurdles." But that all began because of a guy named Clarence Smith. He's gone now, but Clarence was one of the greatest athletes who came out of Norristown High School. That was Jimmy Smith's (The Organist) younger brother. Josh and Clarence were very, very close. Josh wanted Clarence to go to college, but he had other things he wanted to do. So Josh pursued his efforts. Josh did not want his parents to work to pay for him to go to school. So Josh had a talent, so he said, "If I run fast enough, I can get a scholarship." Josh had several. Thus, for those reasons, after Rittenhouse, Josh had done won the districts and everything. He had taught himself how to run the hurdles. But Josh was involved in a lot of other things such as being a pole vaulter and long jumper. It wasn't long before Culbreath's love affair with the hurdles began to take root:

> We had a little strip in the back of Rittenhouse. It was cinder. I taught myself how to run. No one taught me. I taught myself. By the time I was in eighth grade, I became very versatile. I was running the hurdles in a meet, but yet I won the pole vault. I had an old bamboo pole. We would land on shavings. We didn't have the big nice soft place to land that they have today.

Culbreath didn't run on the track team his first year in high school because the coach wanted him to compete in the pole vault. He said he wanted to run the hurdles and actually defeated the team's top runners in an impromptu race that he ran barefoot, but the coach had made up his mind.

Culbreath said that when he returned to the team the next year, the coach called him over and said he wanted him to stay on the team that year. "My senior year, I said I wasn't going to let anyone get close to me," Culbreath recalled. "I think I ran the second fastest time in the country for the two-hundred-yard low hurdles. May 19, 1951, I hit the ninth hurdle, rolled over, and then high-jumped over the tenth hurdle and still took third place. If hadn't hit that ninth hurdle, I probably would have set a record."

Josh's hard work, training, and determination was taking off as a star track-and-field athlete—he was a state high school champion and was a three-time national 440-yard hurdles champion, setting a world record in that event. At Norristown Area High School, Culbreath won the PIAA state championship in the 200-yard hurdles. "It's something that every athlete experience when you have found out you have some talent and you go for what's out there," Culbreath said.

Josh trained hard and made a shoeless sacrifice. "I made sacrifices and trained hard, but I loved to run. I felt free, with no one on the track except me. My edge consisted of combining the natural speed of a sprinter with developing the stride of a six-footer," he says.

He ran barefoot on the cinder track as a sophomore in high school because he couldn't afford track shoes. Yet he still beat all the juniors and seniors. In his senior year, he captured the state crown in the low hurdles after finishing second the year before.

Josh was the only sibling in his family that ran track. Being the youngest of five, he had three sisters and one brother. Josh's brother, Ernest, was quite a standout boxer. He went to the Golden Gloves. He got that far. After Ernest left school, he went and joined the Navy. He caught a portion of the Second World War coming out of Indy. Two of Josh's sisters went to college. They became dental hygienists. All three of his sisters married dentists—all three. That was something else. Josh thought he wanted to be a lawyer, but other things came around. However, his education was first. Morgan State offered him a scholarship, and he accepted. He had scholarship offers galore but wound up at Morgan in 1951 at the insistence of his sister, who was impressed by the photos of Morgan track stars Art Bragg, George Rhoden, and Sam La Beach that she had seen in Ebony magazine.

"She called Morgan's coach, Eddie Hurt, for an interview," Culbreath said. "I went to get her off my back." That's where Josh became who he is today, he believes, because he had a great inspirational coach by the name of Eddie P. Hurt. Morgan State had a thousand students there at that time. Josh fondly reflects, "My coach was an extraordinary man. His name was Coach Eddie P. Hurt. He was a very tiny man. He weighed maybe about 100 pounds. A hundred and fifty pounds would be too much for him. But he had coached a lot of guys and what he did made the history books. He made history."

Running the race, Josh's legacy begins in the whirlwind of track and field. Josh Culbreath first took hurdling seriously when he was attending Morgan State and won the AAU in 1953, 1954, and 1955. Josh Culbreath was an all-American national hurdling champion at Morgan State University in Baltimore. Kudos to Josh's sister, the next chapter tells the story how it all began with Josh's monumental track career at Morgan State as "The Flying Four."

*****

5

It Doesn't *Hurt* at Morgan State

Let The Games Begin—Josh's Legacy Track Beginnings at Morgan State College:

He turned us into men…
                    —Dr. Josh Culbreath ('55)

Edward Hurt

Inducted: 1975, coach

Born: February 12, 1900 - Brookneal, Virginia
Deceased: March 24, 1989

A long-time athletic administrator at Morgan State College in Baltimore, Maryland, Edward "Ed" Hurt served as the school's athletic director, head football coach, and head track coach during his forty-year tenure beginning in 1929. His football teams won fifty-four straight games, and his track teams were just as awesome with such world-class athletes as George Rhoden, Elmore Harris, and Art Bragg among his charges. In all, Morgan State athletes won eight national collegiate individual titles and twelve National AAU championships under his tutelage. A graduate of Howard University, Hurt became head track coach at Morgan State in 1929 and built the school into a national power. He was on the coaching staffs at both the 1959 Pan American Games and the 1964 Olympic Games.

Education
Undergraduate: Howard (Washington, DC)

Occupations
Coach
Athletic director

Cousin Josh and Morgan State University's Track and Field Teams are recognized and acknowledged in a book written by Arthur

R. Ashe, Jr., *A Hard Road to Glory: A History of the African-American Athlete Since 1946*. In Mr. Ashe's book, he states the following:

- In June 1950, the first National AAU meet held at a Black school was at Morgan State College.
- *1956: The XVIth Olympiad at Melbourne, Australia*—Josh Culbreath of Morgan State captured a bronze in the 400-meter hurdles. Culbreath was AAU champion in 1953–55. In 1957 at Oslo, Norway, he set a world record of 50.5 seconds in the 440-yard hurdles. He was Black America's first premier intermediate hurdler.

Edward "Eddie" P. Hurt became the head track coach at Morgan State College in 1929. When the CIAA conference still stood for "Colored Intercollegiate Athletic Association," Coach Hurt reportedly said, "We had a heck of a problem getting started; there is no question about that." At that time, the small Black colleges competed with one another and received little national attention. Hurt said, "It was hard to get recognition, especially in track and field, and we just never had a chance to compete against the better schools. When we first started trying to improve our program, nobody knew we were alive."

Coach Hurt started developing a premier program developing athletes and character. He built Morgan State into a power dynasty. In 1948, Coach Eddie P. Hurt, put together a relay team of Sam LaBeach, John Crooms, William "Bill" Brown, and Bob Tyler. The team won the Class B Mile Relay Championship of America race at the Penn Relays. Their time was just as fast as the winning time for the Class A race won by New York University. The following year, Morgan was invited to compete in the Class A race against the best in the country.

Realizing that Morgan had the makings of greatness, Coach Hurt asked Samuel LaBeach if there were any other great runners in Jamaica that would be interested in attending Morgan.

LaBeach gave the name of his friend, George Rhoden.

In 1949, history was made when the foursome of Samuel LaBeach, Bob Tyler, Bill Brown, and George Rhoden broke the Penn Relay record, but was disqualified on a disputable charge.

By 1950, Morgan State's track team was drawing national and international attention due to the impressive showing at the Penn Relays. The same group came back in 1950 and broke the Class A Mile Relay Championship of America race record at the Penn Relays that stood for fifty-six years. Many elite track athletes, attracted by Morgan's increasing notoriety, came to the school because of the popularity of its track team during that era. The team continued to win at the prestigious Melrose Games in New York City and other meets throughout the country. The Historic Four ran a 3:09.4 at the Los Angeles Coliseum Relays, which was two seconds off the World Record. Morgan State College gained widespread recognition. *Sports Illustrated, Time* Magazine, *Ebony Magazine* and the *Afro-American Newspaper* featured the team in their publications.

The foursome became goodwill ambassadors for Morgan State College both nationally and internationally.

During the 1950s, Coach Edward P. Hurt's freshman mile relay team also won at the Penn Relays. Coach Hurt also had a cadre of sprinters, all capable of running the 100 in 9.6 seconds and below. Examples of some of these sprinters, in addition to Art Bragg and others mentioned before were Ken Kave, Dickie Waters, Paul Winder, Byron LaBeach, Lawrence Griffin, Linwood Morton, Bobby Gordon, and many others.

Because of the popularity of this outstanding team, many great sprinters were attracted to Morgan. Art Bragg won the 100-yard dash at the 1952 and 1953 Penn Relays. Josh Culbreath won the 400-meter hurdles at the Penn Relays in 1953, 1954, and 1955. Robert McMurry was the NCAA 400-yard champion and ran a 45.8 at the Penn Relays. Bob Barksdale won the high jump in 1955 and 1956, while George Dennis tied Barksdale in 1955 and won in 1957. Lance Thompson won the Penn Relays Long Jump in 1952.

Due to Morgan's outstanding track-and-field achievements, the school was awarded the opportunity to host the national AAU Relay Championship of America. Morgan won the 1600 Relay in a time of 3:09.7—just one and five tenths of a second off the world mark set by a United States All-Star team in the 1932 Olympics. Dan Ferris, Executive Secretary of the Amateur Athletics Union (AAU) and guardian angel of track and field in the US gave high praises to the Morgan Bear Relay team.

A quote from an article in the *Afro-American Newspaper* in 1950 stated, "Dan Ferris was among the 3,500 spectators that witnessed the first championship meet on a Historic Black College campus and told the *Afro* reporter, 'Coach Hurt and his Morgan associates cannot be praised enough for the work they have done here. That is an excellent aggregation. It matches anything I have ever seen representing a college in nearly 40 years of track.'"

Coach Hurt's presence was legionary, players wanted to go the extra mile, they didn't want to let him down. He was a father figure to the athletes. He and "Mom Hurt"—his wife, G. Beatrice Hurt—took the kids into their home during non-competition times. His influence is why guys went to Morgan because Coach considered the athletes his kids. You can still hear him say, "Run from there at the 100 mark." Hurt was awarded with many honors, including in 1975, he was the first Black coach inducted to the USA Track and Field Hall of Fame.

Death and Legacy

Hurt died on March 24, 1989. His memorial service was held one week later on the campus of Morgan State University. His interment was completed at the Arbutus Memorial Park in southwest Baltimore County, Maryland. Hurt was survived by his wife, Beatrice, one brother and three sisters. In addition to the Hurt Gymnasium, named in his honor in 1952, a scholarship fund was established in the name of Edward and Beatrice Hurt and the "Eddie Hurt Invitational Track Meet" is held annually at the university.

*****

The Story of Geraldine Beatrice "Mom Bea" Reid Hurt

While Eddie was running the successful stadium effort, Bea became the surrogate mother of the scores of youths who were away from their homes for the first time. The Hurt on-campus home was turned in to a WELCOME haven.

She got word out that any young student who was experiencing lonesome problems could drop in for a visit. As a consequence, Mrs. Geraldine Beatrice (Reid) Hurt became "Mom."

She sewed on buttons, closed holes in socks, and occasionally cooked a warm breakfast for kids who obviously were not relishing the dining hall meals that are typical of those prepared under normal college conditions. Eddie had the Morgan sports effort thriving.

"Mom" supplied the wherewithal—a bounty of future world-class stars.

George Rhoden, anchor on a two-time Penn Relays foursome and himself, a medal winner in the 1952 Olympic Games, formerly headed a Medical Center in Green Valley, California.

Bob Brown, center and captain of teams in 1955–56, was a popular dentist in Indiana; Willie Lanier captained and gained line-backer status with the NFL Kansas City Chiefs.

Bighouse Gaines, retired athletic director at Winston State University and a member of the Basketball Hall of Fame. Josh Culbreath, another Olympian, was athletic director at Morehouse College. Sam LaBeach, Byron LaBeach, Bill Taylor, etc., in Morgan's halcyon years in track, and Roy Cragway was football stardom.

Meanwhile, a story within a story was in progress.

Culbreath let it be known that he was Bea's favorite because she invited him to ride with her at the 1999 homecoming parade.

"No way," screamed Gaines. She chose him to avoid the loneliness on campus in an earlier Christmas holiday break by picking him to drive her and Eddie to Toledo, Ohio, where he was to be honored.

"On our return trip," says Bighouse, "we ran in to a storm at Wheeling, West Virginia, and had to book into a hotel. I was treated overnight first class, and we resumed the journey the next morning."

Neither, however, gave thought to Cragway, who made no claims to favoritism. Yet it was he to whom she gave her own nod—a place in her family—allowing and encouraging him in his pursuit to marry her niece, "Billie."

Mrs. Hurt passed away on December 28, 2003. She was 101 years old.

Mrs. Hurt was Morgan's "Mom," and she left a rich legacy. She nurtured and inspired many for whom her memory will never fade. She was Morgan State University's oldest living graduate, and the apron strings behind Morgan's sports program.

Geraldine Beatrice Reid Hurt was a graduate of the Class of 1931, was trained as an educator and in home economics, was the widow of Morgan's legendary coach Eddie P. Hurt who died in 1989. As the wife of the athletic director and football coach, Mrs. Hurt was the needle and thread who patched her giving generosity known by scores of Morgan athletes as "Mom" or "Mother Hurt." Years after they graduated from Morgan, former athletes still continued to visit her.

According to Nina Dobson Hopkins ('78), who is director of the Counseling Center at Morgan and a longtime friend of Mrs. Hurt, her big heart extended to athletes of other schools as well. During the time of segregation, a Virginia football team was in Baltimore to play Morgan right around Thanksgiving, but there was no restaurant that would serve them food on Thanksgiving Day. "She had her husband go get them and bring them all to her house for a home-cooked meal," Mrs. Hopkins said. Mrs. Hurt told Mrs. Hopkins that she remembered the days when there was no running water at the Morgan campus, and the only water came from a well.

"I was shocked," said Mrs. Hopkins.

During World War II, Mrs. Hurt used to write 50 to 100 letters a week to Morgan students who were drafted or enlisted. "She did it by herself, not even with a committee," explained Mrs. Hopkins, "because she wanted to make sure they had mail from home."

Those Morgan athletes she nurtured over the years included Clarence E. "Bighouse" Gaines, who was named an all-American football player and was elected to the College Basketball Hall of Fame for his long and successful career as coach and athletic director at Winston-Salem State University. Others included running back Otis Troupe, Roy Cragway; basketball legends such as "Rap" Wheatley, Powell Sheffy, "Sugar" Cain, and "Boo" Brown; runners like Josh Culbreath, who went on to became the athletic director at Morehouse College in Atlanta, Bob Tyler, Art Bragg, Sam and Byron LaBeach, and 1952 Olympics 400-meter gold medalist, George Rhoden.

Bea Hurt was a member of the Morgan Women, the Alpha Delta Chapter of Alpha Kappa Alpha sorority. She was also an avid bridge player and played every Saturday night with a group known as the Bridgettes.

Mrs. Hopkins said that Mrs. Hurt was very health conscious and mixed up various ingredients into concoctions to cure whatever was ailing her or her friends. "I was almost afraid to tell her if I didn't feel well, because she'd make up some concoction. She even attributed her incredible memory to some concoction she took which had garlic and herbs in it."

She was a co-founder of the Morgan University Women (MUW), initially formed as a group of wives of Morgan faculty, but eventually growing to include women who worked on campus. The MUW found coats for students who didn't have any, helped the faculty prepare for a lecture, and generally took care of matters around the campus.

Truly, Mrs. Hurt was an amazing, incredible, remarkable woman.

Coach Edward P. Hurt and Bea Hurt vacation during the 1950s.

*****

WE ARE THE CHAMPIONS—FLYING FOUR TRACK TEAM

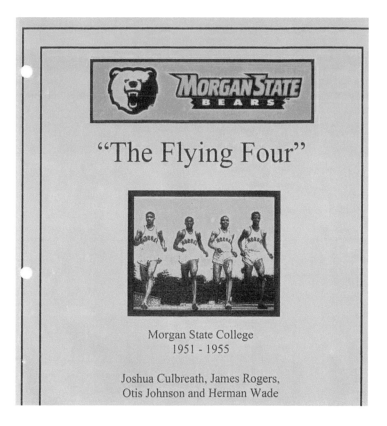

"The Flying Four"

Morgan State College
1951 - 1955

Joshua Culbreath, James Rogers,
Otis Johnson and Herman Wade

In 1951, Coach Hurt recruited James Rogers, Otis "Jet" Rogers, Herman Wade, and Joshua Culbreath. Culbreath was an important cog in the Morgan State relay teams which came to prominence in the 1950s. Iconic and pioneering African-American sportswriter Sam Lacy, who was the first black member of the Baseball Writers Association of America, dubbed the team "The Flying Four" and "The Speed Merchants." In 1953, The Flying Four went on to break the Central Intercollegiate Athletic Association (CIAA) Mile Relay mark set by their 1950 predecessors, Morgan's Historic Four, with a new time 3:11:3. Morgan won the Penn Relays' 4x100 relay four years in a row from 1953 to 1956 and also won the 4x220 relay in 1953. During their four seasons, this foursome won thirteen national championships, twenty-six major titles, and three records. The Flying Four is the only team that ever won the national AAU Championship three years in a row with the same team members. This team set a new record each year in New York and won five relay titles at Penn Relays Championship of America. They won meets at Boston Garden, Madison Square Garden, Boston Athletic Association, Knights of Columbus, Milrose Games, New York Athletic Club Championship, the Baltimore Amateur Athletic games, the Philadelphia Inquirer Games, and the Washington Evening Star Games.

They were inducted into the Morgan State University Athletic Hall of Fame in 1985 and the CIAA Athletic Hall of Fame in 2013.

"They called us 'The Flying Four,' and we kicked everyone's butt," Culbreath said. "We won every championship from Madison Square Garden to the Boston Garden."

FLYING 1-2-3-4

Morgan State's Quartet: Herman Wade, Otis "Jet" Johnson, Jimmy Rogers and Josh Culbreath

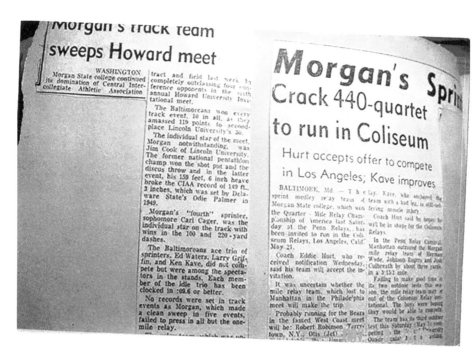

Photo courtesy: Jimmy and Brenda Rogers

Cousin Josh was always known to say in his competing events, "They called us 'The Flying Four,' and we kicked everyone's butt." On March 9, 2021, I had the pleasure meeting with Morgan State's Flying Four Jimmy Rogers and his beautiful wife, Brenda. According to Jimmy Rogers when I had met with him, he told me no, it was the "A-word." LoL!

James "Jimmy" Rogers, No. 3

James 'Jimmy' Rogers, born and raised in Blakenburg, West Coast Demerara, Republic of Guyana, attended high school in Georgetown, Republic of Guyana where he excelled in running on a grass track. In 1949, Rogers won the 100, 200, 400 and 880 yards in the National Championship of Guyana. In the 400, he ran forty-nine seconds, the fastest ever in the history of that event. Rogers was put on the USA radar when he competed against the US Team members Herbert McKenley and George Guida in the Relay Carnival in Guyana. In the 400, Rogers was leading 200 yards into the race when the referee disqualified him, and the favored McKenley went on to victory. Impressed with Rogers showing, McKenley, from Jamaica running for US Team, told Rogers that he should consider running in the States.

McKenley told Coach Eddie Hurt, and Rogers later became the second Guyanese to be recruited to run in US. Rogers ran varsity track for Morgan State for four years (1951–1955), where he was the recipient of many track honors. He was a member of the "Flying Four" Mile Relay Team for four years (1951–1955), where he ran third leg all third years. Rogers, along with Jet Johnson, won the Penn Relays 4x100 Relay (third leg) three years straight in 1953, 1954, and 1955, and the cup was then retired for that event. They also won the 4x220 Relay in 1953 at the Penn Relays. In addition, Rogers was the CIAA 440-yard Champion (1953–1955). Rogers was a member of the American team that traveled to Norway, Denmark, Sweden, and Finland in 1953.

Rogers was a member of winning relay teams in the 440 and 880 (1952–1955). Rogers ran third leg on the National Mile Relay Indoor Team in 1954 and 1955 helping his team win national prominence. While at Morgan, Rogers became a member of the Alpha Phi Alpha fraternity and the Beta Kappa Chi honorary science fraternity. During his undergraduate years, he held the position of president of the Chemistry Club in 1955 and the International Club in 1954 and 1955. Rogers graduated with a BS degree in Chemistry, went on to Meharry Medical College, and he is now a retired physician of urology. Dr. Rogers is an active member of the Alpha Phi Alpha Fraternity Philly Alumni Association and is a lifetime member of Morgan's "M" Club. Dr. Rogers is married to Dr. Brenda Rogers, and they reside in the Philadelphia area. They are the parents of James Rogers II, Mary Rogers, Dr. Marissa Rogers, Marc W. Rogers, the late Jackie Rogers, and have six grandchildren.

Did you know? Jimmy came over to Morgan State from British Guyana, South America, on a full track scholarship. Coach Eddie Hurt heard about Jimmy's running talents and said, "If you can get him, we will take you." In two weeks, Jimmy arrived at Morgan State and was established as one of the Flying Four. Although Jimmy was concerned about segregation in the US, he was encouraged by his parents to pursue his education in the United States. Jimmy's mom told him, "You came to America to get an education, not to tell the people how to run their country."

Otis "Jet" Johnson, No. 2

Otis "Jet" Johnson, born and raised in Philadelphia, Pennsylvania, graduated from Benjamin Franklin High School in 1951 where he was 1951 Philadelphia City Champion in the 100-yard dash and the 220-yard dash. Johnson was captain of both the football and track teams and earned a full scholarship to Morgan State for both sports. Johnson ran varsity track for Morgan State for four years (1951–1955) and was a member of the varsity football team for two years (1951–1955). He was a member of the "Flying Four" Mile Relay Team for four years (1951–1955) when he ran second leg all four years.

They won the Penn Relays' 4x110 Relay three years straight in 1953, 1954, and 1955 and retired the cup for that event (second leg). They also won the 4x220 Relay in 1953 at the Penn Relays. Also, Johnson was a record holder of the sixty-yard dash at the Indoor Baltimore Olympic Club Meet three years in a row, and he was the sixty-yard dash Champion—South Atlantic Indoors, of which the record remains standing.

Legionary Track Coach George Eastment, Manhattan University of New York, once said that Johnson is "the best second leg man in the history of the Mile Relay Team" of his day. Johnson graduated Morgan State with a BS in health, physical education, and recreation. After college, Johnson was a member of the All-Army Track Team that toured the country. Johnson had a thirty-nine-year career with the federal government.

Johnson is a lifetime member of Morgan's "M" Club. In retirement, Johnson had bit parts in the HBO films *Boycott* and *The Wire*; the box-office film *The Sentinel* (starring Michael Douglas); and the television show and movie *Homicide Life on the Streets*. Throughout his life, Johnson has dedicated his time to the community as a member of the Summer Aid Program. Johnson served as coordinator, working with high school students to encourage them to stay in school. Johnson is a consultant for Willingboro, New Jersey's Recreation Department and on staff at the school district for handicapped students. Johnson is an avid tennis player and instructor and also introduces tennis to children as young as three years old. He lives in Willingboro, New Jersey, with his wife, Lucille, and he is the father of two daughters, Lisa Johnson Dean and Lynn Johnson.

Herman "Bitsy" Wade, No. 1

Herman "Bitsy" Wade, born and raised in Pittsburgh, Pennsylvania, graduated from South Hills High School where he was a four-sport letterman. He won the City of Pittsburgh Basketball Championship as the starting guard. In track, Wade won the 400-yard run in 1949; and the high jump and the 120-high hurdles in 1950 and 1951. He was All-City elected in football. In baseball, he pitched on the high school team, and prior to college, he was talented enough to pitch on the old Negro Leagues' Homestead Grays team, just as the league folded from the impact of Jackie Robinson breaking the color barrier in the majors. In 2007, Wade was inducted into the South Hills High School Hall of Fame. Wade entered college and ran varsity track for Morgan State for four years (1951–1955). He was a member of the "Flying Four" Mile Relay Team for four years (1951–1955) where he ran leadoff leg all four years. Wade was CIAA Champion and won awards from the Philadelphia Inquirer and the Washington Star. Wade also competed in the 220, the hurdles, and the high jump. Wade lost only one race in three years of national competition and earned many individual awards. He qualified for Olympic Training in 1956 but elected not to compete. While at Morgan, Wade was on the Dean's List and became a member of the Alpha Phi Alpha Fraternity. Wade is a lifetime member of Morgan's "M" Club. After Morgan, Wade completed his graduate work at both North Carolina State, and at Fayetteville State University.

Wade retired from the United States Army with the rank of lieutenant colonel, after serving twenty years. During his tour of duty, Wade received three bronze stars, the Army commendation medal, and the Vietnamese Ranger citation. He was a Special Forces-trained Airborne Ranger Instructor. In 2004, Wade authored the biography of Coach Hurt, *Run from There*, in tribute to the influence of the national rise of the Black athlete in the 1940s and 1950s. Wade lives in Denton, Texas. He is the father of Air Force officer and commercial pilot Kevin (1957), musician and music instructor Anthony (1956), physical therapist Rhonda (1967–2001), and the grandfather of nine grandchildren.

Did you know? I had a conversation with Mr. Wade over the phone as he talked about his memorable Flying Four running days and his 1-2-3 teammates. He told me, "I was the lead off" and "Jimmy was the fastest man" of the team. I can understand that with Jimmy being no. 3, blowing their competitors in the dust, leading the way for Josh to breeze in an anchoring win for the entire team. Herman said before all their race against their competitors, Josh would always say to his 1-2-3 team, "Okay, guys, give me a little bit to work with." Mr. Wade told me a little laughable story about Charlie Jenkins: "We ran against Charlie. He made us sick. You got Charlie Jenkins chasing you," Wade said. The Flying Four proved their point—it doesn't *hurt* at Morgan State because Herman told me, "It took strength and energy to jump those hurdles."

Joshua "Josh" Culbreath, No. 4

Joshua Culbreath, born and raised in Norristown, Pennsylvania, graduated from Eisenhower Senior High School (now known as Norristown High School) where he began running the hurdles. By 1951, he was Pennsylvania's state high school champion in the low hurdles.

Culbreath ran varsity track for Morgan State Team for four years (1951–1955). He was a member of the "Flying Four" Mile Relay Team for four years (1951–1955) where he ran anchor leg all four years. He was the USA Outdoor champion in the 400-m hurdles for three consecutive years 1953, 1953, and 1955. He was a three-time winner of the event in the Penn Relays during the same years. After his graduation from Morgan, Culbreath served in the United States Marine Corps from 1956–1958, and he competed in the 1956 Summer Olympics in Melbourne, Australia, in the 400m hurdles, where he won the bronze medal. He won several military and NATO track-and-field medals, and he set the world records in the hurdles in 1956 and 1957.

Culbreath later earned a master of arts degree in education from Temple University. He later became the track coach at Central State University and the athletic director at Morehouse College. Culbreath served on the boards of many organizations, has been the recipient of many awards, such as Letter of Citation from the late President Eisenhower, and the mayor of his hometown proclaiming "Joshua Culbreath Day" in his honor for defeating the Russians in the USA vs. USSR first track event, which was held in Philadelphia in 1959. Culbreath was a lifetime member of Morgan's "M" Club and the Kappa Alpha Psi fraternity. Culbreath died on July 1, 2021, in Cincinnati, Ohio.

HALL OF FAME INDUCTION HONORS

- The Flying Four were inducted into the Morgan State University Athletic Hall of Fame in 1985

- The Flying Four were inducted into the CIAA Athletic Hall of Fame in 2013

THE FOURSOME ACHIEVEMENTS

- Won thirteen National Championships
- Credited with twenty-six Major Titles
- Three-time 4 x 440 (Mile Relay) CIAA Relay Champions 1952, 1953 and 1955
- Two-time 440 yard CIAA Champions 1953–1955
- National 4 x 440 AAU Relay Champions 1955
- National AAU Indoor Mile Relay in 1954
- Two-time Mid-Atlantic 4 x 440 AAU Champions 1954 and 1955
- USA Team—European Tour 1953
- Dominated AAU National Indoor Championships for three consecutive years 1952, 1953 and 1955
- Dominated the Indoor One-Mile Relay
- Went undefeated in winning seven (7) indoor meets a year for three years
- Averaged 3:18 0-2 for the mile relay—one of the fastest running times and ranked as one of the top five in the country
- Broke CIAA Indoor Record at 3:18:0 of the Morgan team who previously held the record at 3:19:0

Dr. Josh Culbreath ('55), a national and Pan-American 100-meter hurdling champion was proud of the athletic achievements and the skills he honed under the watchful eye of Coach Hurt. But Dr. Culbreath was most impressed with the impact Coach Hurt had on developing the character of him and scores of other athletes. Culbreath's photo is displayed in the exercise room of Hurt Gym. Living at his former residence in Las Vegas, Nevada, he was contacted and said, "He molded thousands of us. Remember, we were all so inexperienced. He turned us into men and gentlemen."

Josh strongly believed in the power of *kismet*, a meaning that leads to control what happens in the future. Josh believed kismet explains his achievements throughout his life. He recognized that "sport determined his destiny." A confident and self-motivated individual, he set seemingly insurmountable goals for himself. Josh did a lot of reading and one of the things he came across was he ran in many places, and one of this word comes from India, *kismet*, and it's like fate—fate what happens to one, what do you become, you become what you want to if you want to do something. You make up your mind to do it. You have a direction you want to go. You waver from nothing in order to achieve what it is that you have is that goal, and that's what he did and he believed in *kismet*. Josh learned from later years he went to India, and he learned more about India, but he was on the right trail and so forth, because he took many things from his learning of people and what have you, and it took him to another stage to another level and *kismet* was one of them and that's what he got there and if things were going to happen there were going to happen here and it did at Morgan State.

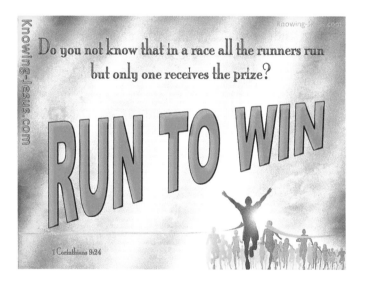

*****

6

There's a Thing Called Education

Josh has advice for student athletes of Norristown today. Josh said,

> Yes, there's a thing called education. You never want to get away from there. That is one of the things I was able to do. I came back to where I was born. Mr. Vincent Farina saw in me as a student when he came from WW2, and he saw me when I was getting ready to go to college. He taught me a lot. When I graduated, he asked me if when I came back to see him and to thank him for helping me and to guide me and to give me encouragement that was the kind of teacher he was. He became the Principal. Then, he went to Methacton and started Methacton School District as a superintendent. But that man inspired me to become whom I came today.

Josh shared the same advice to his own children when they pursued sports growing up. Josh said,

> Well, I had a son who became known as a long-distance cyclist. His name was Khaliq.

He did it because he wanted to do it. He and a buddy flew to California and they rode their bicycles from LA back to Delaware; from Maine to Florida; across Pennsylvania and across North Carolina. He was an active member of Suburban Cyclists Unlimited and The League of American Bicyclists. Sorrowfully in 2001, Khaliq lost his life when he was struck by an automobile while crossing a street to observe the cyclists racing in the Tour de France in Strasbourg, France.

Josh's other son Jahan went on to try and follow into his foot paths. Jahan is Josh's youngest son. He became a hurdler. He went on to Wissahickon High School, and he ran on a state championship team, indoor and outdoor, and he ran the hurdlers. So Jahan followed in his father's foot paths and he got scholarship and went to college. He also was inducted into the Hall of Fame with his college out in California. Josh was also inducted into the Hall of Fame by Morgan State in 1975. Father and son were also honored at the greatest sports festival in the world, The Penn Relays, one of the greatest relays in the world. "I got a big thrill running the Penn Relays where my father's name is on the Wall of Fame," he said. Jahan was an all-American 400-meter hurdler who set the school and conference records while competing in such prestigious meets as the Penn Relays outdoors in Philadelphia and indoors at the Melrose Games in Madison Square Garden in New York City. Jahan said, "He taught me everything I know about track." Jahan reflects his father was no joke when it came to training hard. Jahan tells a memorable story beginning his sophomore year in high school his dad got his sons up each morning at 4:00 a.m. to train on an indoor track made of dirt mixed with oil to hold down the dust.

"When you finished, you either had to put your sweats in a garbage bag or wash them right away because the smell was so bad," said Jahan.

"My dad loved 600-meter hurdle runs, and he'd always beat me the first 300 meters. At the end of 400 meters, the regular race distance, you are totally exhausted. But he'd tack on 200 more meters with five hurdles to get over. I'd get a short rest and then do repeats of the whole 600 meters.

"Dad always told me it takes three things to succeed in track and in life—focus, hard work, and sacrifice."

Also, Josh received a lot of recognitions in his hometown thanks to one of his mentorees Ernie Hadrick, who he had the pleasure of trying to coach and everything else. Josh said Ernie had a lot of potential and that is a satisfying thing there, and that would lead to him trying to go to college the same way that I did through sports.

*****

Josh talks about his proudest achievements, acknowledging there are several, but the thing is like each step has to be touched and climbed. In high school, it was state champion; in college, it was winning an American title. But before that, everything started when you get to the Penn Relays because it is the largest relay in the world. Close to home, Josh started right there running the 440-yard hurdles because he didn't even know what it was like. Josh was a freshman when he got third the first time he ran them, and it was three years after that he won them. There were only three of them in the history of the relays to win them three times in the row. There was a guy named Eugene Beatty in 1931, 1932, and 1933; and Charlie Moore from Cornell (1949, 1950, 1951). Still, there's three of them that have done that. Josh loved being one of the accomplishments. But each step that Josh got was a step further, and he just didn't know how high he was up until he did it. Josh became the American champion three years in a row; and then he became the Pan-American Games Champion in Mexico City. Josh trained without being acclimated to high altitudes. Josh went, and he was one of the first ones to run the 400-meter hurdles. "I won." Josh had not run the hurdles in a year. But Josh was American Champion three times, Pan American champion in Mexico once, and then the second one was in Chicago the Pan Am games and Josh defended his title. But that was a journey in itself because of the high altitude, and the games being held there in '68 found that it did a great deal of harm to a lot of people. But we learned a lot more from high altitude versus that rare air and distances; it took its toll. More about that story further in the reading.

Going back to the Olympics, some of the other achievements Josh accomplished was the ultimate win of the bronze medal. Josh said, "I got a bronze medal which I cherish as a gold," because when you make it to the Olympic Games, there are no other tasks that you want. There isn't anything else higher than making it to the games because you are representing your country. Josh was representing his country just like he was representing where he was born, Norristown High School, Morgan State. It was a college, and then a university, and each time it was another stepping-stone. And so you couldn't go any other higher than making the Olympic Games because it was worldwide; it was started hundreds of years ago in Athens, Greece. Josh basks that he ran in the place where the Olympic Games had begun. He set a record there on that track, which he did not think could be done because it was not an oval track in Athens. But the year he went there, there's a feeling that you had of thousands of years ago that this took place 600 BC, and here, they had these athletes coming. Josh competed there, and he felt this was the epitome of track and field because this is what they had done in this particular place, Athens, Greece, the birth place of the Olympic Games and it didn't get any better than that. Noted earlier, I told you Josh was the embodiment from Mt. Olympus! Josh was three-times American champion, two-times Pan-American champion, and then Penn Relays three times, and there are only three of us who has ever done that feat in the world. "But these are the things that I just cherish because I came from a little place a little Borough called Norristown, Pennsylvania."

*****

As a hometown hero representing Norristown, Pennsylvania, shining in the spotlight, you would wonder what was life like after the Olympics and the successes might come along and open many doors of opportunities. Josh sarcastically said, "Well, you called it success; it still was work that had to be done. I was too old to run. So, I ended up being the first Black schoolteacher in secondary schools in Norristown. That was an achievement."

Josh liked being the first doing a lot of things, but he paid the price for it. But Josh thought it was great because again, Mr. Vincent Farina (his history teacher who had been wounded during WW2) had told Josh you have a college degree. Now, Josh had a political science degree; he did not have any teaching degree. Mr. Farina told Josh to take the test, go down to Temple University, "and they have a program that we are going to institute here starting this year," and that was called ITPCG program which meant Intern Teaching Program for College Graduates. So Josh was in the first class at Temple University that, if he finished this course to work on his master's degree, he would be eligible to teach school. Josh passed the test. Josh went to Temple University, and he got his master's degree, and last year was the fiftieth year that he had graduated from Temple University. But that is how Josh got in to teaching and he earned the right to teach. But he did a lot of things outside. Josh had a chance to give back and to teach and help other students along the way, "and one of them, I'm proud to say, is here at Norristown Area School District and that was Ernie Hadrick. I had a lot of guys before him and I had a lot after them."

Mentoring and training a lot of student athletes through his life and career fosters responsibility and relationships to prepare student athletes for their community service as role models and what it has on their community or to their community. Josh responded, "You have to experience of trying to find out how it is to get along with people, and when you do that and you have the ability to talk, and you have the knowledge of anything that you feel strong about and enjoy, you can give back an awful lot as well as learn. You're learning all the time. Just a conversation alone you become inspired that you want to do something that you may have been afraid of but somehow you have courage to do."

Josh was the shortest hurdler in the world, and every guy he ran against looked down on him. Some of them made some unsavory remarks to Josh and said, "Wow, how did you get the American championship?" and that inspired him even more. "I'm saying that as an example because there are so many things that can take you off the wrong track so easily. Stay focused and believe in your dreams, and your hopes, and your aspirations."

Life after track was over with and starting a family, Josh was busy so much doing so many things. Josh had the pleasure when he ran for each time when he was teaching school. Josh also was still running, and he was still contributing to everything else, and it was wonderful. Josh was the first Black teacher in his school to teach in secondary schools in Norristown and at Rittenhouse Junior High, where he, along with his elder sister and the other four, had gone, and that was a great honor. Teaching was a great profession.

Josh's father never went to school. "He was the eldest boy of eleven children. He learned how to read and write from his brothers and sisters. He stole my mother—that's called elopement—so she had gone to seventh grade. In those days, it could be done, but they were both sticklers on going to school, and therefore, I had most of the family went to college and graduated. Then, we had to try and utilize and inspire in others to do so in our own children. I took my talents everything that I had learned from my teachers and I still used them to reach out to others today. I'm still involved in many things as an advisor to the USA Track and Field. I joined a fraternity. I came back home and seeing guys like Ernie Hadrick and seeing the interests that was there. It rubbed off because he also has tried to do the things that I tried to instill in him and many others."

Josh explains his memorable coaching experience at Central State University. Josh responded, "Central State. I have done so many things."

Josh set the bar high where he and his track team were able to go to the White House. An experience he will never forget. "Wow, that was quite a thing. But I got there because of Central State University. I was a coach there, and as a result I had done something that a lot of coaches have not done, but they wish they had. I had won ten national titles within eight years. Then they wanted to know—a lot of people—"How did you win ten national titles?' and so forth that way. Well, my men and women won the indoor national title, and we won the outdoor national title; and therefore, I had won those, say, ten championships within eight years, and it was one of the biggest things that happened. So as a result, with this, they said, 'Hey, you have to go to the White House to meet the president on that one.' So, we went to the White House Rose Garden to meet Mr. Clinton, the president of the United States. That's how we got to the White House and it was an honor."

Working in the real-world, Josh explains, "I have taught school, I had gone to school, I worked for industry—private for a steel company in personnel. I worked for some years where my father had spent thirty-eight years. I was the first Black in personnel there. But there was a first in everything that you were doing, and you set by example. So I enjoyed it, and I did a lot of things. But there were other things I was interested in. I loved teaching school, I loved being with the kids, and I loved being track coach, and I could teach them what I did not have. They had better facilities and everything else; and now, I don't regret anything that I had done in my life. I enjoyed it because it led to another stepping-stone and I had a chance to deal with young people. I loved working with young people. As I went to Central State, I had done a lot of things prior to that time. I had traveled."

*****

7

You Earn That Right

When I won the American Championship, it led me going into Europe to compete against their champions, and I defeated every champion that I ran against and I was very fortunate. I was undefeated until the Olympic trials. Then, that led me going into Melbourne, Australia, for the Olympic Games in 1956. I almost did not make that team because there was a very freak incident. I had graduated from Morgan in 1955 and I entered and was accepted in Law School in University of Colorado in Boulder. I had runned there and I had won my American title there. I had a sister [Helen Clarissa Culbreath Noel, fondly called "Lynn"] who was a leading TV commentator out of Denver at that time, and of course, she was just delighted to know that I was going to law school there being closer to her because she felt better. We haven't seen each other for a while. Then, I had to drop out of law school because we have a strict ruling in how to make the United States Olympic Team. It's opened, because I had been an American champion three years in a row does not put you on the Olympic Team like it may have done maybe in 1900 or 1904. Here, you had to earn that right.

Our system in the United States is the hardest system for, say, making a US Olympic Team. What you had to do was first of all that year you had to run a qualifying time in order to try and get to that Olympic trials and if you were out of school you ran for a club. If you were out of a club and you were with the Armed Forces, you had a process of elimination. That means that the Army had to have a process of elimination with all their guys if you were in Europe, Asia, or Africa, and you were good enough, they flew you back to the United States, and here you would have a process of elimination against your fellow other guys in the Army who were based here in the United States and you came from different parts of the world. This is how big it is. Then, it was a process of elimination. From there, when you got to what we called a process of elimination and then it boils down to the first three for each event. Then you had these three guys had to be selected from the Army and the same thing happened to the Navy people. I was in the Marine Corps. I dropped out of law school, I enlisted in the Marine Corps and why I did it at that time was a big mistake. Because I went to boot camp at Parris Island. Parris Island was known as one of the training centers that makes Marines, "Boot Camp." We had two of them, one was in California. If you went in California, it was like we called your Hollywood Marine. But if you went to Parris Island, which was swamp with a lot of mosquitos and everything else, you had to be a real Marine went to Parris Island. If you want to be a Hollywood Marine, you go to California. I was in the Marine Corps, and I was America's Hope. We had the Cold War between Russia who's the greatest, and I was the hope for the 400-meter hurdles, and here I was in boot camp and I had six weeks only. I had not run since I had won the championship in 1955. I went to law school, and I couldn't train too much, and I dropped out of law school. Now I am in the Marine Corps, and I have not run in nine months. How can I make it? And believe me, you don't be picked and say that you are the greatest you are on the team. *You earn that right.*

So I had to run in the process of elimination when I dropped out of law school, I went back and I said, "Well, I got to go back home," and I said, "I can't do anything right now so I may as well enlist in the United States Marine Corps," and I did. They sent me to Parris Island, and they found out that since I was undefeated and I had been the American champion three years Pan American Games champion they said, "Where am I?" and they found me in boot camp, and they snatched me out and told me, "You're going to Quantico," which is Marine Corps headquarters Virginia, and they said, "You have three to four weeks to get in to condition to try out for the United States Olympic Team."

Hard? It was. Because I had not run since August in competition of '55. So in 1956 of June, I think it was the trials. They put me back in Quantico, Virginia, and I had exactly five weeks to get back in top shape to run. I won all Marine Corps championships, and I won all the service championships, still process of elimination of three people each time, and then when I got to the Olympic trials, I had some young boys who were waiting for me. One of them was Glenn Davis from Ohio State. The other one was

Eddie Southern from the University of Texas. We were in the finals process of elimination. Well, in order to make that Olympic Team, I had to break the world's record. I also, these two guys broke it also—Eddie Southern and Glenn Davis. But we were the ones—Glenn won it (new world's record), Eddie was second (also under the record), and I was third (just two-tenths short of the record). That was how we made the Olympic Team process of elimination. Not what you had done during the time of all those years of being consistent and being an American champion—"It was the time to be ready." So I ended up making it. The process was we came back after June, we had to wait and be training because the Olympic Games were held in Melbourne, Australia, and their summer months happened to be in November. So from June, I was still in the Marine Corps so I could run, and I ran in Europe, and I ran against everybody who wanted me and I was "kicking their tail" because I had to be ready. I wanted to make sure when I got ready to go to Melbourne, Australia, that we were going to be ready. We had three meets when they assembled the team in California and we ran in Oregon, we ran in the rest of the other two meets, we ran in California, and at the time there were no jets flying you. We went by prop plane from Los Angeles, we stopped into Honolulu, and we stayed there for about three days in Hawaii because the planes would not go that far without "petrol." So, we had to go from there we went to the Fiji Islands to refuel and then to Melbourne, Australia, and finally to the Olympic Games. "That's how the journey went and believe me when you got there you knew

that you were meeting the best in the world at
the Games."

As Josh arrives in Melbourne, he has a mail call. He looks over,
along with US Olympian teammate, Chicago's Ira Murchison:

MELBOURNE MAIL CALL—Norristown's Josh Culbreath, left, looks over
his mail after his arrival in Melbourne with the U. S. Olympic team. At the
right is Ira Murchison, Chicago, who is a top hopeful for Uncle Sam in the 100-
yard dash. Culbreath's specialty, the 400-meter hurdles, will be run next Saturday.

*****

I had the pleasure of receiving from a Quantico Public Affairs specialist who shared with me the original *USMC 1956 Olympian Press Releases* provided by the history division at the Marine Corps University. What you are about to read is the original press release story written by Staff Sergeant John Mahoney penning the words spoken by Josh. The drawn lines signify unreadable handwriting from the original authentic USMC 1956 Olympian Press Release shown on pages 117–124.

Joshua Culbreath

A former enlisted man in the Marines and a track star in the 400 meter hurdles took first place in that event in the dual USA-USSR track meet held in Philadelphia, July 1959. His winning time for the event was 50.5 seconds. Culbreath was a member of the 1956 Olympic team which participated in the games at Melbourne, Australia. He placed third in the 400 meter hurdle event. Culbreath enlisted in the USMCR in March 1956 for three years of active duty. He was released to inactive status in March 1959. He and world record holder in the javelin throw, 1st Lt Al Cantello, USMCR, were teammates at their local high school in Norristown, Pennsylvania, and represented Marine Corps Schools, Quantico, Virginia, in the 1956 International Military events and the Olympic games in Melbourne, Australia.

Quantico, Va., Dec. 18, 1956—"As I stood there on the Victory Stand with Glen Davis and Eddie Southern I had a proud feeling run through me which I'd never felt before. As we stood there, they raised the American Flags (one for each of us), then played the Star Spangled Banner. Nothing, I believe, can ever replace our National Anthem to make one proud he's an American and everyone of our American athletes who took that Victory Stand will bear me out on that."

These were the words of Josh Culbreath of Quantico, the third place winner in this 1956 Olympic 400 meter hurdle event Josh a Pfc. stationed here at Quantico returned home yesterday from Melbourne.

Looking as bright as ever, the cheerful, 5-7, 137 pounder had nothing but praise for the treatment he and his teammates received abroad.

When Josh left for California to train with _____ team he carried his Quantico track suit _____ committee had _____ they were encouraged to wear their college colors _____ men were, or still are, college students. Josh with _____ in him, wore the Quantico track suit with the name ___ across the front.

Following the training period, the team was split _____ up ____ groups for the trip to Australia. Josh's group left _____ two day stop at Hawaii before continuing on to Melbourne. They finally arrived Nov. 9, a beautiful day with temperatures in the high 70's.

The weather however didn't last long and the Americans, as well as everyone else, had a week of training in mud, rain and cold weather.

Josh said, "I never ran a flight of hurdles until the day of the Olympics. I was afraid with the rain, mud and cold (temperatures were in the 30's) I'd pull a muscle or something."

When asked about the relationships among nations, Josh came back with, "Everyone agrees we got along famously. We traded pins which each country had for the purpose and a little bit of small talk."

"Anatyin Lutuyev, the Russian who had held the world's 400 meter hurdle record would come out everyday and watch us practice. He's count the number of steps we'd take between the hurdles. I often wondered when he had time to do his own training," Josh continued.

As it all turned out, poor Lutuyev should have trained more than he watched because the Americans took their first sweep in this event with the Russian finishing fourth behind Josh.

Knowing how everyone is interested in why Josh clocked such a poor time after leading the field in the quarter and semifinals, I asked him. "No excuse, but for the first time since 1952 my legs tightened up on me. I think it was because we ran the semi and finals the same day. As a matter of fact withing two hours of each other. I just couldn't get loose after the semi-finals."

That's easy to understand, seeing how Josh is so much smaller than his teammates who hit over the 200 pound mark.

"I'm not through yet though," says Josh, "I'll be back in 1960 because I feel I left a job undone."

With the heart this little runner has we know that he will, and we're looking forward to the 1960 Olympics.

MARINE CORPS SCHOOLS, QUANTICO, Va., Oct.2--Champions like fighting men are made not born.

It's a man's will to be the greatest, hard train- ing and a few breaks. Marine Pvt. Josh Culbreath wanted to become an Olympic champion ever since he can remember and this year he has his chance to become the world's greatest 400 meter hurdle king.

Josh was born and raised in the little coal town of Norristown, Pa., on Sept. 14,1932, to Jesse and Anna B. Culbreath. He attended Norristown High School, Morgan State College and the University of Colorado.

The young trackster started out in the track world as a high jumper, then a pole vaulter before he found himself best qualified as a hurdler. In 1948 as a junior in high school he placed second in the state championships and won the 200 yard hurdles the following year. He also was proclaimed the second top high school hurdler at 200 yards in the country.

Finishing high school, Josh entered Morgan State College in Baltimore, Md. Here he was to meet Edward P. Hurt, considered to be one of the world's greatest track coaches. Under Hurt, the young Norristown boy began to gain recognition. He won the National AAU title twice and as a sophomore gained his greatest title up to that time winning the ICAA 120 yard high hurdles.

In the next few years Josh made two trips to Europe where he ran his best race in his life up to that point with a 51:3 for the 400 meter hurdles at Tornia, Italy. He came back to this country to win the Penn Relays and set a new record of 52:4.

Ireland proved to be a great country for the stawart hurdler as he set a new mark of 53 flat on a green track for the 400 meter hurdles. Next came Scotland and he set a new record there also with a 52:8 on a banked off track.

Last year, Josh really began to come into his own. He won the Pan-American Games Mexico

City title in the 400 meter hurdles with a 51:5. This also set a new Latin American record.

Military service was calling Josh now so he enlisted in the Marine Corps going to Parris Island for his recruit training. But before he took up his military duties he made another trip to Europe and won another National AAU title.

Although he didn't get much time for training his track muscles in boot camp, Josh said the physical training program helped him keep in great shape.

He arrived at Quantico shortly before the All-Marine Track and Field Championship (May '56). He didn't have much time to work his track muscles loose but a two a day training schedule was enough to enable him to set a new Marine Corps record and to go on and set a new Inter-Service record in Los Angles.

Josh still had a long way to go before he was to hit his top form however. But he did well enough to place third in the Olympic Trials with a 50:4 which was the world record before Glenn Daivs and Ed Southern broke it in placing first and second respectively.

Following the Olympic Trials he traveled to Berlin with the Armed Forces team in a NATO meet. There he set a new German record of 51:1.

The young Marine is now preparing for the greatest race of his life but he'd like to point out one thing. "I have to place a lot of credit on my Quantico coach, Lt. Tom Rosandich and the fact I had the use of such a wonderful track to prepare myself for this Olympic year."

Josh feels that sports and for him track has had a bearing on making him a better Marine also. The high competitive spirit which helps a man both in the world of running and combat needs a mentally and physically conditioned man. Through his Marine training and track training, he feels he can qualify better as a defender of his country.

*****

Joshua Culbreath

A former enlisted man in the Marines and a track star in
the 400 meter hurdles took first place in that event in the
dual USA-USSR track meet in held in Philadelphia, July 1959.
His winning time for the event was 50.5 seconds. Culbreath
was a member of the 1956 Olympic team which participated in
the games at Melbourne, Australia. He placed third in the 400
meter hurdle event. Culbreath enlisted in the USMCR in March 1956
for three years of active duty. He was released to inactive
status in March 1959. He and world record holder in the javelin
throw, 1st Lt Al Cantello, USMCR, were teammates at their local
high school in Norristown, Pennsylvania, and represented
Marine Corps Schools, Quantico, Virginia, in the 1956
International Military events and the Olympic games
in melbourne, australia.

August 1959   - USMC - enlisted service No. 1592292

Courtesy the original USMC 1956 Olympian Press Releases
provided by the history division at the Marine Corps University.

QUANTICO, VA.

Olympic Star-Josh Culbreath
by SSgt.John Mahoney
FOR IMMEDIATE RELEASE

file

QUANTICO, Va., Dec.19 1956 "As I stood there on the Victory
Stand with Glen Davis and Eddie Southern I had a proud feeling
run through me which I'd never felt before. As we stood there,
they raised the American Flags(one for each of us),then played
the Star Spangled Banner. Nothing,I believe, can ever replace
our National Anthem to make one proud he's an American and
everyone of our American athletes who took that Victory Stand
will bear me out on that."

These were the words of Josh Culbreath of Quantico, the
third place winner in this 1956 Olympic 400 meter hurdle event.
Josh a Pfc. stationed here at Quantico returned home yesterday
from Melbourne.

Looking as bright as ever, the cheerful, 5-7,137 pounder
had nothing but praise for the treatment he and his teammates
received abroad.

(more)

PFC - US MCR
3 yr enlistment
March 56 to March 59.

118

When Josh left for California to train with the ...
team he carried his Quantico track suit ....
committee had sche.... ... ...
they were encouraged to wear their college colors as ... ...
men were, or still are, college students. Josh, with ... ...
in him, wore the Quantico track suit with the name Quantic... ... ...
across the front.

Following the training period, the team was spl... up in to ...
groups for the trip to Australia. Josh's group left Nov 5 ...a, a
two day stop at Hawaii before continuing on to Melbourne. They
finally arrived Nov.9, a beautiful day with temperatures in the
high 70's.

The weather however didn't last long and the Americans, as
well as everyone else, had a week of training in mud, rain and
cold weather.

Josh said, "I never ran a flight of hurdles until the day
of the Olympics. I was afraid with the rain, mud and cold(temperatures
were in the 30's)I'd pull a muscle or something."

When asked about the relationships among nations, Josh came
back with,"Everyone agrees we got along famously. We traded pins
which each country had for the purpose and a little bit of small
talk."

"Anatyln Lutuyev, the Russian who had held the world's 400 meter hurdle record would come out everyday and watch us practice. He's count the number of steps we'd take between the hurdles. I often wondered when he had time to do his own training," Josh continued.

As it all turned out, poor Lutuyev should have trained more than he watched because the Americans took their first sweep in this event with the Russian finishing fourth behind Josh.

Knowing how everyone is interested in why Josh clocked such a poor time after leading the field in the quarter and semifinals, I asked him. "No excuse, but for the first time since 1952 my legs tightened up on me. I think it was because we ran the semi and finals the same day. As a matter of fact withing two hours of each other. I just couldn't get loose after the semi-finals."

That's easy to understand, seeing how Josh is so much smaller than his teammates who hit over the 200 pound mark.

"I'm not through yet though," says Josh, "I'll be back in 1960 because I feel I left a job undone."

With the heart this little runner has we know that he will, and we're looking forward to the 1960 Olympics.

THE OLYMPIAN LEAP

INFORMATIONAL SERVICES
MARINE CORPS SCHOOLS
QUANTICO, VIRGINIA

Josh Culbreth Olympic Star

by SSgt John Mahoney

FOR IMMEDIATE RELEASE

MARINE CORPS SCHOOLS, QUANTICO,Va.,Oct.2--Champions like fighting men are made not born.

It's a man's will to be the greatest, hard training and a few breaks. Marine Pvt.Josh Culbreath wanted to become an Olympic champion ever since he can remember and this year he has his chance to become the world's greatest 400 meter hurdle king.

Josh was born and raised in the little coal town of Norristown, Pa.,on Sept.14,1932, to Jesse and Anna B.Culbreath. He attended Norristown High School,Morgan State College and the University of Colorado.

The young trackster started out in the track world as a high jumper,then a pole vaulter before he found himself best qualified as a hurdler. In 1948 as a junior in high school he placed second in the state championships and won the 200 yard hurdles the following year. He also was proclaimed the second top high school hurdler at 200 yards in the country.

1951

Finishing high school, Josh entered Morgan State College in Baltimore,Md. Here he was to meet Edward P. Hurt, considered to be one of the world's greatest track coaches. Under Hurt, the young Norristown boy began to gain recognition. He won the National AAU title twice and as a sophmore gained his greatest title up to that time winning the ICAA 120 yard high hurdles.

In the next few years Josh made two trips to Europe where he ran his best race in his life up to that point with a 51:3 for the 400 meter hurdles at Tornia, Italy. He came back to this country to win the Penn Relays and set a new record of 52:4.

Ireland proved to be a great country for the stawart hurdler as he set a new mark of 53 flat on a green track for the 400 meter hurdles. Next came Scotland and he set a new record there also with a 52:8 on a banked off track.

Last year,Josh really began to come into his own. He won the Pan-American Games title in the 400 meter hurdles with a 51:5. This also set a new Latin American record.

(more)

122

Military service was calling Josh now so he enlisted in
the Marine Corps going to Parris Island for his recruit training.
But before he took up his military duties he made another trip to
Europe and won another National AAU title.

Although he didn't get much time for training his track muscles
in boot camp,Josh said the physical training program helped him
keep in great shape.

He arrived at Quantico shortly before the All-Marine Track
and Field Championships. *(MAY 56)* He didn't have much time to work his
track muscles loose but a two a day training schedule was enough
to enable him to set a new Marine Corps record and to go on and
set a new Inter-Service record in Los Angles.

Josh still had a long way to go before he was to hit his
top form however. But he did well enough to place third in the
Olympic Trials with a 50:4 which was the world record before
Glenn Daivs and Ed Southern broke it in placing first and
second respectively.

Following the Olympic Trials he traveled to Berlin with the
Armed Forces team in a NATO meet. There he set a new German record
of 51:1.

The young Marine is now preparing for the greatest race of his life but he'd like to point out one thing. "I have to place a lot of credit on my Quantico coach, Lt.Tom Rosandich and the fact I had the use of such a wonderful track to prepare myself for this Olympic year."

Josh feels that sports and for him track has had a bearing on making him a better Marine also. The high competitive spirit which helps a man both in the world of running and combat needs a mentally and physically conditioned man. Through his Marine training and track training, he feels he can qualify better as a defender of his country.

*****

124

Three Americans versus the three great runners from Russia everywhere in the world, and we were very fortunate. I was the first one up. This was on a cinder track not all weathered wise or anything and it gets dugged up. But we all qualified in our heats. We were separate. We didn't have to run against each other because we had the fastest times in the world. We did not have to run as hard with us being seated against each other. But then we had to come to those finals. The three of us from America had made the finals. In the finals were the great Russian Yuriy Nikolayevich Lituyev. He was favorite also be one of the great ones. A guy named Dave Lean from Australia was in it, and a guy named Gert Potgieter from South Africa, and the other three were Glenn Davis of America, Eddie Southern of America, and Josh Culbreath; and they put me in the worst lane. Lane 1 which they had run like ten thousand meters the day before. This mean it was a cinder track which was just dugged up because you had all these guys running in the same lane and that was Lane 1. You did not want to be in Lane 1 which was a cinder track all chewed up. Where I was and I had to run it because I had been selected to run in Lane 1. Well, I ran and it was not one of my greatest. I run easy running 50 points something in times which was under the Olympic record. But in the finals, I had everything going against me, but I was able to try and stay up and then come up and fight back the last, say, ten yards; and it was America 1-2-3 Glenn Davis, Eddie Southern, and myself. The first clean sweep of the Olympic Games was won by the hurdlers. We again won the same thing; the 110-meter high hurdles was won by America 1-2-3. That was the Olympic Games, and it was quite a run, but it was not my best race. But it got me to become an Olympian and get a medal.

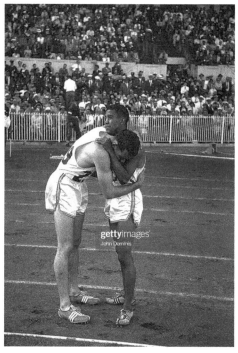

"Clean sweep" Josh Culbreath and Eddie Southern embracing at the Summer Olympics after crossing the finishing line.

*****

How it all went down during the final, the six lanes were fairly even, with Lituyev pushing the backstretch to gain a slight advantage going into the final turn. That was swallowed up during the turn as Davis surged, leading Eddie Southern and Gert Potgieter off the turn. Davis expanded his lead over Southern from 2 meters to 5 meters down the home stretch for the win. Over the final barrier, Potgieter caught his trail leg on the hurdle which knocked him off balance. He was able to take two more strides then did a face plant in the middle of the track. On the inside, Josh Culbreath was able to cruise by for bronze, completing the American sweep. Josh timed in 51.6, one-tenth of a second faster than Russian, to give Americans first sweep in event since 1920.

On the stand for the medal presentation, Davis reached down from the champion's pinnacle and rubbed a hand through Culbreath's hair. "Let's repeat this in 1960 at Rome," he said. Culbreath grinned broadly.

To this day, Culbreath is irked that he drew the inside lane, which "was like a beach" from the churning by runners' feet in the previous event, the 10,000-meter run.

Still, he managed to finish third behind Davis and Southern, giving the United States its first sweep of the Games. A photo of the three appeared as the centerfold in *Life* magazine as they stood on the victory stand.

"When I got back to Quantico, the commandant congratulated me because I had my index finger on the seam of my sweat suit during the national anthem," Culbreath said. "He said I was the only one standing tall." When you put your index finger on the seam of your trouser that is standing tall as a Marine.

Which is why the following clipping is the perfect definition for who Josh Culbreath really is:

REPORT OF U. S .MARINE CORPS
Maj. James K. McCreight

THE basic prerequisites necessary to become an Olympic champion closely parallel those required of a successful military leader. The same abilities are encouraged and developed, i.e., leadership, loyalty, courage, physical fitness, teamwork, the ability to think clearly and quickly come to a decision and last, but far from least, discipline.

Fully recognizing that the Olympic Games represent the epitome of athletic competition and realizing that organizing and supporting the United States Olympic Games Teams is an "all hands" job, the Marine Corps has put forth every reasonable effort to fulfill its share of responsibility in supporting the United States Olympic effort.

Active athletic programs offering an unlimited variety of events are conducted at each separate command throughout the Marine Corps. Competition progresses from the intramural level to organized league play with other Armed Services teams and culminates in the world wide Marine Corps athletic championship program. This program, which is continuously available to every Marine, regardless of where he may be stationed, readily lended itself to an extensive Olympic development program and provided every Marine with the opportunity to train for possible Olympic competition.

For the competition format the men's 40-m hurdles competition started with six heats, where the fastest two from each heat qualified to one of the two semifinals groups. The three fastest runners from each semifinals group advanced to the final.

400-Meters Hurdles, Men

Date	23–24 November 1956
Status	Olympic
Location	Melbourne Cricket Ground, Melbourne, Victoria
Participants	28 from 18 countries
Olympic Record	50.8 / Charlie Moore ▦USA / 21 July 1952
	50.8 / Charlie Moore ▦USA / 20 July 1952

Coming in to 1956, the top American was Josh Culbreath, AAU Champion in 1953–55 and Pan-American Champion in 1955. The world record holder at the beginning of the year was Soviet Yury Lituyev with 50.4 set in 1953. Lituyev had been second at the European Championships in 1950 and 1954 and was the top European in 1956. But two young Americans took up the intermediate hurdles in 1956. Glenn Davis was a top 200/400 runner at Ohio State and won the US Olympic Trials in a world record 49.5, narrowly defeating Eddie Southern, still only a junior, who ran 49.7. In Melbourne again established his superiority, winning the final by 7/10ths over Southern, with Culbreath completing a US medal sweep, Lituyev trailing in fourth. South Africa's Gert Potgieter had been in the medal hunt until he fell on the last barrier, finishing last.

Pos	Nr	Athlete	NOC	R1	SF	Final	
1	278	Glenn Davis	USA	51.3 (1 h1)	50.7 (2 h1)	50.1 (1)	Gold
2	279	Eddie Southern	USA	51.3 (1 h2)	50.1 (1 h1)	50.8 (2)	Silver
3	277	Josh Culbreath	USA	50.9 (1 h3)	50.9 (1 h2)	51.6 (3)	Bronze
4	282	Yury Lituyev	URS	51.6 (1 h5)	51.8 (3 h2)	51.7 (4)	
5	257	David Lean	AUS	51.4 (2 h1)	51.4 (2 h2)	51.8 (5)	
6	274	Gert Potgieter	RSA	52.0 (2 h5)	51.3 (3 h1)	56.0 (6)	

Round One (23 November 1956—14:30)
Top two in each heat advanced to the semi-finals.

Heat 3

Rank	Name	Country	Result
1	Josh Culbreath	United States	50.9
2	Guy Cury	France	51.6
3	Jaime Aparicio	Colombia	52.0
4	Tom Farrell	Great Britain	52.7
5	Muhammad Yaqub	Pakistan	53.1
6	Tsai Cheng-Fu	Chinese Taipei	54.6

Semi-Finals (23 November 1956—17:40)
Top three in each heat advanced to the final.

Group 2

Rank	Name	Country	Result
1	Josh Culbreath	United States	50.9
2	David Lean	Australia	51.4
3	Yuriy Lituyev	Soviet Union	51.8
4	Ilie Savel	Romania	52.0
5	Harry Kane	Great Britain	52.7
6	Ioannis Kambadelis	Greece	53.8

Final (24 November 1956—17:10)

Rank	Name	Country	Result
1	Glenn Davis	United States	50.1
2	Eddie Southern	United States	50.8
3	Josh Culbreath	United States	51.6
4	Yuriy Lituyev	Soviet Union	51.7
5	David Lean	Australia	51.8
6	Gert Potgieter	South Africa	56.0

Men's 400 metres hurdles
at the Games of the XVI Olympiad

Venue	Melbourne Cricket Ground
Date	November 23–24
Competitors	28 from 18 nations
Winning time	50.1

Medalists

1	Glenn Davis		United States
2	Eddie Southern		United States
3	Josh Culbreath		United States

The Closing Ceremony of the Melbourne was poignant and new to the Olympics. At the Closing Ceremony, the competing nations had been represented previously only by a flag bearer and the name standard bearer. But an Australian boy named John Ian Wing had written to the Melbourne Organizing Committee and suggested a change. He proposed that the athletes march in as a group, without regard to nationality or sport, to show how the athletes of varying nations had come together during the two weeks of the Olympics. As the final march of the athletes occurred at the Closing Ceremony, the Australian crowd serenaded them with the mystical Scottish hymn, "Will Ye' No' Come Back Again?" The Official Report noted, "A wave of emotion swept over the crowd, the Olympic Flame was engulfed in it and died; the Olympic flag went out in tears, not cheers, and a great silence. This, more than any remembered laurel of the Games, was something no-one had ever experienced before—not anywhere in the world, not anywhere in time."

Charles Dumas

Jash: Do you remember This meet.

Man With Seven Feet

(Reprinted, with permission of the publishers, from the October, 1956, "World Sports" Magazine, of London.)

"Go on out and jump seven feet and get it over with," exclaimed Mrs. Nancy Dumas, a Compton (California) housewife, to her son, Charles, late on the afternoon of June 29 this year — the night of the high jump in the USA Olympic Trials at the Los Angeles Coliseum.

Not that Charley was nervous; he just seemed fidgety and anxious to get into action. "Guess I might as well," he drawled as he got up off the sofa to leave the house.

When Charley arrived at the Coliseum, his coach, Herschel Smith, was not to be found; he had Dumas' competitor's ticket in his pocket but was late in reaching the stadium.

Anxious to get into his Compton College track suit and start warming up on the field, Dumas went to a ticket window and paid three dollars to get in, then found his way down to the field, where he was recognized. In a short while he was in and out of the dressing room and back on the field getting ready for his event.

There was plenty of excitement that night, for Glenn Davis had just set a world record of 49.5 secs. for the 400m. hurdles, with Eddie Southern and Josh Culbreath right behind him at 49.7 and 50.6; the 100m. world record had twice been equalled ... and soon everybody was out of the high jump except Charley Dumas.

Charley had one miss at 6 ft. 9 ins. (2.06m.) and muffed his first try at 7 ft. ⅝ in. (2.15m.); but the second time he went over without touching the bar, and the 34,126 crowd, acclaiming the first man to clear 7 ft., began going a little crazy. Everybody except Dumas. Charley just walked off the field calling it a day, and said that some other time he would go higher.

Ernie Shelton, most consistent of all jumpers over 6 ft. 10 in. (2.08m.), not only saw another man beat him to the magic 7 ft.; he failed to qualify for the USA team. He missed at 6 ft. 9½ in. and, hours later, in deep despondency:

"High jumpers tend to become 'screwballs' because theirs is the toughest of all athletic events, emotionally. I can't fathom this Dumas. He's too orthodox. He doesn't do anything more abnormal than go into a trance. He never talks. He just concentrates quietly. Among high-jumpers I have known, he's an emotional giant."

Dumas stands 6 ft. 1 in. (1.85m.) tall and weighs 179 lb. In 1955 he set an American high school record of 6 ft. 9⅜ in. (2.07m.), though in a non-prep-school meeting he leaped 6 ft. 10¾ in. He never jumps in practice, except early in the season; he just runs and jogs a little. And in early season he runs the low hurdles.

He approaches the bar with a short run from the left, comes almost to a complete stop right under the bar, lifts his spiked right foot with an amazing initial kick, goes up like a coiled spring off his left leg and rolls over the bar.

The night he leaped 7 ft. he wore, for the first time, track shoes made in Germany of Australian kangaroo skin. There are those who say the kangaroo was still in the left shoe when Dumas took off!

"This initial lift, his spring and the fact that competition never worries him constitute Charley's secret," says Coach Smith, the man who directed Cornelius Johnson to an Olympic title in 1936.

Those qualities, plus his "7 ft." reputation, now stamp Dumas as the undeniable favorite for the high jump in Melbourne.

*****

8

High Altitude Against Dignity

The Olympic Flames never died out for Cousin Josh. Prior to the 1956 Melbourne, Australia, Olympics, Josh participated in the 1955 Second Pan-American Games, Mexico City. What amazes me is Josh was setting records participating in huge events such as the Mexico City Pan-American Games where he was one of 2,583 athletes representing twenty-one nations participating in the second celebration considered as Second Pan-American Games.

Athletes vs. Altitude

At Mexico City, competitors in the Pan-American Games met an unexpected foe. In the rarefied air 7,600 feet above sea level, they are being felled by anoxia.

While a powerful U.S. team at the Second Pan-American Games toppled records and captured most of the available gold medals, scores of finely trained athletes were being toppled by the Mexico City air—or rather lack of it. There is an online video with Josh reliving a flashback of his memorable story he won the Pan-American Games in Mexico City in high altitude and how he had to gasp for air to a young man who loves and respects veterans by the name of Tyreke who is a Warrior Heartbeat. Josh explains in his words, "…when you have not been acclimated to weather and train in it you find out it is difficult to run in it because it is a short of breath, you are in high altitude and the air is thinner. But we don't have time to train to go for how you become acclimated to that climate. We had to run in it knowing that it was hard and knowing that the air was thin." In the rarefied 7,600-foot atmosphere, well-conditioned young men from the lowlands dropped like flies. The games became a battle against altitude, and the only effective weapons were tanks of oxygen. The story is the American team entered this battle strangely unprepared. Again, Josh said they did not have time to train to the climate conditions. There is a photo of Josh carried on a stretcher after collapsing crossing the finishing line at the Mexico City Pan-American Games. Some athletes arrived in Mexico a week before the games, time to acclimatize themselves; others did not get there until shortly before their events. U.S. team physician, Harry R. McPhee, drew an obvious conclusion: next time any U.S. athlete compete at such altitudes, they should arrive on the scene at least 10 days early. That much time at least is necessary to get used to diluted air.

The following are a list of athletes describing how they were impacted, including Cousin Josh:

Edgar Friere (Brazil) clutches his side as he gasps for air.

Cynthia Mills (Jamaica) crumples after 60-meter dash.

Frank Rivera (Puerto Rico) collapses after 800-meter.

Josh Culbreath (U.S.) is carried off after hurdles win (see photo)

When he went on to win gold in Mexico City, pictures of him collapsing after crossing the finish line prompted him to enroll in law school at the University of Colorado so he could train in high altitude.

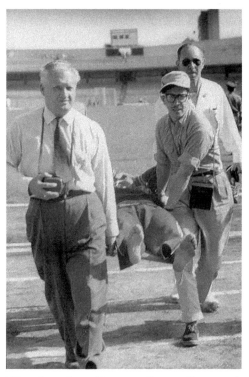

1955 Second Pan-American Games collapse after crossing finish line winning the gold in Mexico City. Josh felt he paid the price once, this time for not being prepared enough to win with dignity.

The point is high-altitude training can benefit elite endurance athletes like runners and swimmers. As elite athletes acclimate to high altitude, they acquire more red blood cells which allow their blood to carry more oxygen. Colorado is known for high, elevated towns and altitudes. Traditionally, elite athletes have lived and trained at high altitudes, such as Colorado Springs, Colorado. "Live high, train low," elite athletes should live and lightly train in high-altitude areas to acclimate their bodies to lower oxygen levels. Josh was focused and prepared as a model athlete to hurtle his obstacle of challenges. With such intense competition, how can elite athletes legally gain a competitive advantage? Ben Levine, MD Internal Medicine-Cardiology and his colleague Jim Stray-Gundersen, MD, researched altitude training for ten years with grants from the US Olympic Committee and USA Track and Field (USATF).

> Our "live high, train low" research is the training platform for most American elite-athlete altitude programs. To benefit, athletes must spend the majority of their time—12 to 16 hours a day—at the sweet spot of around 8,000 feet above sea level. If they get too much higher, they can develop altitude sickness, lower plasma volume levels, and suffer inadequate sleep patterns. Training should occur around or below 4,000 feet above sea level. Research is inconclusive as to exactly how long an athlete must train low for optimal benefit, though it is critical to conduct all high-intensity efforts at low altitude.

Therefore, Josh and "athletes entered the competition unprepared for the serious effects of altitude poisoning, thus in the rarefied air 7,600 feet above sea level, scores of finely trained athletes from the lowlands dropped like flies wounded after battle. However, despite the altitude problem, world records were broken, and as a result, the sports festival gained tremendous prestige and world prominence." Ain't no stopping him now, and four years later Josh went on to participate in the Third Pan-American Games held in Chicago, Illinois, Soldier's Field during August 27 to September 7, 1959.

*****

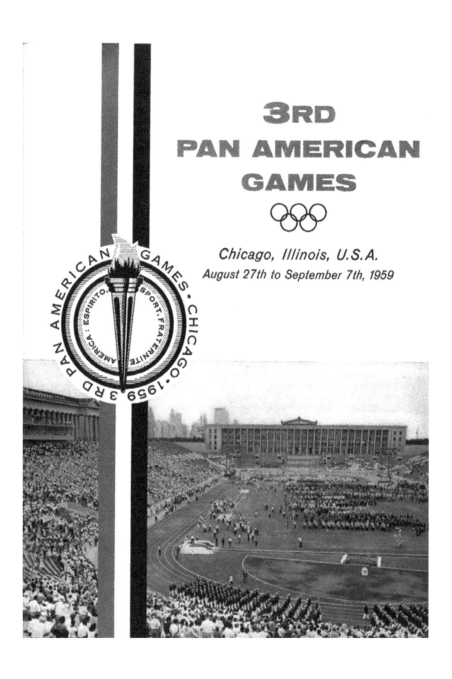

3RD
PAN AMERICAN
GAMES

Chicago, Illinois, U.S.A.
August 27th to September 7th, 1959

United States Gold Medal Winners

1959 PAN AMERICAN GAMES

CHICAGO, ILLINOIS

ATHLETICS—MEN
(Track & Field)

DONALD G. BRAGG
  Pole Vault
DYROL JAY BURLESON
  1500 meters
PHILIP YATES COLEMAN
  3000 meter Steeplechase
JOSH CULBREATH
  400 meter Hurdles
WILLIAM SOLON DELLINGER
  5000 meters
CHARLES EVERETT DUMAS
  High Jump
DAVID ALLAN EDSTROM
  Decathlon
ALBERT W. HALL
  Hammer Throw
HAYES WENDELL JONES
  110 meter Hurdles—400 meter Relay
JOHN JOSEPH KELLEY
  Marathon Run
THOMAS JOSEPH MURPHY
  800 meters
OTIS RAY NORTON
  100 meters—200 meters—400 meter Relay
WILLIAM PARRY O'BRIEN
  Shot Put
ALFRED A. OERTER, JR.
  Discus Throw
ROBERT ADDISON POYNTER
  400 meter Relay
BUSTER LARRY QUIST
  Javelin Throw
IRVIN ROBERSON
  Broad Jump
WILLIAM G. WOODHOUSE
  400 meter Relay

Josh Culbreath

"At the opening ceremonies of the 1959 Games at Soldier Field, the Third Pan American Games were opened by Dr. Milton Eisenhower, brother of the president, with a sparce[sic] crowd of 40,000—the smallest in Pan-American history. There were twenty-five nations and 2,263 contestants taking part in the opening day festival."

Other local track greatness such as Ira Davis and Al Cantello competed in the games. Josh bounced back with dignity when taking gold again at the Pan-American Games in Chicago:

400-METER LOW HURDLES—Josh Culbreath, a 27-year-old school teacher from Morgan State, retained the title in record time of :51.2, beating Dick Howard of New Mexico U. by a tenth of a second. Cliff Cushman of Kansas took the bronze medal in :53.0.

1,600-METER RELAY—The West Indies four-yard victory over the USA in the record time of 3:05.3 was one of the highlights of the Games. Mal Spence (:46.9) picked up three yards on Eddie Southern. Brother Mel Spence (:46.7) lost two yards back to Josh Culbreath. Basil Ince (:45.7) barely held off Jack Yerman in a scorching leg. Then George Kerr (:46.0) broke it up, winning by four yards over Mills.

Oops, he did it again! Josh sets new Pan-American record:

400 METER HURDLES
FINAL RESULTS — SATURDAY, AUGUST 29

Place	Name of Contestant	Representing	Time
1	JOSH CULBREATH	UNITED STATES	51.2*
2	RICHARD HOWARD	UNITED STATES	51.3
3	CLIFTON CUSHMAN	UNITED STATES	53.0
4	Anubes Ferraz	Brazil	53.4
5	Ulises dos Santos	Brazil	53.4
6	Victor Maldonado	Venezuela	53.4

* New Pan American record (old mark was 51.5 set by Culbreath, USA, 1955).

SEMI-FINAL QUALIFYING TRIALS — FRIDAY, AUGUST 28

Semi-Final No. 1	Time	Semi-Final No. 2	Time
1 Josh Culbreath, USA	53.2	1 Richard Howard, USA	53.5
2 Victor Maldonao, VEN	54.1	2 Clifton Cushman, USA	53.5
3 Anubes Ferraz, BRZ	54.4	3 Ulises Dos Santos, BRZ	53.8
X Guido de Jesus, PR	DNF	4 Gabriel Roldan, MEX	54.5
X H. M. J. Echeverry, URU	DQ	5 George Shepherd, CAN	55.6
		6 Armando Betancourt, CUB	TNA

DNF—Did not finish.   DQ—Disqualified after false starts.
TNA—Time not available.

Cousin Josh was also amid of women track and field greatness listed in meter relay events below (including Willye White, Martha Hudson, and Shirley Crowder) who represented the United States, where these women endured an intensified training program for Women's Team leading to eight gold medal triumphs:

400 METER RELAY
FINAL RESULTS — WEDNESDAY, SEPTEMBER 2

Place	Nation	Team Personnel	Time
1	UNITED STATES	ISABELLE DANIELS, WILMA RUDOLPH, LUCINDA WIL-LIAMS, BARBARA JONES	46.4*

400-METER RELAY — USA (Isabelle Daniels, Wilma Rudolph, Lucinda Williams and Barbara Jones), :46.4 (record).

Daniels   Rudolph   Williams   Jones   White   Hudson   Crowder

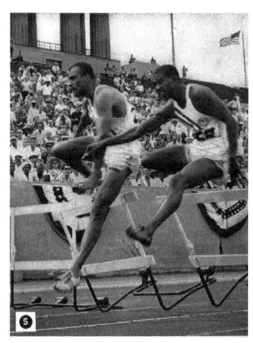

Richard "Dickie" Howard (left), and Josh Culbreath, both of USA,
drive for the tape in the 400-meter hurdle finals, the former winning.

Gibson

Even tennis great Althea Gibson was credited first US Gold Medal in Women's Tennis. Althea Gibson, the former US and Wimbledon queen, came out of a "temporary" retirement to win the single's title—the first ever for the USA in the Pan-American women's tournament.

9

Iron Curtain Victory Accolades by P'E No. 34

Josh's story continues on and on. Forever—there is no ending defeat. Upon his arrival back home to Norristown, Pennsylvania, he was remembered and met with cheers, tears of great jubilation, celebrations by his family and friends, and media frenzy. Cousin Josh was in all the newspapers locally by the Norristown *Times Herald*, chronicled by sports editor Red McCarthy; *The Philadelphia Inquirer*; he even appeared in *Time* magazine featured standing on the Olympian block along with his US track team buddies 1-2-3.

From his former home in Las Vegas, Culbreath recalled his trip down under in the Melbourne Olympics:

> It was something. I had to prepare myself for it. I read books about Jesse Owens. I got to know him. I'm still on his board in Chicago. Jesse was an inspiration. He was one of the emissaries. He went to Melbourne with us. People like him and Joe Lewis were people we looked up to. When he talked to me, I was the shortest hurdler in the world, but I was ranked number one in the world. Yuriy Lituyev was ranked number one in the world in the metric system.

Josh Culbreath, left. He's seen here with "Skag" Cottman and Jesse Owens (on right) at a sports banquet in Philadelphia. *Courtesy of the Skag Cottman family.*

Time magazine article titled, "Best Ever," reported the trials were probably the greatest display of mass US track-and-field prowess in history, and the US had the greatest team it has ever sent to the Olympics. In six events, US athletes ran faster and jumped higher than any other American ever had before. In three of the events, they exceeded what any other man had ever done anywhere. One of them was the 400-Meter Hurdles.

> Until 9:30 on the first evening of the trials, the world record of 0:50.4 was held by Russia's Yuriy Lituyev. Forty-nine and a half seconds later, two Americans had broken it and a third just missed it. The finish: Glenn Davis of Ohio State, University of Texas' Eddie Southern, and Josh Culbreath of Maryland's Morgan State College and the US Marines.

Culbreath said that he was on the first USA versus USSR team to visit the communist country:

> The first time we went there was in in 1958. It was the first time a team went behind the iron curtain. The first time they came to America, it was 1959. All the Big Five coaches picked my teammate to win and me to get last. They all picked Dickie Howard to win. My coach, Edward T. Hurt, from Morgan State, picked me to win. Dickie and I ran the eighth, ninth and tenth hurdles together, and then I just took off. It was held at Franklin Field at the University of Pennsylvania.

History in the making, Josh confronts the Iron Curtain during his 1959 race competition against the Russians at the height of the Cold War.

> If you thought Rocky Balboa and Ivan Drago's fight was Philadelphia's main contribution to the Cold War, think again. That feat belongs to a different Philadelphia icon—Franklin Field. On July 18, 1959, male and female athletes of

the United States and Soviet Union gathered at the home of the Penn Relays to engage in a good-spirited, yet highly politicized, track and field competition. In 1959, Josh was on the American team in the first USA-USSR Track and Field Dual Meet during The Cold War, held at Franklin Field. Yet, in July 1959, Franklin Field was the epicenter of the world as these two rival nations competed. According to the *Journal of Sport History*, the meet in Philadelphia included two athletes from each country in all men's and women's Olympic events.

Josh ran in the midst during a historical moment of the Cold War which was an ongoing political rivalry between the United States and the Soviet Union and their respective allies that developed after World War II. The Cold War was waged on political, economic, and propaganda fronts and had only limited recourse to weapons. Between Russia and the United States, he ran against the Russians in 1959 at Franklin Field winning the gold in the 400-m hurdles at 50.5. La Salle College graduate Ira Davis ran a leg in that 4x100 relay. Another La Salle graduate, Al Cantello, took the javelin result at 262'5" (79.99 meters). On July 18, 2019, it has been sixty years ago on this day, Philly was the center of US-Soviet Union tensions. The Semper Fi Marine and legend Olympian Champion that he was, Josh once again fought the good fight on Franklin Field battleground and won the race from a tense and changing relationship during the USA-USSR Track and Field Dual Meet Series. It's no surprise along the way he always remained "a fierce but friendly competitor, well-traveled and interested in other cultures, Culbreath would speak to rivals in their own tongue and then say, 'I'm gonna whip your butt,' in English, while they still smiled and nodded."

By all means, locals Culbreath and Cantello's defeat of the rival nation Russia hit the presses in *Norristown Times Herald* sport wave headlines Tuesday, July 14, 1959, by *The Sport Show* editor, Red McCarthy:

Cantello, Culbreath Give Norristown Rare Distinction
World-Renowned Athletes Provide 'Community Double' Vs. Russia

World travelers Josh Culbreath, left, and Al Cantello 'come home' to represent United States in track meet with Russia this weekend at Franklin Field. Photo was taken a year ago when the Norristown athletes qualified in Bakersfield, Calif., for first USA vs. USSR meet in Moscow.

(AP Wirephoto)

Do We Realize
The Grandeur
Given Hometown
By Josh and Al?

Here is an excerpt of Red's editorial remarks behind the "grandeur" of Josh and Al:

It is tremendous, then, the stature that Al Cantello and Josh Culbreath have given Norristown through their athletic and goodwill exploits—and countless hours of sacrifice for arduous training.

It's a stature not bounded by the territorial limits of this vast nation, but a stature of worldwide significance—Cantello, the current world record holder in the javelin throw, and Culbreath, the former world record holder in the 440-yard hurdles.

They are two young men who, while not using the airlanes with consistency of a Secretary of State, nevertheless probably have outdistanced the diplomatic brief-case carrier, with competitive and goodwill visits to every continent on the globe—always carrying the address 'Norristown, Pa.' behind their identification.

Josh proved he was no jive turkey with the Russians because during his time running with the Philadelphia Pioneer Club, he also made the March 30, 1958 *NY Times* headlines in an article "CULBREATH WINS DASH" at a race in Ankara, Turkey:

CULBREATH WINS DASH

Bragg Victor in Pole Vault in Carnival at Ankara

ANKARA, Turkey, March 29 (*P*)—Josh Culbreath of the Philadelphia Pioneer Club raced 200 meters (about 220 yards) in 23.6 seconds today on a track so slippery from a day-long drizzle that he almost fell on his face at the start.

Despite the poor weather conditions approximately 2,000 fans watched the first events of a two-day athletic carnival. Later Culbreath romped 400 meters in 54 seconds.

Don Bragg, a former Villanova pole vaulter, was the biggest United States attraction with a leap of 14 feet 9¼ inches.

Harry Bright of New York was second in the 800-meter event, won by Fahir Ozguder in 1:56.3. George King. New York A. C. miler, was fourth behind Ekrem Kocak, who triumphed in 4:03.5 in the 1,500 meters.

The Americans' visit here was co-sponsored by the United States State Department and the Amateur Athletic Union.

*****

150

Come and read all about it! Josh's name gained celebrity status with news coverages of the Olympic Games as he was captioned locally back home in the front of *The Norristown Times Herald* sports section headline pages. He was starring in the sports newspapers and being interviewed by old-school Norristown's notable sports editor, Red McCarthy. Red McCarthy recognized Josh many times in one of his *The Sport Show* articles as "In Australia with The World's Best," "Godspeed to Our Local Olympians," and on the day in Melbourne, November 24, 1956, "Culbreath Finishes Third in Olympic 400-Meter Hurdles...Josh Timed in 51.6, One-Tenth of Second Faster Than Russian, to Give Americans First Sweep in Event Since 1920." Red wrote an intense write-up regarding that headline how America's 1-2-3 won the 400-meter hurdles:

> Glenn Davis, 21-year-old Ohio State sophomore from Clinton, Ohio who set a world record of 49.5 seconds in the U.S. trials, led a 1-2-3 American sweep in the 400-meter hurdles, the first sweep in the event since 1920.
>
> Davis set a new Olympic standard of 50.1 seconds and Eddie Southern of Dallas who finished second tied the old mark of 50.8 set by Cornell's Charlie Moore in 1952. Josh Culbreath, a Morgan State College grad from Norristown, Pa., completed the U. S. parade by finishing third in 51.6 seconds, just one-tenth of a second ahead of Russia's Yuri Lituyev.
>
> It was the same order of finish for the Americans as it was at the Olympic trials in Los Angeles last Summer.
>
> Back home in Norristown, Pennsylvania, Josh's parents, Mr. and Mrs. Jesse Culbreath, 822 Smith Street, when informed by *The Times Herald* of Josh's finish, the Culbreaths were naturally sorry their son didn't win, but were very pleased and happy to hear he placed third. Pete Lewis,

Culbreath's track coach at Norristown High, was also elated and was particularly pleased that Josh beat Yuriy Lituyev, the Russian.

November 22, 1956 was the Olympic Opening Games in Melbourne, Australia, and Red McCarthy wrote a sports article headliner in The Times Herald titled, "Warm Sunshine Greets Opening of 1956 Olympic Games," dated Thursday, November 22, 1956. McCarthy received a note by Josh and penned in his storyline "… The feelings of all athletes in this greatest of all international sports spectacles may be gleaned from the brief note arriving in the mails for this desk yesterday—dateline Melbourne, Australia, from Josh Culbreath: 'I have been training vigorously. Time is drawing nigh. A dream in a dream, and a dream of a lifetime! Regards to all, and please say a prayer that I can do my best. Thanks—Josh.' Certainly, a sincere, and humble, request. Win, place, show or lose, the athlete beseeches the Almighty to only help him do his best."

Another sports headliner written by Red in *The Times Herald* on Friday, November 23, 1956:

Culbreath Leads Hurdle Qualifiers at the Olympic Games in Melbourne

Nov. 23—The American trio of Josh Culbreath, Glenn Davis and Eddie Southern marched ahead in the 400-meter hurdles toward Saturday's semi-finals and finals. Culbreath, from Norristown, PA., won the fastest heat in 50.9 seconds, only one-tenth off the Olympic record.

Davis, of Clinton, Ohio, won his heat in 51.3, and Southern, of Dallas, Tex., won his heat in the same time.

Qualifying behind Culbreath, who has been trying to shake a cold, in the third heat of the day were Guy Cury, of France, clocked at 51.6, and

Jose Paracio, of Columbia. Even with a cold Josh can singe a win in a heated race.

Thanks to Red McCarthy's coverages on Josh's Olympic track legacy, it jubilated excitement of proud Norristown residents throughout the years and even today by a man who left an impact in the sports world of hurdling in track and field.

*****

After a whirlwind dream come true, breaking world records, winning golds and a bronze medal, hailed as an Olympian Champion, Josh eventually returned home from Melbourne, Australia, to Norristown, Pennsylvania, and once again, Josh was headlined in *The Norristown Times Herald* along with another local Olympian Al Cantello: "President Sends Congratulations to Cantello, Culbreath;" "Community Celebration Climaxes 'Day' for World Champion Athletes;" "Day of Tribute Starts with Service Club Luncheon." At the Service Club Luncheon held at the Valley Forge Country Club, athletes Josh and Al were honored as Norristown's two victors for the USA in the recent international track and field meet with the Soviet Union. All smiles, they were greeted by Pete Lewis, who started them off as their coach at Norristown High; Judge Alfred L. Taxis, Jr., who presided at the luncheon, and Red McCarthy, sports editor of *The Times Herald*, toastmaster.

Day of Tribute Starts With Service Club Luncheon

Sept. 15, 1959

Norristown's two victors for the U.S.A. in the recent international track and field meet with the Soviet Union were all smiles when greeted by Norristown service clubs at a luncheon yesterday noon at Valley Forge Country Club. Left to right are: Pete Lewis, who started them off as their coach at Norristown High; Cantello, Culbreath, Judge Alfred L. Taxis, Jr., who presided at the luncheon, and Red McCarthy, sports editor of The Times Herald, toastmaster.

(Times Herald Photo)

President Sends Congratulations to Cantello, Culbreath

Salute Cantello and Culbreath Tonight—Military Parade Highlights Program at Roosevelt Field

Met with more accolades, Josh was greeted by and personally met with Hail to the Chief! Josh was recognized and congratulated in person by President Dwight D. Eisenhower. The personal congratulations of President Eisenhower highlighted an almost day-long community tribute to Norristown's two world prominent athletes, Lt. Al Cantello and Josh Culbreath.

The president's message was delivered by Douglas R. Price, special assistant to Eisenhower at the White House, during a climaxing program at Roosevelt Field. John B. (Jack) Kelly, Jr., Olympic oarsman, member of the prominent Philadelphia family, was also a guest speaker.

Cantello, who shattered world record for the javelin throw in June held in Compton, California, and Culbreath, who broke the world record for the 440-yard hurdles in 1957 in Oslo, Norway, were saluted by their friends and neighbors for the stature they have achieved for Norristown in the eyes of the world.

It was a huge fanfare hoopla for the athletes honored with a joint service club luncheon at Valley Forge Country Club. Later, they had paid a visit to children of the Montgomery County School for the Physically Handicapped, then addressed the study body at their alma mater, Norristown High School, at a special assembly arranged by Principal Lewis V. Kost.

The gala celebrations carried on with hosting a "Cantello-Culbreath Day" which had marked the first official community tribute to the two young men who gave Norristown the distinction of being the only community in the nation to provide the United States two winners in men's competition of the recent international track and field meet with Russia.

Their achievements, however, have been worldwide for a number of years. For the record, Culbreath, a medal winner in the 1956 Olympic Games in Australia, broke the world 440-yard hurdles record in 1957 in Oslo, Norway. He was the 1955 Pan-American Games 400-meter hurdles champion in Mexico, and two weeks ago, broke the Pan-Am record in successfully defending his title in Chicago. That is crazy amazing.

As for Cantello, he was currently a lieutenant in the Marine Corps and had attained many collegiate and national honors in the javelin throwing event. He reached the acme of his competition the past June when he threw the javelin 279 feet to break the American record, then threw it 282 feet, 3 ½ inches for the greatest throw ever made by man in one of the world's oldest sport—spear-throwing.

DID YOU KNOW?—Both of these young men have traveled far and wide since their graduation from Norristown High School, carrying the name of Norristown in all corners of the globe. In addition, to traveling under AAU supervision for international competition, both have been selected on numerous occasions by the U. S. State Dept. to conduct clinics on foreign soil.

Inspiration describes these two esteemed great men of high regard. They are a reflection of stamina, courage, and unselfishness. They are a shining great example of standing icons with commitment to success for any challenges they face.

*****

Salute Cantello and Culbreath Tonight—Military Parade Highlights Program at Roosevelt Field

An informal dinner at the Valley Forge Hotel preceded the program at Roosevelt Field. Keynoted with a military parade into Roosevelt Field, an open-air program affords Norristown the opportunity of paying tribute saluting its world prominent athletes, Josh Culbreath and Al Cantello. The community-wide salute to two native sons, both of whom have established world track and field records next to their names. A motor cavalcade, headed by United States Navy Band, US Marine Color Guard and Marine marching unit, US Army drill team, US Army Reserve units, Combat Support Co., First Battle Group, 111th Infantry, Twenty-Eighth Division, Pennsylvania Army National Guard; C Company, First Battle Group, Nuss-O'Hara—Todd Post, VFW Drum and Bugle Corps; Norristown Post Catholic War Veterans' State Championship drill team, Segmor VFW Post, Willow Grove drill teams; Boy Scouts of America, Valley Forge Council, Lafayette District took the party from the hotel and will lead the cavalcade from the hotel travelling East on Main Street to DeKalb, North on DeKalb to Fornance, West on Fornance to Markley, South on Markley to the program at Roosevelt Field, where it was met by other military and veterans' units for a grand parade into the stadium. A squadron of helicopters from the Pennsylvania National Guard also were expected to participate dipping in salute over Roosevelt Field during the early evening.

In prefacing the personal message from President Eisenhower, Price said he was particularly pleased "to have the opportunity to represent the White House here tonight as a way of stressing the importance which President Eisenhower attaches to competitive sports as an integral part of our way of life."

The President's message in full:

"It is a pleasure to send greetings to the citizens of Norristown assembled in honor of their fellow citizens, Lt. Albert Cantello and Mr. Josh Culbreath.

"In their performances at the recent track and field meet with athletes from the Soviet Union, these two champions brought honor to their community and to their country. Their fine state of training, competitive spirit, and largeness of heart, provide a splendid example to all."

Congressmen Join in Tribute To World Champion Athletes

Borough Leaders, Service Clubmen Say 'Thanks' for World Prominence Given Norristown by Josh 9/15/59 Culbreath and Al Cantello

September 15, 1959 it was headlined in the papers,

CONGRESSMAN JOIN IN TRIBUTE TO WORLD CHAMPION ATHLETES
Borough Leaders, Service Clubman Say "Thanks" for World Prominence Given by Josh Culbreath and Al Cantello.

Norristown service clubs, Rotary, Lions, Kiwanis, A.B.C., Exchange and Junior Chamber of Commerce, paid their respects to Lt. Al Cantello and Josh Culbreath during a luncheon at Valley Forge Country Club. The scheduled speaker, Congressman John A. Lafore, Jr., was unable to attend because of Congress being in its final day of its 1959 session. However, he did forward a telegram of congratulations and tribute to the two world prominent athletes. Later during an informal dinner at the Valley Forge Hotel, John G. Schett, president of the Central Montgomery County Chamber of Commerce, was the toastmaster.

Andrew A. Malane, manager of the Valley Forge Hotel, rolled out the hotel's new red carpet for dignitaries and gave the Cantello-Culbreath entourage the distinction of receiving the hotel's first 'red carpet welcome.'

The telegram sent to Congressman Lafore to Burgess Merritt W. Bosler, general chairman of the observance committee:

"Since receiving your kind invitation, I have been looking forward with great anticipation to attending your community ceremonies honoring Norristown's two outstanding athletes, Josh Culbreath and Al Cantello, who accomplished such magnificent feats in the U. S. A. versus Russia meet, this bringing honor and glory, not only to themselves, but to their home town Norristown, the State of Pennsylvania, and the nation.

"Most unfortunately, Congress is in the last hours of its 1959 session just prior to adjournment when vitally important legislation is being given final consideration; and as your representative in Congress, it is absolutely necessary that I remain in Washington during these closing hours to look after your interests as my constituents.

"Will you, therefore, please convey to the good citizens of Norristown and to the two distinguished athletes, Josh Culbreath and Al Cantello, they have gathered together in honor my deepest regret at not being able to be with you on this momentous occasion which would have given me as much real personal pleasure.

"The recent victories of these two world famous athletes at the dual track meet in Philadelphia have, I believe, particular importance because these triumphs, great as they were in themselves, have even more significance since the competitors were Russians whose ideology recognizes and credits only the strong and the proficient. These young men representing us and our way of life are symbolic of our country's strength, and their actions have shown the Russians our strength in the only way they understand.

"Will you please extend to Josh Culbreath and Al Cantello my warmest and heartiest congratulations on their outstanding athletic prowess and accomplishments, together with my sincerest best wishes for their future success and well-being."

JOHN A. LAFORE, JR.,
Representative in Congress,
Montgomery County, Penna.

Senator Hugh Scott sent his congratulations:

I sincerely regret the pressure of Senate business, as the Session nears its end, prevented me from making plans to join with you and the Community of Norristown in honoring Josh Culbreath and Albert Cantello.

Norristown is to be commended for this fine recognition in proclaiming "Cantello-Culbreath Day." These two fine athletes have brought honor and renown not only to the Community, but to the State of Pennsylvania and the nation.

Will you please extend to them my personal congratulations and very best wishes.

HUGH SCOTT,
US Senator.

*****

10

Flying High in India

The closing ceremonies and celebrations were not the end of the road yet for Josh who continues to keep ticking like a stopwatch. Josh was like the definition of a handheld timepiece designed to measure the amount of time that elapses between its activation and deactivation. It never ends for him. From the Olympic podium to the global populous country in South Asia, the halo of the Olympic rings continues to shadow the following of Josh's journey to the globe of India.

"India can have winning athletes."

After the Olympics, Culbreath continued running in military competition throughout the 1950s and in to the 1960s and recalled details of one particular visit to India.

"When I went to India, I wanted to see if what I had read was true. I lived in the villages, and I saw the most wonderful people, caring people. Maybe they didn't have a lot, but they were willing to share it with you," he said. Josh loved to tell stories of his travels and his running career. He trained one of the best athletes of India, Milkha Singh, who was called "The Flying Sikh" in India. He was a great runner from India.

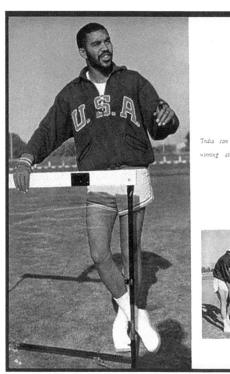

Josh instructing Indian coaches at the National Institute of Sports.

"REGARDLESS of what many others may think, I tell you this: given the training and much-needed encouragement, Indian athletes would fare far better at Olympic meets than they have so far done. And this is possible within a couple of years."

Joshua Culbreath, 30-year-old American Olympic star, was speaking. Josh is at present in Bangalore where he is coaching the Indian track team for the 1962 Asian Games, scheduled to open in Jakarta, Indonesia, on August 24.

In his home town of Norristown, Pennsylvania, Josh Culbreath is a teacher in a school for mentally retarded children. For the past year, home for Josh and his wife and their two children has been Patiala. In the massive Motibagh Palace, which now houses the National Institute of Sports, the American track champion has been training Indian athletic coaches under an assignment from the Rajkumari Sports Coaching Scheme. He expects to continue his work in India for another nine months.

The desire to encourage Indian athletes is uppermost in Josh Culbreath's mind. "I'm told," he says, "that India is a poor country, that many of its people are undernourished. That may be true. But, I'm told that, because of this, India can't have winning sportsmen. That's not true.

"What is more needed here is motivation, a change of attitude toward competitive sports. Get rid of excuses and develop the determination to win."

The Culbreaths are not the only foreigners residing at the Institute. As Josh says, it's a real United Nations in miniature. "Here we are a United Nations in *peace,* working for *peace,*" he emphasizes. The teaching staff include, qpartfromJosh, another American, one Iranian, one Australian, an Englishman, two coaches from the USSR, and a badminton specialist from Malaya.

Josh is now retired from competitive sports. "I have had my laurels," he says, "the best laurels a runner can dream of. And I feel my legs becoming faster and faster

JOSH CULBREATH   Continued

each year. But I don't have to run all through my life."
That is why he is in India, trying to impart some of his
knowledge and technique to others.

India is where Josh Culbreath wanted to coach and
he wanted it enough to decline several offers to teach in
Africa. Josh saw Milkha Singh and other Indian sportsmen
in action at the 1956 Melbourne Olympics, where he
himself ranked third in the 400-metre hurdles and won a
bronze medal. There he was convinced that Indian
athletes have a great potential in international sports.
Since then—and particularly since his first visit to India,
on his way to Tokyo for the 1958 Asian Games—he has
been determined to return to this country and work with
Indian athletes.

A NATIVE OF Pennsylvania, Josh blazed a trail of
spectacular achievements for about fifteen years in
national and international sports. He remained, from
1948 to 1951, the world's 400-yard hurdles champion.
Two years ago he broke his own record with a 51.2
seconds timing by winning the 400-metre Pan-American
Games championship at Chicago. Another outstanding
event of his career was winning the 1951 Pennsylvania
State championship in 200-yard low hurdles, which
earned him number two ranking for that event in the
United States. His achievements are numerous in several
other track events, including high and broad jumps,
100, 200 and 400-yard dash events and relays.

Surprisingly, all this Josh achieved with a pair of
deformed feet. He was born with an extra bone in each
foot. Only recently he underwent corrective surgery.
Another aspect of his career deserves mention and has
a special relevance to India. Josh's own life has been a
denial of the popular notion that academics and athletics
are incompatible. He himself has always been good at
his studies and was graduated with honours both from
high school and college, taking a Bachelor of Arts degree
in political science. He completed courses for a master's
degree in education at Temple University in Philadelphia,
before departing for India last year.

Life at Patiala is an active and strenuous one for both the trainees and the teaching staff of the Institute. Josh conducts lectures in the morning from seven to nine-thirty and in the afternoon between three-thirty and six. In the afternoon sessions, he conducts his practical work with trainees on the field and performs as he instructs. He does not want his students to accept any idea or theory on trust. He feels he must himself demonstrate what he wants to explain, and he does it with a facility and a seriousness that can be expected only from a master athlete.

The Institute, Josh thinks, is unique in Asia, providing scientific coaching as a means of raising the standard of sports and games. Though it commenced functioning only on March 28, 1961, it already shows great promise. Apart from having ample accommodation for class rooms and laboratories for its future development, the Institute is laying out numerous playing fields—several of them turfed for cricket, hockey and football—a cinder track, clay and lawn tennis courts.

For the time being only those trainees are admitted who have had experience in bona fide coaching assignments. Josh says: "It's a grand idea to teach the teachers first—when they are really qualified, their students can't be poor, and gradually these teachers and their students will jointly work to raise the standard of sports throughout the country."

Josh's athletic training course at Patiala covers fifteen events, each lasting eight days. The main events in his course are 100, 200 and 400-metre dashes, 110-metre high hurdles, 400-metre hurdles, and pole vault.

But Josh Culbreath does not view his assignment as all work. He applies the same energy as on the field to learning as much as possible about India, its customs and traditions. His love for India is genuine and emphatic. He has named his infant son Ranga, after his old friend and the Institute's present deputy director Mr. T. D. Ranga Ramanujan. His elder son, four-year-old Qalil, speaks quite a few words in Hindi with an impeccable accent. "I want them to assimilate as much as they can of this country," Josh tells, "This experience is a part of their heritage." Since he is at Patiala, Josh has also grown a beard. "Why not? I'm in the Punjab. It seems so natural to me. And, frankly, I've always hated shaving."●

Josh training Indian athletes, including Milkha Singh, far left, for Asian Games.

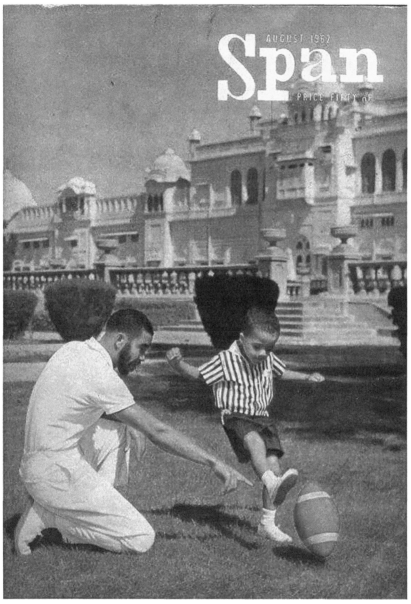

August 1962: The cover: Josh Culbreath gives his young
son his first lessons in American Football.

Josh trained one of the best athletes of India, Milkha Singh, who was called "The Flying Sikh" in India. He was a great runner from India. Josh trained Indian athletes for Asian Games.

The first independent sports star of independent India, Milkha Singh, dominated Indian tracks and fields for more than a decade in his speed and consciousness, setting multiple records and winning numerous medals. "Flying Sikh," according to Pakistani records, he was born in Govindpura, Punjab, British India on November 20, 1929. He won the commonwealth games individual athletics gold medal. The President also conferred the Padma Shri award on Singh, who was most remembered for finishing fourth in the 400-meter final at the 1960 Olympic games.

In 1958, he broke the 200m and 400m records at the Cuttack national games.

He also represented the country at the 1964 summer Olympics in Tokyo. He set an Olympic

400m record at the 1960 Rome Olympics, winning a gold medal at the 1958 commonwealth games and the 1956 Asian games.

He also won gold medals in the 1958 and 1962 Asian Games. He represented India in the 1956 Summer Olympics in Melbourne,

It was a race in Pakistan in 1962, where he defeated 100-meter gold medalist Abdul Khaliq at the Tokyo Asian games, where he was dubbed "The Flying Sikh" by Pakistani president Ayub Khan.

His life story was made into a movie *Bhaag Milkha Bhaag* (Run, Milkha, Run) that was released in 2013.

Singh died on June 18, 2021, at the age of ninety-one in Chandigarh, India.

*****

11

The Master Plan

The master plan was in the horizon on Josh's agenda. Josh participated in a number of Masters Road Race Series and was headlined numerous times in the *National Masters News*. Competition never held this Olympian down from retirement. He participated in track-and-field events at the Masters, competing against other forty-plus athletes. Circling an about-face return into the States, Josh filtered his steps to "the Flower City" Rochester, New York, June 26, 1982, participating in the 14th Annual Eastern Regional Senior/Masters track and field meet at Fauver Stadium. The National Masters was declared a huge success due to help from its sponsors like: Cola; Seven-Up; Diet Seven-Up; Nike; and Penn Mutual.

Dick Withrow, president of the Greater Rochester Track Club, thanked the parent Seven-Up company of St. Louis and the Seven-Up Bottling Company of Rochester.

Representing Seven-Up were 1956 Olympic 400-meter hurdle bronze medalist Joshua Culbreath, and Warren G. Jackson, former nationally ranked high jumper (1948–52) and minority affairs consultant to Seven-Up.

Culbreath won the 45–49 400-meter hurdles in 62.5 and finished second to Haig Bohigian of Tarrytown, New York, in the 100-, 200- and 400-meter dashes.

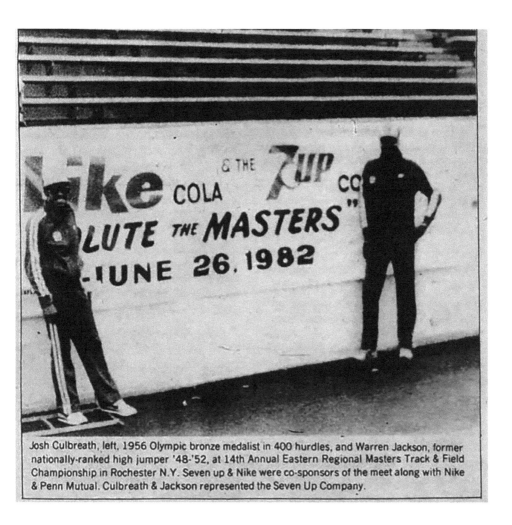

Josh Culbreath, left, 1956 Olympic bronze medalist in 400 hurdles, and Warren Jackson, former nationally-ranked high jumper '48-'52, at 14th Annual Eastern Regional Masters Track & Field Championship in Rochester N.Y. Seven up & Nike were co-sponsors of the meet along with Nike & Penn Mutual. Culbreath & Jackson represented the Seven Up Company.

Clicking his winged Hermes heels all the way to Wichita, Kansas, Josh tailwinds to participate in the September 1982 National Masters T&F Championships in Wichita.

Olympic medalists Josh Culbreath, left, and Bob Richards meet at 1982 National Masters T&F Championships in Wichita. Culbreath took 2nd in M45 400H (61.54), while Richards won M55 pole vault (11'0") and took seconds in the shot and discus.

Sportsfoto by John Allen

*****

A man of steel and determination, I would not call out Josh as no spring chicken. Josh's numerous health setbacks and his remarkable recoveries was a further testament to his indomitable spirt, his will power, and faith. I suppose during his childhood days growing up in the South when he had a rapport with the chickens, he was fearless. He figured out how he can take away the eggs from the chickens without the chicken hawks coming after him. Josh knew how to escape and evade obstacles. He was an overcomer, and he triumphed over tribulations. You can't stop the inevitable—and if you want something, you have to train for it. Train he did, and the results were remarkable. He was a true Olympian once again protected by the power of kismet. The following story explains.

V World Veteran's Track & Field Games, September 23–September 30, 1983

Sri Chinmoy opened the V World Veteran's Track & Field Games, San Juan, Puerto Rico, at Hiram Bithorn Stadium with a silent meditation. Over 2000 masters athletes from 47 countries competed in the event. He also wrote the Games' official anthem, as well as competing in the Games.

Remember Him?

Olympic hurdler Josh Culbreath (right) chats with United Nations meditation leader and masters sprinter, Sri Chinmoy, left, at the recent V World Masters Games in Puerto Rico. (Photo by Dhananjaya)

"At 51, Josh Culbreath Takes to the Olympic Hurdles the Second Time Around." The New York Voice, Saturday, October 22, 1983.

"At age 51, 400-meter hurdler Josh Culbreath has triumphed over four major auto accidents and a bout with the bottle to win his second Olympic bronze medal.

Culbreath won his first bronze medal at the 1956 Melbourne Olympics: his second came at the recent 1983 World Masters Olympics, held in Puerto Rico. The Games were attended by over 2000 men and women from 47 countries and included over 20 former world Olympians.

'It's a miracle Josh is running at all,' said his former world Olympics coach, the current masters 100-meter world record holder Payton Jordan. 'He's walking around with a 3" metal tube in his lungs and 2" missing from his left hip that they took to repair a paralysis in his spine. He's a true champion in all ways!'

Culbreath himself tells of his steel-willed determination in over-coming the paralysis of his left side that saw him working endless hours relearning how to walk. Pain led to a bout with the bottle, and by the late 1970s he had ballooned from 145 pounds to 180 pounds. Then he read an article on Jordan's success in masters running…

'I solidly back the Masters competitions every chance I can,' Culbreath said. 'The competition gives encouragement, motivation and inspiration to the older runner. It gives longevity to their lives. It gives hope to the younger athletes, too; they see they'll have an avenue for competition as they get older.'

Sri Chinmoy, the masters athlete who conducted the opening meditation at the Olympics, supported and expanded on Culbreath's views. 'The Masters Games are most significant,' he said. 'Look how athletes such as Josh are helping and encouraging each other. Such joy they are both giving and receiving!

'These athletes,' he continued, 'have learned through years of often painful experience that true happiness comes from transcending their own previous limits, and this does not preclude helping others do their best as well...'

Sri Chinmoy, June 5, 1987:

> "Brave runners, my heart is all gratitude to you. The English dictionary houses the word "impossibility," but your life-history-book does not include the word "impossibility." You live not only in the world of possibility, but also in the world of inevitability.

*****

Colorado's high elevation may have knocked him down, but he was one of "over 200 athletes who braved snow and frigid temperatures to travel to the Lake Erie Open Masters Indoor Track and Field Championships, January 8, 1984, hosted by the Over the Hill Track Club and sponsored by the Seven-Up Company." His noted performance as a "1956 Olympic bronze-medalist, Josh Culbreath, Philadelphia Masters, was a winner in both the 45y hurdles (6.7) and the 440 (63.7)."

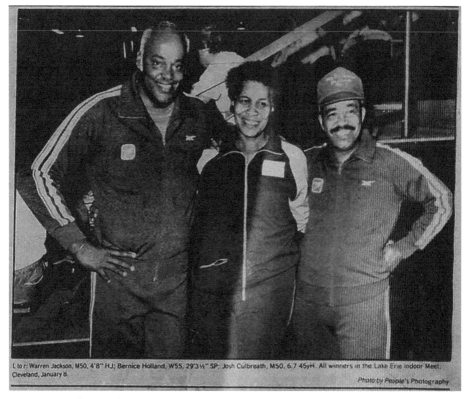

L to r: Warren Jackson, M50, 4'8" HJ; Bernice Holland, W55, 29'3½" SP; Josh Culbreath, M50, 6.7 45yH. All winners in the Lake Erie Indoor Meet, Cleveland, January 8.

Photo by People's Photography

Left to right: Warren Jackson, M50 4' 8" HJ; Bernice Holland, W55, 29' 3 1/2" SP; Josh Culbreath, M50, 6.7 45yH. All winners in the Lake Erie Indoor Meet, Cleveland, January 8.

April 1984, the sixty-eighth issue of the *National Masters News* headlined, "MIDWEST INDOOR DRAWS 160."

The second edition of the TAC Midwest Regional Masters Indoor T&F Championships at the University of Cincinnati on February 26 brought together 160 athletes from nine states and Canada. In all, 101 masters fieldhouse records were set by all age groups.

In the much awaited M50 300y duel between Missouri's Dr. Lee Blount and Philadelphia's Josh Culbreath, Blount edged ahead to win in 36.8 over Culbreath's 37.5.

He also competed in the Men's Long Jump Final:

```
LONG JUMP FINAL    50-54
1. Josh Culbreath           PP        16'9"
   (16'9"-16'3¼"-P-P)
2. Larry Steinrauf          Boo       16'7"
   (F-15'6"-16'1"-16'7")
3. Bob Jones                DM        16'7"
   (15'6"-F-P-16'7")
4. Burt Saidel              DM        16'0"
   (16'0"-14'7"-P-15'1")
```

June 1984, the seventieth issue of the *National Masters News* headlined, "300 COMPETE AT UCLA." in Los Angeles, April 28–29, "sixteen former Olympians joined over 300 other age 30-or-over athletes for the First Annual Olympic Legends Masters Track and Field Meet on the new Olympic track at UCLA's Drake Stadium."

Josh had hopped a plane and notched the M50 hurdles at UCLA's Drake Stadium on Sunday, April 29 in 64.0:

```
M50
Josh Culbreath          64.0
Joe Murphy              66.5
Will Robinson           68.1
```

September 1984, the seventy-third issue of the *National Masters News* highlighted Josh, as a newcomer, enjoyed two marvelous days weather-wise participating in the 50-odd Masters on July 7 and 8 for the 1984 National Decathlon Championships at the new IUPUI Stadium in Indianapolis.

> In the M50 age group, Leon Trout, 50, Union, NJ, was the champion, tying a meet record in the hurdles. Bruce Hescock, 50, Bethany, CT, finished second. Former 400m Olympic hurdler, Josh Culbreath, 51, Gwynedd, PA, finished third, setting a 400m meet record with 57.6.

*****

12

Overcoming Racial Barriers,
Obstacles, and Adversity

Ira Davis

Hate has no home here. Josh reflects on his trials and tribulations of racial barriers he faced during
his travels and running years as a record-holding
Olympian. A Marine veteran serving his country
he was disregarded. Even those front-door qualifications were met with direction to the end of the
line. As you read through Josh's biography you will
read about his challenges he had to endure.

Like storytelling Josh, another Olympian
standout by the name of Ira Davis had a story

to tell. Ira and Josh were athletic mates during Chicago's Third Pan-American Games in 1959 at Soldier Field, and in Philadelphia's 1959 Penn Relay Games between Russia and The United States first USA-USSR Track and Field Dual Meet during The Cold War. La Salle College graduate Ira Davis ran a leg in that 4x100 relay. Another La Salle graduate, Al Cantello, took the javelin result at 79.99 m.

Smelling the roses at times are not always peachy creamy. Ira has a compelling, as he sees it: the "ability to realize that there is a story to be told." "The story is not always told in a timely fashion, and lots of times the stories that can be told are not always available for minorities to reflect on. I have a story probably like every other black man…"

In 1959, he was chosen to partake in a good-will tour to Africa. Ghana. Nigeria. South Africa. Rhodesia. He recalls approaching customs in Johannesburg: "Josh [Culbreath] and I were the only two blacks on the team. The coaches were White, the other athletes were White. We got up to go through customs to get on the plane thinking everything is fine, no big deal, I'm an American. I went to the front of the line, Josh was behind me, the rest of the team behind us, and customs made me get out of line. They made Josh get out also. They made us go to the back of the line. We were supposed to be stars, but still we were not accepted in a lot of ways."

This continued on to Rhodesia (modern day Zimbabwe) where the pair were warned that they might not be able to stay in the hotels. Although this didn't transpire, they do remember going to get haircuts and coming back to reporters and cameramen in the lobby. One man showed them a newspaper headline that read Davis and Culbreath Denied Haircuts, "which was not true, so we had to explain what had happened and how we were received graciously and whoever owned the article was lying." That reporter was fired and put out of the country.

Davis would go on to have a notable national team career when opportunity for the triple jump presented itself, which was not a lucrative life-style. He was making three dollars a day repre-senting the USA. To support his wife and chil-dren, he persevered through workforce obstacles (including a bid-rigging attack by a white com-petitor) to become one of the most successful minority business owners in the Delaware Valley at the time, owning development and moving companies worth millions.

Davis reflects on his path—the highs and lows, the triumphs and injustices. He defied expectations and broke barriers as an athlete, as one of the first black track and field head coaches of a major white university (when he took over at La Salle in 1976), and as La Salle's first black Hall of Athletes inductee.

From all of this, Davis asks for reflection. He wants student-athletes to think about Black History Month, on those who have come before them and on the impact that can be made on those who come after. Understanding that there is an enduring power in the story that you can write.

*****

Josh faced another low episode and he continued to fight injus-tice in his own way.

Sometimes he paid the price, but he kept on proving his point.

Such was the case when he was summoned from the campus of Morgan State in Baltimore for the 1955 Pan-American Games in Mexico and met up with the team in Houston.

Culbreath and his fellow black teammates were not allowed to stay in a fancy hotel, instead being put up on a local Army base.

When the same hotel arranged for the athletes at the Army base to have steak dinners brought in, Culbreath refused.

"They said, 'Oh no, you can't do that,' … I said, 'Oh, yes I can, and you don't what to get me started,'" he recalled, shaking his head from side to side, still displaying a combination of disbelief in the scenario and pride in his stance.

"And they didn't," he added. "They knew better."

*****

There is another story told by Australian long-distance runner Allan "Al" Lawrence. He won a bronze medal for Australia in the 1956 Summer Olympics. Al has written a book called *Olympus and Beyond (A Story of Life, Sport, and Love on Four Continents)*. In his book, he shares a titled story in chapter 31—"August–September 1957 European Tour"—"Just Call Me Jack" about Cousin Josh. Al explains he arrives for competition in Gothenburg which is the second-largest city in Sweden. He arrives at a hotel when the meet promoter, a Mr. Stromberg, arrived from the railway station where he had picked up a small American team, which included Josh Culbreath, the bronze medalist in the 400-meter hurdles in the Melbourne Olympics.

Stromberg announced to Al that he would be running a special 5,000 meters against Gordon Pirie, the 1956 Silver Medalist, and current world record holder at 3,000 and 5,000 meters, and T. P. Togersen of Denmark, who ran both the 5,000 and 10,000 meters in Melbourne.

Al checked in and went to his room, not, however, before he first had a visit with Josh Culbreath, the American intermediate hurdler, whom he met in Melbourne.

Later, during their stay in the hotel, apparently Al explains there was a riff of serious arguments between Mr. Stromberg and Gordon Pirie regarding Pirie's uncooperative attitude not running in a 5,000-meter race against a competitor. There was a full-scale shouting match in the hotel lobby, and Al states he was chatting with Josh Culbreath and witnessed the whole exchange. Finally, Gordon shouted that he and his wife were checking out of the hotel and returning to Malmo. This made Mr. Stromberg even more furious. So Al, Gordon, and his wife escaped, and the three of them made their way quickly across a park and flagged a taxi to the railway station, where Gordon bought two tickets to Malmo. Al arrived back at the hotel—it was in uproar with small search parties searching the premises and making inquiries among the hotel's athlete-occupants. The Piries flight had not gone unnoticed, however, Josh Culbreath has seen the three of them fleeing across the park outside the hotel and was enjoying the furor the Pirie's departure was causing.

Although Al was questioned by the "Little King" (Mr. Stromberg) about Gordon's possible whereabouts, he seemed to have escaped major suspicion of complicity in the Pirie's "flight for freedom." Al learned that Josh Culbreath had no love for promoter Stromberg, either.

> "I was invited to run my specialty, the 400-meter hurdles, but when I arrived here I was told by Stromberg that I was also going to run the Open 400 meters, as well! I can't complain to anybody, and I can't do anything about it myself." At the time, I never asked Josh the obvious question, why not?

Later, Josh told me that Black touring athletes faced different and more difficult obstacles to overcome than their White counterparts.

*****

Sharing their journeys

Glance, Culbreath among those able to break down racial barriers through athletics

By ROD HARWOOD • Sports writer

Three-time Olympian Harvey Glance and Community Colleges of Spokane hurdles coach Linda Lanker, who also coaches at Coeur d'Alene High School, were members of coaching staff for the United States team at 2006 Junior World Games in Beijing, China. Glance and Josh Culbreath, right, a bronze medalist in the 1956 Summer Olympics, are the keynote speakers at the "It's About Time" human rights student summit Monday at Coeur d'Alene High School.

COEUR d'ALENE — They have dedicated their lives to taking on the world — world class, world records, world best — clearing social, political and economical hurdles to chase a dream.

They come from different eras within the same vision and now they come together in the Inland Northwest to see if sharing their experiences might help make the world a little better place.

United States Olympian and former world record holder Josh Culbreath was part of the American sweep in the 400-meter hurdles at the 1956 Melbourne Games. He later set the world record in the 440-yard hurdles in 1957 in Oslo, Norway.

Three-time Olympian Harvey Glance was a member of the American gold-medal winning 4x100-meter relay in 1976 at the Montreal Games. The 16-time All-American equaled the 100-meter world record twice in 1976.

Culbreath, who earned a master's degree from Temple and a bachelor's in political science from Morgan State, and Glance, the only black head coach in University of Alabama history, will be the keynote speakers at the "It's About Time" human rights student summit Monday at Coeur d'Alene High School.

"What Martin Luther King Jr. was doing (with the civil rights movement), I was doing things of that nature in sports," said Culbreath, who won his bronze medal in 1956 while long-time friend and mentor Jesse Owens looked on from the stands as President Dwight D. Eisenhower's personal representative.

"A lot of young people don't realize what we went through. Here I was a three-time (AAU) national champion, but in the South, we had to go in through the back of a restaurant. I think athletics opened a door. Jesse would tell us, all we want is an opportunity. All we wanted to do was represent our country."

Heavyweight champion Joe Louis and Owens took those initial strides for Culbreath and others to follow. Glance, who is considered the greatest sprinter in Alabama state history, continued the time line.

Glance, a three-time Olympian and gold medalist, became vice president of USA Track and Field in 1988. When his track career came to an end, he went on to become the head coach at Auburn until 1997, then became the head track coach at Alabama.

He wasn't without his own trials and tribulations. Glance was a team captain on the U.S. Olympic team that was forced to boycott the 1980 Games in Moscow.

"I want to talk about what I think is one of the most important facets in life, which is education," said Glance, who was the fastest man in the world in 1976 when he held the world record for the 100-meter dash and the world record in the 100-yard dash in 1978.

"Jesse Owens was my idol, not so much because of the running part, but because of his life. Almost every generation gets caught up in its own generation and forgets about those that come before them. When you talk about the history, there was a color barrier that had to be broken and people took a stand and made that happen. They raised consciousness and brought attention to it and made it easier for guys like myself.

SHARING

from B1

"It's about education and raising consciousness that when somebody's going through a struggle even though you have nothing to do with it, you can help change that."

Where Glance did not experience segregation or the "whites only" signs, Culbreath did. He remembers not being allowed in movie theaters in St. Louis despite having won three national championships, as well as being the first black man to compete in Florida.

Culbreath, who is also a United States Marine, says in spite of it all, one of the proudest moments in his life was standing on the podium in Melbourne with gold medalist Glen Davis (50.29) and silver medalist Eddie Southern (50.94) and seeing three American flags go up as they played the national anthem.

"I was holding my medal in one hand, but you could see, in the Marine Corps, your index finger would be in the seam of your trousers and that's where my index finger was because, being a Marine, I was going to stand tall," said Culbreath, who ran 51.74 that day to win the bronze.

Glance was a coach on the 2006 World Junior team that competed in Beijing and will return on the coaching staff of the 2008 U.S. team. He is beginning his 10th season as the head coach of the men's track team at Alabama.

"I am the first and only black head coach in University of Alabama history in 170 years of athletics, so we've made great strides," said Glance. "I did not live during the time of white and colored bathrooms, but I know of that. If you're not directly affected, then you probably can't relate.

"But that's why it's important to know the history, that it existed and it can still exist if people's minds are not like.

"I'm in hopes that we're better off today and that's what this is about."

"It's About Time" is the theme to Monday's student summit on the national holiday recognizing Martin Luther King Jr.'s efforts. The summit, free and open to the general public, begins at 1 p.m. at CHS.

'The Martin Luther King of athletics'

JASON HUNT/Press

Josh Culbreath speaks during the Student Summit at Coeur d'Alene High School on Monday.

Rising above the hate

Athletes share how hurtful behavior drove them to new heights

By LUCY DUKES
Staff writer

COEUR d'ALENE — Harvey Glance had the choice of giving up when people threw bottles at him as he ran.

He could have stepped back when he faced racism.

Instead, he became a 16-time All-American, three-time Olympian, a gold medal holder and 100-meter dash world-record holder.

"I became the fastest man in the world, driven there by people who wanted to pull me down," said Glance, now the head coach of the men's track and field team at the University of Alabama and coach of the United States track and field team at the 2008 Olympic Games in Beijing.

Glance, Josh Culbreath and a dozen or so other athletes shared their experiences at the Student Summit on Monday at Coeur d'Alene High School. The summit celebrated the role of athletics in promoting racial equality.

Culbreath and Glance were the keynote speakers at the event, attended by about 100 people and organized by the Human Rights Education Institute. Breakout sessions with various athletes followed their talks. The two also spoke at a Human Rights Education Institute sports-oriented fundraiser later in the day.

see SUMMIT, A5

Josh's Sunday school teacher Mrs. Lillian Bright encouraged Josh to be in the church program plays. He was a small boy for his age at that time. A few years later went by, and Josh was much older. He said to Mrs. Bright, "Why do you always want me to be in the same plays doing the same thing? I'm older now."

Mrs. Bright said to him, "Josh, you do such a good job, and because you speak so well, you make people stop, look, and listen to you, and everybody cannot do that."

THE PRESS Tuesday, January 22, 2008 A5

SUMMIT

from A1

Culbreath was a bronze medalist in the 1956 Olympics in the 400-meter hurdles, and was a 440-yard hurdles world record holder. He has coached many Olympic athletes and has been described as the "Martin Luther King of athletics."

Williams

During the breakout session, he talked to those gathered around him about what it was like to be the first black athlete to compete in South Africa, waiting in line with his team at customs and being sent "into the back."

"It hurt," Culbreath said. "We had stood in line with other people, but we weren't regarded as other people."

Culbreath also told those listening on Monday that when he ran, he represented Americans, and believed he was entitled to American freedoms.

He told them that at one point he was a champion athlete, but wasn't allowed into a movie theater because of the color of his skin.

Those who heard the two speak said they were grateful to learn about their experiences.

"I thought it was really interesting how the things that were supposed to hurt only drove them further," said 16-year-old Matt Harlow, a student at the high school.

The event showed that racial discrimination is still present, but that it's becoming less of a problem, said 17-year-old Jay Eborall, another Coeur d'Alene High School student.

NIC Athletic Director and Student Summit emcee Al Williams said the panel of athletes was "tremendous."

"I'm just in awe of their experiences," he said.

*****

Gratitude

There are many Unsung Black Olympian track-and-field athletes from our past sport's history worth celebrating. These forgotten Black Olympians named in chapter 3 who were groundbreakers need to be resurfaced and recognized.

One early morning, I was watching *The Tamron Hall Show* hosting an episode called "Stories of Gratitude." An aha moment by Tamron's topic directed me back to my writing of Cousin Josh's sports biography surrounding the same perspective. Josh's sports biography is an expression of gratitude. It is important to acknowledge his and many other past Black Olympic track-and-field athlete's vital life journeys. Their training of mental and physical exercises prepared them to compete for rivalry competition. Undergoing intensive workouts showed on the track and field through the spikes of their footwear pounding into the track lanes crossing the finish line to victory. Those impactful events were gripping moments we need to commemorate.

In the past, everything had its place. During this period time, Cousin Josh and his fellow Olympian teammates were surrounded by the civil rights movement of segregation in the '30s, '40s, and '50s. These athletes who traveled on the road encountered and suffered biases when told there was no housing to reside in during their travels as Olympians. Even when they were not traveling, they ran into these things. They did not have special privileges because they were all Black. In an oral history lesson, my cousin Josh told me of the prejudices which they encountered. They were refused entrance into restaurants to be served and refused entry into movie theatres. In some situations, when honored by established organizations and at luxurious first-class hotels, they had to enter by the back door because they were Black, regardless. When the late Jesse Owens went to a well-known lavish hotel in New York City to be honored after winning four Olympic gold medals, he had to go by the back door. Also, in high school, they were told they would never measure up with a college degree.

In time, the sounds of the crowds in the stadium become quiet. Despite these negative experiences, they recognized themselves as proud Americans. They cherished the moments by hearing the national anthem playing as they stood on the Olympic victory podium representing their country and savoring every precious minute that comes to an end. It is an experience of a lifetime.

Later in life, the realism of the civilian world sets in. When these Black Olympians came home, most people focused their mentality on them as Olympian athletes. People did not realize these athletes were accomplished with advanced collegiate and professional degrees. A vast percentage of them emerged successfully with their lives. They became graduates of distinguished colleges, universities, and graduate schools. They became prominent doctors, lawyers, vice presidents in corporations, scientists and inventors, orators, educators, served in the military, and some became Hollywood entertainers.

Another story about a brilliant scientist and inventor was the late Dr. Meredith Gourdine. Dr. Gourdine was an Olympic silver medalist in the long jump who competed at the 1952 Summer Olympics in Helsinki, Finland. After graduating from Cornell University, he became a scientist and inventor. Dr. Gourdine invented *Incineraid*, a system that dispersed smoke from buildings and fog from airport runways. Dr. Gourdine was awarded *over thirty patents* during his career. In 1994, Dr. Gourdine was inducted into The Engineering and Science Hall of Fame. They did not want to be perceived as athletes or jocks. They are more than just athletes. They are deep-rooted established leaders. These Olympian athletes performed a lot of community service to everybody who crossed their path. They wanted to use and articulate their experiences and talents to pass on to the next generation of youths and young athletes.

After the Olympic games, Cousin Josh and his fellow past Unsung Black Olympian friends became mentors, leaders, and contributed humanitarian services to their communities. They implemented a change in the community with acts of teachings to children and trained young athletes who had become Olympians. Their contributions were selfless and humble. All of these are true stories and more to be told. These are all the things that make Cousin Josh and these incredible Unsung Black Olympians heroes, not as Olympian jocks. It is important to remember and recognize Cousin Josh and his Olympian friends during their groundbreaking moments—setting history and excelling in their events at the Olympic Games. Forever these world-class athletes will leave an imprint of exciting memories of our time in sports.

Embrace their heroic epic moments. These are the people who lift us, and they opened doors like the shining light of the Olympic flames that all things are possible, and we owe them a debt of gratitude.

13

"Pop"

Despite all the obstacles Josh encountered throughout his life, his strength and determination have allowed him to thrive. Through his later years he took on his next leap as a Track Team Coach. During his coaching career, he started training young talented track athletes honing their athletic skills to become Track & Field Olympians such as Sayon Cooper, Deon Hemmings and Neil de Silva. Josh was affectionately known as "Pop" by his athletes. Here is the story of Sayon Cooper who reflects about Josh as his college coach who told him he was good enough for the Olympics.

Hanging with Mr. Cooper: Liberia's Track Team Coach

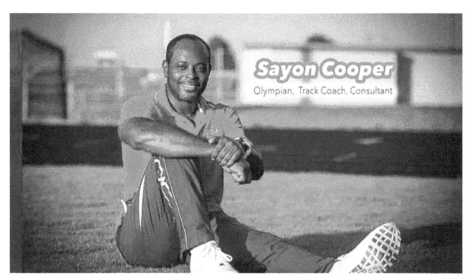

JUNE 13, 2018, MANSEEN

"Liberia was going through a war and I was proud to represent my country. I was proud to show that there was still hope for us."—Sayon Cooper

Humble Beginnings

Grow up. Become a soccer star. The typical Liberian boy aspires to reach these two milestones.

Before heading to Rio, Liberia's track team coach, Sayon Cooper sat in his office at the Morehouse School of Medicine and reflected on how his soccer dreams turned into track and field success.

"I didn't know anything about going to college for free on a track scholarship," Sayon Cooper admits.

His track career began, almost accidentally, during the end of his sophomore soccer season. Sayon's high school soccer coach insisted he find a way to stay in shape until the new season began. That summer, Coach Godrey Moore transformed Sayon from a striker into a sprinter. In 1992, His undeniable speed got him lots of attention at Seneca Valley High School. It had only been a few years since the teenager left his grandmother in Liberia to join his parents and younger siblings in Maryland, USA.

Coach Cooper confesses, "I wanted to be like my father. He played soccer, but not professionally." Instead, the young runner took on his mother's athleticism. "My mother ran track and played basketball. She was very good," he adds.

Indeed, his mother's athletic genes opened huge doors.

"First my high school coach told me I could go to college for free. So, I set my goals on that. Then my college coach [1956 men's 400m hurdles Olympic Bronze medalist Joshua Culbreath] told me I was good enough for the Olympics. So I set my goals on that," Cooper explains.

Success in Track and Field

He leans back in his chair and laughs at how clueless he was about his talent and the opportunities it would provide. As Coach Cooper continues the conversation, he subconsciously runs through a list of names—coaches and agents who impacted his career. Coach Culbreath. Coach Kitley. Paul Doyle. Coach Seagraves. The list goes on.

Each name acts as an investor contributing to Cooper's impressive accomplishments at Central State University, Abilene Christian University, two Olympics, and several World Championships.

"When you have a calling, God has a way of pulling you towards it," Cooper says. I've always wanted to expose athletes to the information and opportunities that my coaches gave me."

*****

Joshua Culbreath a.k.a. Pop
Sayon Cooper

The following reflections on Pop by Sayon Cooper were composed during his airplane trip home from the 2020 Tokyo Olympic Games.

The first time I walked in his office, I knew it would be a beginning of something special. I noticed his smile, which brightens the room and his voice as sharp as a master Sergeant in the military. It was if he had met me before.

The wall was somewhat intimidating as I saw a picture of a man going over a hurdle. That picture was taken at the 1956 Olympic Games in Melbourne, where coach Joshua Culbreath (whom I will referred to as Pop; will explained later) earned himself an Olympic bronze medal.

Coach Culbreath quickly became more than a coach to me, as I made a daily stop at the end of my school classes each day. We would talk about his life experiences on how he became a United States Marine, an Olympic bronze medalist, a father, and an educator. It was these moments that motivated me to think about life after college and my purpose in this world.

He made me believe I could achieve anything in life if I put in the work and believe that in due time, those goals and dreams would become a reality. In addition, he made it clear that nothing in life was handed to you on a silver platter. His strategy is you go and take what's yours and don't make excuses for your short comings or when a goal was not achieved initially. You get back up and keep fighting, because all champions experience failures, but it's about learning from your mistakes and moving forward, he used to say. It was that moment I decided that I wanted to be an Olympian like Pop. He would say "don't be like me, be better than me". What a powerful saying that kept my drive going when there were challenges or slight setbacks along my Olympic journey. I used to say to myself, if Pop can do it, so can I.

During my freshman and sophomore years at Central State University, my biological father and I were not on good terms. Pop played a significant role in making things right with my father. Pop would share his relationship with his father and how beneficial it was to him; however, he made it clear that eventually things would work itself out, and that I should never feel embarrassed to say sorry when in the wrong. Pop was right! My relationship with my father eventually improved over the years, and today, we have moved passed those early conflicts and misunderstanding. It all came down to communication and expressing what I felt on the inside. Pop was great at communicating with his athletes. He was that father you never had. I felt so comfortable to discuss anything (good or bad) with him because I trusted him.

My achievements as an athlete came developed during my days at Central State University and many hours spent with Pop. I became an Olympian in 1996, which was my junior year.

After my junior season at Central, the University lost its athletic track scholarships. Pop called me to the office to share the news. He said he was going to Morehouse College, and I was welcome to come along with him. In addition, he said I can get you to any college in the

United States base on your track and academic performances. I initially had Arizona State, Texas Christian University (TCU), Abilene Christian University (ACU), and UCLA on my list.

It came down to two (2) schools, ACU and TCU. Abilene Christian University took all my credits and would allow me to graduate on time. TCU wanted me to go an additional semester, which was not in my future plans. My college roommate at the time (Ayodela Aladefa) and I visited Abilene and we immediately knew that was our next and final stop for our undergrad experience. That college year was the best year of my collegiate season, as I became a National champion in the 55m, 100m, and 200m. I also ran on our national championship 4 x 100 and 4 x 400m relay team (indoors and outdoors). Later that year in 97, I represented Team Liberia at the World Championships in Athens, Greece and missed advancing to the 100m Finals, finishing 12th in the World at 100m, and quarter finals in the 200m.

In 1998, I graduated with an Industrial Technology degree. Fast forward to present day, I am happily married to Tangi Cooper, and a proud father of 5 girls. I also enjoy spending time with other family members, especially my mother, Elizabeth Tubman White, my dad T. Romeleus Cooper, God mother Theresa Foster Sydnor, siblings (Alaric Diggs, Keania Cooper, Rocelia Cooper, Tre Childress, and Adama Diggs when he's around).

I recently attended my fourth Olympic Games (2 as an athlete and 2 as a coach).

These things were possible because Pop took the time to make a difference in his athlete's lives, including mine. I will always be grateful and thankful for being his son from another mother. And to Jahan Culbreath, Camille Culbreath, and other family members, I thank you dearly for sharing Pop with us. He truly made a lifetime impact in my life and may God bless his soul forever.

*****

Deon Hemmings winning the 1992 college women's 400m
hurdles for Central State at the Penn Relays. Her first of two
Penn Relays wins. Photo courtesy: "courtesy Penn Relays."

Deon Hemmings was another Olympian Josh trained under his watch developing a 400m hurdler. Josh moved on to instruct young people around the world in track and field. Hemmings was the first ever Jamaican woman to win an Olympic Gold when she won the 400m Hurdles at the 1996 Olympics in Atlanta, Georgia breaking the Olympic record which stood to 2004. Hemmings also won two silver medals at the 2000 Olympics Sydney Games in the 400m Hurdles and 4 × 400 m Relay (together with Sandie Richards, Catherine Scott-Pomales and Lorraine Graham).

Josh was known as "Pop" to his athletes. Well, "Pop" was no joke because

when Deon Hemmings, a female runner from Jamaica, said she didn't want to run anymore at practice, Culbreath offered to help her to pack her bags.

She stayed, and went on to win a gold medal at the 1996 Atlanta Olympics (where three of his other athletes also competed) and two silver medals at the 2000 Sydney Games.

A male runner with Olympic pedigree, Neal de Silva of Trinidad and Tobago, was actually sent home but welcomed back when he "became a man."

De Silva, who placed seventh at the 1992 Barcelona Olympics, paid the price.

Culbreath, his coach, proved a point.

*****

14

Sports Chatter Memories in Las Vegas

Vegas, "The City of Lights," was where Josh had resided as his former residence during the early beginnings of the twenty-first century. Culbreath was a regular in Las Vegas on Fox Sports radio with partners primary CBS Sportscaster Radio Network host Rich Perez and Minnesota Vikings Joey Browner from 2002–2005 while all three represented CMX Sports and Entertainment.

During their casual meetings at the M Resort Hotel in Las Vegas, Rich engages in several interview sessions from 2008 thru 2009 with Josh. Josh employs his oratory skills to Rich with his telling stories of past Olympians he personally encountered during his running days as an Olympian, with athletes he remained brotherly and "big brother" friends with, such as Jesse Owens, Wilma Rudolph, Willye B. White, and Bob Woodruff. Here are Josh's stories about these unforgettable athletes spoken to Rich in his exact own words:

Josh interview by Rich Perez at the M Resort Hotel in
Las Vegas. Courtesy photo: Cynthia Culbreath

June 28, 2008—Dr. Joshua Culbreath and Rich Perez Talking of Willye B. White

Josh takes time to talk about the great late
Willye B. White and her accomplishments. He
goes on to tell his story and tribute to his old
teammate Willye B. White. One of the greatest
athletes of all time. Willye made five Olympic
teams. The first time she made one was in 1956
in Melbourne, Australia.

"I was on that team, she was on that team,
and another young girl was on that team by
the name of Wilma Rudolph. Where did this
inspiration come forth for this young lady to
try and become as devastating as she did? Let's
turn the pages of history for a moment. Willye
B. was an extraordinary athlete as a child from
what I heard. She could always run and jump.

209

As a young girl, of approximately about ten years old I heard that she was beating girls who are in high school and a few who made freshman in college. She wasn't the exceptional athlete. Well, we had people that may have inspired her like Jesse Owens and being from the Chicago area he did a lot. I remember reading about him a great deal, and I learned from talking to him and being on the board of the Jesse Owens Foundation in Chicago. What it was to have an opportunity to know this man. Willye got to know him as well. We somehow feel that what the greatness association breeds a simulation, and truly this you have to respect. Willye learned a great deal. She was encouraged I'm sure by Jesse. But there was also a lady by the name of Alice Coachman. Alice Coachman was born in Georgia but went to an historical black school in Tuskegee. She went on to become the first black woman to win an Olympic gold medal in 1948 in London in the high jump. So, Alice Coachman has gone down in the history books because she was one of the first, and with that alone, a woman like Willye wanted to do many great things. Five Olympic teams, 20 years of training diligently, but never giving up and imagine she almost made six. She missed the long jump, I heard, by maybe a quarter of an inch. That was history in itself. But we can never forget what she has done. She has been truly a landmark and a guiding angel to many of the young athletes, not the black athletes and the females alone, but to the world. She was a good-will ambassador, she was loved, and she taught how it was to be competitive because she told me about a little place in Mississippi. It was a pleasure to being her big brother as I was called until the day she passed. It was a pleasure being able to talk about her. My teammate and friend with a great deal of love; and to Willye B., she will always be remembered on anything that happens in buildings and everything else throughout Chicago and The United States will be well deserved because she indeed is worthy of any recognition from her travels throughout the world. What an ambassador. To Willye, we wish her well. Godspeed."

*****

JUNE 28, 2008—DR. JOSHUA CULBREATH AND RICH PEREZ TALK OF JOHNNY WOODRUFF

Dr. Joshua Culbreath 1956 Olympic Athlete and Humanitarian in Las Vegas June 2008 talking of the greatest run in history made by the great 1932–1936 Olympic athlete in Track and Field Johnny Woodruff where Woodruff actually stopped in a race and still won…

Rich interviews Josh reiterating their talks about the great Johnny Woodruff and some of the accomplishments that he did during his lifetime. Josh told Rich a phenomenal story about how he stopped in a race. Rich asks Josh to reflect on that and it's a story that needs to go on the rest of our lives and beyond us. Here is Josh's story about Johnny Woodruff in his own words:

Josh recounts a telling story about "Johnny was one of the greatest athletes of all time." Johnny was born in a little place called Connellsville, Pennsylvania outside Pittsburgh. I had the pleasure of going to see John before he left us to go on to a bigger and better place. He passed away on October 30, 2007 in a place called Fountain Hills, Arizona and left his widow Rose. He was one of the greatest inspiration. Johnny as an athlete in Pittsburgh was an exceptional athlete. He was approximately six-feet-six. They called him "daddy long legs." "Long John" was the name he had, and he was an exceptional athlete. He was a freshman at The University of Pittsburgh when he made the 1936 Olympic Team that went to Berlin. He was a half-miler. Johnny was one individual that people knew he was going to be an exceptional athlete. He had natural ability. In attending at school in Pittsburgh I found out about him through his roommate by the name of Erwin "Ersy" Brown who was born in a little place called Norristown, Pennsylvania. Mr. "Ersy" Brown was my scoutmaster, and he had won a state championship for Norristown High School in Pennsylvania by himself. He had scored enough points to win the state championship in track. There was a guy by the name of Mr. Charles Blockson whose son became one of the great Black Historians in the world. His father contributed to his points in that winning the championship. Johnny and Mr. Brown became very, very close friends and inseparable. John made the Olympic team and went to Berlin. He was the only black man in the finals of 800-meters in Berlin. Everyone knew he was the man to beat. John took everything in stride. He knew he had to get out there because these guys were going to play games on him. The games they were going to play—box him in—because he's the one we have to beat him if we can keep him out and keep him in the box one of us could win, and that was the strategy. Well, they did just that. They boxed John in. He couldn't get out. They had just passed the 40-meter when the bell rang, two laps to the 800 meters. John knew if he tried to use his elbows that he would be disqualified for disrupting the other runners, and also tried to get out illegally because he couldn't get two strides ahead. So, what did he do? John stopped! He stopped! Never in history have a man done this in any race. So, when he did, he was spiked twice by runners who were coming fast. When he did this, then he gracefully moved out into outer lane. Now, he had approximately

300 meters to go and he has to catch up from a standing start. Never done before. But he went down the back stretch little by little he pulled up and pulled each one of the guys in a little at a time one yard here one yard there. When he came down off of a curve into the home stretch John Woodruff was in about four position. From here, he called upon everything that he had and everything that he had trained for because this was the big one, and as he came and posted last 50-meters he gave them this explosive kick that people had never thought would be humanly possible after stopping in a race. John Woodruff not only passed everybody, he not only won the Olympic gold medal, but he set a new Olympic record. That's what you call one of the greatest feats of all time. It was outshadowed only by Jesse Owens four gold medals. That's why people never heard about the great John Woodruff who was one of the greatest middle-distance runner in the world. I did a tape on him that he gave me his life story, and at one time, John supposedly broke the world indoor record for a mile, but he was never recognized. They never recognized also he held the world's record for 880 he had broken it but there was a discrepancy somehow between a white runner who had run on the same track and given a world record with John broke on the same track, but he was they stated it may have been a little short. The great John Woodruff will always be remembered by me because I loved him for the man that he was, and he was my friend.

Josh ends his telling story about John to Rich Perez. Rich concludes his interview thanking Josh teaming together for ten years in Vegas.

Rich commends Josh for being such a great humanitarian, and so glad Josh reflected on that story about Johnny Woodruff.

John Woodruff and the Nazi Olympics:

> Adolf Hitler embraced the Berlin Olympics as a chance to demonstrate his theory of the superiority of the "Aryan" race. John Woodruff was motivated to shatter that myth.
>
> "We destroyed his master race theory," said the 800-meter gold medalist.

Josh was right in telling his story about his friend Johnny Woodruff, who stopped in his 800-meter race during the 1936 Berlin Olympic Games. A 28-minute must-watch YouTube documentary video by TribLIVE, Olympic Oak: The story of John Woodruff, the 1936 Berlin Olympics & the roots of Athlete Activism chronicles the gold-medal victory of the Connellsville native. It is an emotional video that explains why Johnny Woodruff stopped in his race. The video expounds on how his heroic act affects sports activism today. As a heartfelt recommendation, every young track and field high school and college athlete (boy, girl, man, and woman), sports enthusiast, and every Olympian in any sport should watch this celebrated documentary. Like Josh, another Olympic great of 99-year-old, Herb Douglas, is the oldest living American Olympic medalist, having won bronze in the long jump at the 1948 London Olympic Games shares his relationship with John Woodruff. Being an athlete is an athletic gift. To be a winner and understand the lesson to become an Olympian, track and field athlete, or standout athlete in any sport of your choosing, you must understand and learn the history of black athletes before us.

*****

July 19, 2009—1956 US Olympian Medalist Joshua Culbreath Discusses Triumphs In Life And Sports With Rich Perez:

Josh Culbreath discusses triumphs in life and sports with Rich Perez at the beautiful M Resort Hotel in Las Vegas, Nevada on July 19, 2009. Dr. Joshua Culbreath one of Americas all-time best athletes and 1956 Olympic medalist discusses great events in track and history makers of his day. Dr. Josh Culbreath is well respected worldwide and tremendous leader in our country.

Rich makes his introductions announcing a lot of things had happened in the past: Tommie Smith, John Carlos, more Dr. Martin Luther King, all the way up to Barack Obama. But not many people know about Jesse Owens and what he accomplished. It really what sets forth the things in motion. Josh responds as follows:

That is why we are talking about Willye B. White being one of the great athletes of all time in five consecutive Olympic Team. Had it not been for Jesse setting the precedent in which he did, we wouldn't have what has come about now. Willye has been an inspiration to more women throughout the world (I think) than any other women because track and field is looked at in Olympic Games as largest contingent and of course it encompasses more events than any other sport. So therefore, with all the team members there and this one young girl tries out for five consecutive Olympic teams and establishing herself in the world as a woman who was a freedom of speech and rights, she was a real leader. We had women in the 1920s, but here you have

a young lady that took the initiative to be concerned about others and wanted other young
people to have the benefit of travelling in getting
an education and trying to make a difference in
which she has done to the world.

Rich chimes in ending the conversation
stating, "Tremendous it has been, Dr. Josh."
Thank you so much for sharing your thoughts on
all these great athletes and these times have been
lost but are memories and you are passing it on.

*****

Dr. Joshua Culbreath Discusses the Heroes of Track and Field's Past with Rich Perez, July 19, 2009:

Dr. Joshua Culbreath sits at an interview with Rich Perez at the beautiful M Resort Hotel in Las Vegas, Nevada. Josh one of America's all-time best athletes and 1956 Olympic medalist discusses great events in track and history makers. Willye B. White and Wilma Rudolph along with great plans for the future based upon the past accomplishments.

Rich introduces, "We're on the subject of Willye B. White whose been such an inspiration to so many people that don't even realize it today their lives are affected because of her." Rich asks Josh to tell his story for everybody how this all began. Here is Josh's story in his words:

Well, Willye B., because of her exploits and her determination and making all these Olympic Teams, there are a lot of people behind the scenes such as Dr. Nell Jackson and Dr. Ritchie because with these ladies there they were able to try and show the world what they were capable of doing. We had enough time with how it was going to be told and how it was all done. But Jesse Owens, like me, had started the ball rolling as far as integration into the sports world because sports people look at it as being something very clean and wholesome. I rather stick with sports as being the intro for having the black athletes and many other minorities now, Latino brothers and also sisters that have achieved because of what Jesse did which led to many of us because I would like mention during that era too, Rich, we had many people during the 1930s and the '40s there were more children named Joe Louis and Jesse than any other time I think in history because they were the only two role models that the colored, Negro, African Americans, black athletes and people had to look up to. But Willye B. came up after that time and she of course established herself with the females which has led to her starting many organizations which exist today. They have a foundation and everything else. Thanks to Dr. Ritchie we have a State Building named in Chicago today named after her. They have a park named after Willye B. and I am hoping that if the 2016 Olympic Games are accepted in Chicago that they'll name a stadium named after her because she has done so much to inspire not only the young children throughout Chicago but throughout the United States throughout the world. She has travelled extensively. She has spoken to many, many people. She missed making her sixth Olympic team in a row by I think about a quarter of an inch in the long jump. So you can see that she was destined to do many great things and there is not enough that I can say about her because with her and Wilma at that time, I was like there big brother in '56 and I was like a protectory of them. They were sixteen years old and to tell a joke which we shared until both of them died was I told them that they always look at me as their big brother and then when they became whoa! Twenty some years of age they became just absolutely gorgeous and so I told them, "I don't want to be your big brother anymore" Lol! But that was a joke until they died.

Rich laughing and says, "That's tremendous, Doc! [laughing] Well I tell you what, Wilma Rudolph and Willye B. White, those are two names that will live forever in the minds of the Olympians and the track and field and all of athletics, all of the people involved. I think it is a tremendous honor to have you sitting here telling us about these two because you had first-hand knowledge of them when so many people never got to meet these people. But you know the grassroots efforts that they started, and I tell you it's been just tremendous both their stores are amazing."

Josh says there is a lot more things to come with some of things that had been done, and the thing is with the Women's Organization have progressed so much as a result of Willye B. We can go on because these are the things that also were inspired like to Billy Jean King for instance. We were playing a major role and she was in tennis of course and Martina Navratilova I had the pleasure of trying to add to her career many years thereafter. But, it is so interesting to find out that a little girl from a little sharecropping area in Mississippi had risen to the world to the top of it in the athletic world and became somebody that people loved.

*****

July 20, 2009—The Civil Rights Movement In Athletics

Rich Perez introduces Norristown, Pennsylvania-born Dr. Joshua Culbreath one of Americas all-time best athletes and 1956 Olympic medalist discusses great events in track and history makers during an interview at the M Resort Hotel in Las Vegas, Nevada.

Rich asks Dr. Josh, "Tell me what led up to all the civil rights movements in athletics." Here are Josh's own words:

Well, it had to be of course as we said before Jesse Owens he tossed the baton like I like to regard myself as one of those guys that helped to do this as well. Willye B. was the woman that did it for the women in particular because of her tenacity and her determination and her outspokenness about world events and there's no doubt about it. Of course, when that happened in '56, she was a part of the big movement that came some years later and that was with Tommy Smith and John Carlos. But she had already established herself as someone to reckon with in the world [and say] freedom of many things of competition of women being comparable to men but she was on that team with Tommy and John Carlos in Mexico City when they raised their hands with the black glove in Mexico in 1968. So, you see she was a part of history still and went on to do other great things and our last Olympic Games was in 1972 in Munich.

So, there of course was historical in itself when the Jewish athletes were murdered.

Rich Perez ends his interview with Josh by saying, "wow, it's amazing Dr. Josh I want to thank you not only for myself, you're a great friend of mine but I want to thank you for all the people watching who admire you as well."

*****

From his personal possessions, I was given one of Josh's DVD medias and was curious wanting to know what was on it. I inserted the DVD on my laptop to listen and discovered in 2010, Josh was interviewed to talk about sports and about great athletes. In his own words, here are his exact words speaking about Willye B. White:

Hi there, my name is Josh Culbreath and I am here to talk about sports and about great athletes. One in particular I would like to mention is Willye B. White. A young lady that played a major role in developing (say my ability) to try to reach young people. Willye B. White, a name that we will remember for a long, long time. This is a young lady I think that brought something to the table, brought something to the party, and left a beautiful impression on the world. I talked to people about her and I explain that it's kismet. Kismet is a word which I had learned many years ago when I had the opportunity to run and later I was asked to come back to their country by the central government of India and kismet was a word that was so powerful that it has remained with me and will until the day I die. It means preordained, destiny. Just my talking about Willye B. for instance, it had to happen. From the expression they use in India it was written upon the wall—so shall it be done. It is written upon the sand, so shall it be done; and it is very true regardless of who you are and what you are. Having the opportunity of meeting someone has already been arranged many years before, that is kismet. Willye B. was a young girl out of Money, Mississippi. Money, Mississippi maybe located down near the Delta. I've never been there. But it's a cute name, Money. It means a lot to a lot of people, and I'm sure this little place where she's from was not a place which was a thriving (say, metropolis) but, she had something to bring from Money to the world. Willye B. was a young girl that had a lot of tenacity, beautiful thoughts like most of us when we were growing up. We wonder what are we going to be when we grow up? What are we going to do? Willye (I think) had learned what the word kismet was at a very early age because surely she demonstrated it. She lived it, and as a result there are hundreds and thousands of young children throughout the world that had profit by knowing her, reading about her, and the things that we hope that she left in her legacy.

A dream without a plan is just a wish. (Willye B. White)

*****

15

The Penn Relays

Franklin Field—one of track and field most iconic settings is noted for being the springboard for a lot of individual careers. It was the first venue that included college, high school, and foreign competitors. It is a place that captures the hearts of track fans everywhere to witness some outstanding record-breaking performers and teams.

Josh Culbreath, Norristown (Pennsylvania) High School '51; Morgan State '55; Quantico Marines '57; Philadelphia Pioneers '60 1953–55 A three-time winner in the 400m Hurdles, Culbreath was an important cog in the Morgan State relay teams which came to prominence in the 1950s. (Head coach:) (Inducted into Penn Relays Wall of Fame: 1994)

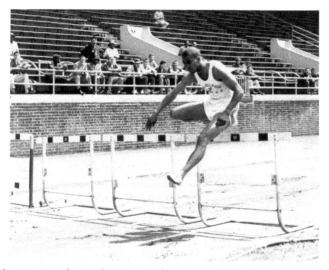

Josh winning the 1960 Penn Relays open 400m hurdles in 1960.
Photo credit: "courtesy Penn Relays."

PHILADELPHIA, PENNSYLVANIA—For any real deal serious track and field muses and sports enthusiasts you know what time it is when the month of April rolls around every year. Commuting by train, bus, on foot, or flying in by plane get ready to be met in The City of Brotherly Love with soft pretzels, cheesesteaks, hoagies, food and souvenir vendors, possible sold-out hotel venues, social outings, and huge crowds up to 100,000 at the yearly ritual of the greatest outdoor sports festival in the world—THE PENN RELAYS! You haven't been to a track and field meet until you've been to the Penn Relays. It is the most widely recognized historic annual relay meet. It is like a three-day weekend homecoming family reunion affair. Crowd surfing and *BANG*! echoes in the air by the sound of the gun for athletes to take off running in their competing lanes. Many grammar school kids, high schoolers, collegians, club runners, masters, Special Olympics, and wheelchair racers will compete in a place that looks as if you're at a main stadium of the Olympic Games Coliseum. You feel the atmosphere is a rushed adrenaline of excitement in seating stands by spectators all over the world who are about to lose their voices for screaming and cheering on their favorite athletes and track teams on the battlefield hosted by University of Pennsylvania's Franklin Field. Past Olympic Champion royalties and star celebrities are even present.

It is an all eyes on you spotlight moment—like being on Broadway—and a moment of a lifetime for all the athletes competing in this world renown carnival event. On any level, these athletes are champions. Win or lose, it will always be story telling memories for the rest of your life. It is an exciting feeling like some of the lyrics by Alicia Keys's best-selling song, "New York":

> Noise is always loud, there are sirens all around and the streets are mean
> If I can make it here, I can make it anywhere that's what they say
> Seeing my face in lights or my name in marquees found down on Broadway
> Even if it ain't all it seems
> I got a pocketful of dreams
> Concrete jungle where dreams are made of... Big lights will inspire you

Those lyrics are the same sentiments for Olympian Champion Josh Culbreath has as a trailblazer athlete. He was the light everywhere he went and he had a "pocketful of dreams." He is lauded as one of the sport's greatest who have competed in the Penn Relays. April 1994, he was inaugurated to be inducted as "charter member of the Penn Relays Wall of Fame along with 15 other inductees who are Mark Belger, Lee Calhoun, Chandra Cheeseborough, Eamonn Coghlan, Ron Delany, Herman Frazier, Charlie Jenkins, Marty Liquori, Herb McKenley, Ted Meredith, Eulace Peacock, Reggie Pearman, George Simpson, Norm Tate and John Woodruff."

"Another reason Culbreath is in the inaugural class of inductees to the Penn Relay Carnival Wall of Fame are the anchor legs, he ran during Morgan State's four-year win streak in the 400 relay. In that circle, he'll be known forever as No. 4. Herman Wade is No. 1. Otis Johnson is No. 2, and James Rogers No. 3. It's the order they passed the baton."

Josh was also a distinguished star member on the Penn Relays Welcoming Committee. As the stopwatch begins to slowly wind down after a worldwide, international energetic running career, but still carrying that Olympic Spirit in his blood, Josh was actively involved every year participating and making his appearances at the Penn Relay events. In April 2019, Josh was one of the

> notable Olympian members on the Welcoming Committee along with fellow Olympic notables Herb Douglas, Charles Jenkins, and Penn Relays Director Dave Johnson. They turned it into "an old home week" when they all celebrated the return of 1956 Olympic long jump champion, USA National Track and Field Hall of Fame member, and celebrated inductee into the Penn Relays Wall of Fame, Dr. Gregory Curtis "Greg" Bell. Dr. Bell made his return to Philadelphia's Franklin Field as the honored guest of the 125th University of Pennsylvania Relay Carnival—he was treated as royalty. Rightfully so. Properly so. He hadn't been back to the Penn Relays from his Indiana home for over a dozen years, and that made it even more of a joyous homecoming celebration. His memories are crystal clear—and they date back to the era when his event was named the broad jump, not the long jump. Dr. Bell extended the Penn Relays record to 25 feet, 6 ¼ inches in 1956, became the Relays' first 26-footer with his win at 26-1 ½ in 1957, and capped it all with a 25-8 ¼ win as a senior in 1958.

Dr. Greg Bell spent fifty years in dentistry and was more than director of dentistry at Logansport State Hospital in Indiana. He was a mentor and advocate for psychiatric patients. On February 19, 2020, he had surgery for heart valve replacement and insertion of a pacemaker. Finally, on May 30, he retired at the age of eighty-nine.

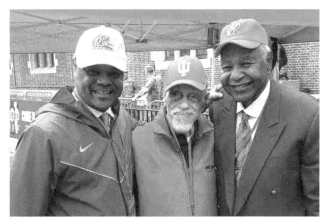

Herman Frazier, Gregory Bell and Charles "Charlie"
Jenkins, Sr. reconnect at Franklin Field
Philadelphia, Pennsylvania.

Look at this candid photo, it is priceless. I get excited when I learn about all of Josh's Olympian posse. Their ongoing brotherhood and sisterhood celebrated connection of it all is overwhelmingly emotional. I think about all their hard work, perseverance, trial and tribulations they all had to go through during their era. I know it was not easy but through it all that is why they are who they are—they are the epitome icons and timestamp of track and field history and greatness. THEY ARE—the for real deal—OLYMPIAN CHAMPIONS.

MOTTO: ONCE AN OLYMPIAN; ALWAYS AN OLYMPIAN
NEVER FORMER; NEVER PAST®

You cannot walk away from those valuable memories. Josh arrived in the world as a predestined winner. He left a laundry list of his athletic and community service legacy including his continued sports involvement on the Penn Relays Welcoming Committee. Josh will most be remembered for being an Olympian Hurdler Champion, a Hall of Famer, a Wall of Famer, serving his country as a Quantico Marine, an international world traveler around the globe, a sportscaster, Pop, a track coach training young track-and-field athletes honing their skills to become Olympians, an educator, a speaker, and a polyglot. He possessed dutifully actions to encourage others to work hard, stay focused, and never give up. He has influenced and paved the path as a positive fabled role model to former local Norristown track and field greats such as Ernie Hadrick, Lawrence A. Livers Jr., Ronald "Legs" Livers and twin brother Don Livers, Tony Darden, and Netta Young-Hughes, as well as countless other athletes from other suburban areas, out of state, colleges, universities, and around the world. He is recognized and renowned by multitudes of former Olympians, boxing, NBA, NFL and other renowned athletes, dignitaries, music artists, TV and movie celebrities around the world. For instance, the similarities of two Olympian athletes Edwin Moses and Sayon Cooper were influenced by Josh. Let's talk about a track-and-field sport—hurdling. Josh Culbreath comes to my mind because Josh and Edwin have likeness. What inspired Edwin about Josh is this man was five foot seven inches tall. He can jump a hurdle like he was a giant. Both are educators and hurdlers. Edwin and I discussed college life from his days at Morehouse. He told me Josh was an inspiration to him because they both attended HBCU. Because his parents influenced him as educators, stellar Olympic track great Edwin accepted an academic scholarship in engineering from Morehouse *College* rather than an athletic scholarship elsewhere. Josh had scholarship offers galore. But at the insistence of his sister and her phone call to Morgan's coach, Eddie Hurt, Josh wound up at Morgan; he received his bachelor of arts degree in political science and a master of arts and education from Temple University. Josh also attended the University of Colorado Law School from 1955 to 1956. Although there was no track at Morehouse, *Moses trained* for the 1976 Olympic trials using the public high school facilities around Atlanta. Josh, during his high school years, learned of his talent in track and field. Josh told his story while he was in high school: "We had a little strip in the back of Rittenhouse. It was cinder. I taught myself how to run. No one taught me." Josh said he wanted to excel at something because he was too small for the major sports. So he looked around for a sport that nobody wanted to do—the hurdles in track and field. Therefore, Josh became known for running the 400-meter hurdles. Josh was one of Morgan State's Flying Four Track Team hurdler hot commodity where he ran anchor leg all four years under his coach Eddie Hurt. Moses competed mostly in the 120-yard hurdles and 440-yard dash. Before March 1976, he ran only one 400-meter hurdles race, but once he began focusing on the event, he made remarkable progress. Moses convinced Hugh Gloster, the president of Morehouse, to grant him $3,000 for the Olympic Trials and support over the summer: "If you give me the chance to go to the Olympics, I will break the world record and win the gold medal." By 1980, Moses had been undefeated for three years, broke his world record, and was preparing to defend his title at the Moscow Olympics. During my discussion with Edwin about Josh, "We both ran the same event—the 400-meter hurdles. Josh is an Olympian, and I am an Olympian," he said. Edwin proved he was a hot commodity, just like Josh. Edwin Moses attended Morehouse College in Atlanta, best known at the time for its alumnus Martin Luther King. As noted, Josh was an athletic director at Morehouse College. A gasp moment of their uncanny similarities—Josh is depicted as the "Martin Luther King of athletics." Like Josh who is an Olympian, Edwin left his competitors in a trail of dust by his remarkable defeats excelling in the 400-m hurdles at the following Olympic Games:

Olympic Games		
G	1976 Montreal	400 m hurdles
G	1984 Los Angeles	400 m hurdles
B	1988 Seoul	400 m hurdles
World Championships		
G	1983 Helsinki	400 m hurdles
G	1987 Rome	400 m hurdles
IAAF World Cup		
G	1977 Düsseldorf	400 m hurdles
G	1979 Montreal	400 m hurdles
G	1981 Rome	400 m hurdles
Goodwill Games		
G	1986 Moscow	400 m hurdles

Edwin also "became the first recipient of USA Track & Field's Jesse Owens Award as outstanding U.S. track and field performer for 1981." Edwin was also the winner of the James E. Sullivan Memorial Award for 1983 as the nation's top amateur athlete. Josh was a friend of Jesse Owens, sat on his board in Chicago, and is posed in a photo with Jesse at a Philadelphia sport's banquet shown on page 145. Likewise, with Sayon Cooper, Josh was his college coach; trained and honed his skills to become an Olympian. Free education, I had mentioned earlier in my storytelling about Josh in this bio, he said, "If you have the sports that are there, you have a choice, and you having the choice to do what you want providing you can do it well enough; and you took those skills that you had and you can make them work for you by going to college free... So, I said, 'I have to do something' and I did. I said, 'If I can run that fast I can get a free education.'"

Similarly, Sayon had admitted, "I didn't know about going to college for free on a track scholarship." As Josh was encouraged to excel in sports under the tutelage by his high school coaches, Sayon affirms, "First my high school coach told me I could go to college for free. So, I set my goals on that. Then my college coach [1956 men's 400-m hurdles Olympic Bronze medalist Joshua Culbreath] told me I was good enough for the Olympics. So, I set my goals on that." Sayon looks back through a list of names—coaches and agents who impacted his career. One of them is Coach Culbreath. The others: Coach Kitley, Paul Doyle, Coach Seagraves. The list goes on. "When you have a calling, God has a way of pulling you towards it," Cooper says. Josh believed in the power of *kismet*. It means *preordained, destiny*. Remarkable similarities by the effects of Josh laid upon Edwin and Sayon are unexplainable. It is too astonishing. Now, that's leaving a mark stamped by a man who truly left an impact on these two renowned Olympian athletes.

Joshua "Josh" Culbreath has truly lived like the Olympic rings full circles of a wonderful, fulfilling great life.

*****

In 2013, Josh was the honorary referee at the Philadelphia
Penn Relays. Standing beside Josh is long-time dear friend
Philadelphia Penn Relays Director Dave Johnson.
Photo credit: "courtesy Penn Relays."

16

The Cherry on Top

On a personal note—Culbreath's list of athletic awards is stunning. The cherry on top of a brilliant whirlwind career, you are about to leap into reading-through the many achievements, accomplishments and recognitions of Joshua "Josh" Culbreath's life and legacy.

Personal information	
Full name	Joshua Culbreath
Nationality	American
Born	September 14, 1932 (age 88) Norristown, Pennsylvania, U.S.
Sport	
Country	United States
Sport	Track and field
Event(s)	400m hurdles
Team	Morgan State College (1952-1955) United States Marine Corps (1956-1958)
Medal record	[hide]
Men's Athletics	
Representing the United States	
Olympic Games	
(B) 1956 Melbourne	400 m hurdles
Pan American Games	
(G) 1955 Mexico City	400 m hurdles
(G) 1959 Chicago	400 m hurdles

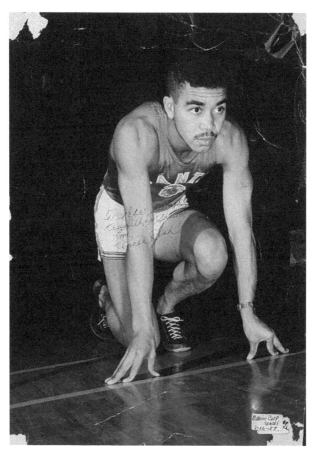

Courtesy: Culbreath Family photo

List of Morgan State University alumni

This is a list of notable alumni which includes graduates, non-graduate former students, and current students of Centenary Biblical Institute (1867–1890), Morgan College (1890–1938), Morgan State College (1938–1975), and Morgan State University (1975–present). Located in residential Baltimore, Maryland, Morgan State is a historically black university and Maryland's designated public urban university. The Morgan State University National Alumni Association is the official alumni organization of the university.

Sports

Name	Class year	Notability
Tim Baylor	1976	defensive back, Baltimore Colts and Minnesota Vikings
Joe Black	1950	pitcher, Brooklyn Dodgers, first African-American pitcher to win a World Series Game, NL Rookie of the Year (1952)
Bill Brown	1951	Track and field – 800 meters – Pan American Games Silver Medalist
Roosevelt Brown	1952	tackle, New York Giants, member of the Pro Football Hall of Fame
Raymond Chester		tight end, Oakland Raiders
Josh Culbreath	1955	Track and field – 400 m hurdles – 1956 Summer Olympics Bronze Medalist
Sijara Eubanks		professional Mixed Martial Artist, current UFC Flyweight contender
Len Ford	1949	end, Cleveland Browns, Pro Football Hall of Fame
Elvis Franks	1980	defensive end, Cleveland Browns, Oakland Raiders, New York Jets
John Fuqua		running back, Pittsburgh Steelers
Clarence Gaines	1945	former basketball coach at Winston-Salem State University, coached most basketball games in college history[citation needed]
Cornell Gowdy	1986	cornerback, Dallas Cowboys, Pittsburgh Steelers current NFL scout
Leroy Kelly	1963	halfback, Cleveland Browns, member of the Pro Football Hall of Fame
Willie Lanier	1966	linebacker, Kansas City Chiefs, member of the Pro Football Hall of Fame
Dave Meggett	attended, but transferred	NFL player
Joshua Miles	2018	offensive tackle Arizona Cardinals
Jack Pierce	1984	Track and field – 110 m hurdles – Olympic Games bronze medalist
Jeffrey Queen	1969	running back, San Diego Chargers, Oakland Raiders, Houston Oilers
Donald Sanford	.	American-Israeli Olympic sprinter
Visanthe Shiancoe	2002	tight end, New England Patriots
Chad Simpson	2008	running back, Indianapolis Colts, Buffalo Bills, and Washington Redskins
Rochelle Stevens	1988	Track and field – 4x400 m relay team – Olympic Games Bronze Medalist
John Sykes	1972	running back, San Diego Chargers
Maurice Tyler	1972	cornerback, Denver Broncos
Bob Wade	1968	cornerback, Pittsburgh Steelers, Washington Redskins, Denver Broncos
Mark Washington	1970	cornerback, Dallas Cowboys
Marvin Webster	1974	center, New York Knicks

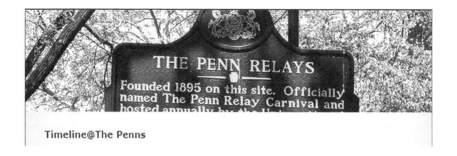

Timeline@The Penns

1949. Cornell's Charlie Moore—a future gold medalist—wins his first of three 440-yard hurdles. Following Moore was another three-time champion—Morgan State's Josh Culbreath (1953–55). There has not been another since.

USATF—USA Outdoor Track and Field Champions: Men's 400-m Hurdles

1955	52.0 (440 yd.)	Josh Culbreath	Morgan St
1954	52.0 (440 yd.)	Josh Culbreath	Morgan St
1953	52.5 (440 yd.)	Josh Culbreath	Morgan St

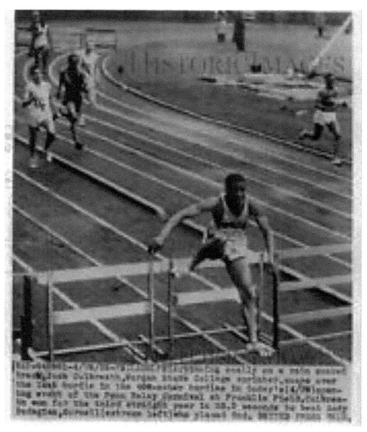

1955 Press Photo Josh Culbreath Wins 400 Meter
Hurdles, Penn Relays Philadelphia.

Hall of Fame

JOSHUA CULBREATH

CLASS:	INDUCTION: 1975
SPORT(S): Track & Field	

Joshua "Josh" Culbreath Born and raised in Norristown, Pennsylvania.

Josh attended the Eisenhower Senior High School. "Josh," who entered Morgan in 1951, is considered one of the all-time great hurdlers at Morgan, as well as in the United States.

Josh was a three-time Penn Relays champion, three-time American champion, and two-time Pan-American Games champion in the 400 meter of 440 yard hurdles. He also ran the anchor leg on Morgan's one-mile relay team, which won several indoor and outdoor championships.

In 1953 at the CIAA Tournament, "Josh," along with Herman Wade, Otis Johnson and Jimmy Rogers, broke the old record set by the

1950 team with a new time 3:11:3. "Josh" also ran the 120 low and high hurdles.

In 1955, in Oslo, Norway, "Josh" won and set a new world record in the 440 yard hurdles with a time of 50:5 seconds.

"Josh," a participant in the 1956 Olympics, was a bronze medal winner in the 440 yard hurdles.

"Josh" was on the Board of Directors of thirteen organizations. He was an administrator with the Equal Employment Opportunity and Affirmative Action Programs, Worldwide Headquarters of Sperry-Univac in Blue Bell, Pennsylvania.

"Josh" was the recipient of many awards. Some of these include: B'Nai B'Rith Brotherhood Award, Letters of Citation from the late President Eisenhower, and the mayor of his hometown proclaimed "Joshua Culbreath Day" in his honor for defeating the Russians in the USA vs. USSR first track meet, which was held in Philadelphia in 1959. A member of the "M" Club and the Kappa Alpha Psi Fraternity, Josh was also an honor student who was well liked by his classmates and many friends.

August 1978—Gala for Olympian "Josh" Culbreath's Induction into The Black Athletes Hall of Fame in the Grand Ballroom of the posh Waldorf Astoria...lavish black-tie dinner...television cameras...host Howard Cosell...big-name entertainment...and wall-to-wall celebrities. Josh is seen in photo: Roy Campanella (seated) congratulate new Hall of Fame members: From left: Floyd Patterson, Frank Robinson, Nat "Sweetwater" Clifton, Joshua Culbreath

Olympian 'Josh' Culbreath enters Hall of Fame

Story and photos by Anne Dewees

It was a night to remember the grand ballroom of the posh Waldorf Astoria lavish black-tie dinner television cameras host Howard Cosell big-name entertainment and wall-to-wall celebrities

The gala was Joshua "Josh" Culbreath's induction into the Black Athletes' Hall of Fame, in the illustrious company of former heavy-weight champion of the world Floyd Patterson; former Harlem Globetrotter and N Y Knick star Nathaniel "Sweetwater" Clifton, and baseball star Frank Robinson

The four athletes joined previous winners Hank Aaron, O J Simpson, Muhammed Ali and Roberto Clemente

Famous Hurdler

Culbreath gained worldwide fame during the 1950s for his ability to run and leap hurdles faster than anyone else in the world. He's ranked second by *Track and Field News* on the all-time list in the 400-meter hurdles. At 5 feet, 7 inches, he's regarded as the shortest hurdler to accomplish so much.

Although he played football and basket-

ball at Norristown (Pa) High School, Josh says he "wanted to excel at something and I was too small for the major sports. So I looked around for a sport that nobody wanted to do.

"Hurdling is complicated, requiring precision, concentration and fortitude. You have to get your steps perfect. If you clip a hurdle you lose six inches from your stride. When you try to compensate 'rigor mortis' sets in.

Trained Hard

"I made sacrifices and trained hard, but I loved to run. I felt free, with no one on the track except me.

My edge consisted of combining the natural speed of a sprinter with developing the stride of a six-footer," he says.

He ran barefoot on the cinder track as a sophomore in high school because he couldn't afford track shoes. Yet he still beat all the juniors and seniors.

In his senior year he not only captured the state crown but also was ranked number two in the country.

Culbreath's hurdling won him a scholarship to Morgan State University. He won

(Cont'd on Page 8)

Above Roy Campanella (seated) congratulates new Hall of Fame members. From left; Floyd Patterson, Frank Robinson, Nat 'Sweetwater' Clifton, Joshua Culbreath.

Below Culbreath in 1957.

Josh was known for his excellent communication skills and as a speaker. Josh used those social skills as Senior Affirmative Employee Relations Representative for Sperry Corp. (now UNISYS) in Blue Bell, Pennsylvania. Read below as he is presented an award by Dr. Frank Fair for providing funds and equipment for the Montgomery County Opportunities Industrialization Center (OIC):

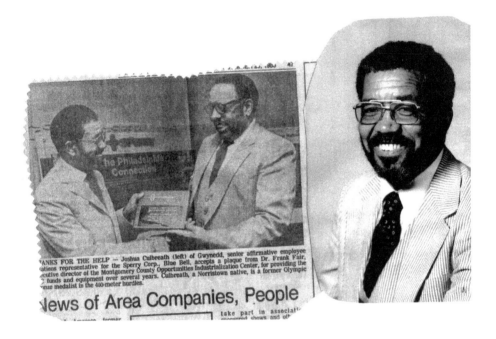

THANKS FOR THE HELP — Joshua Culbreath (left) of Gwynedd, senior affirmative employee relations representative for the Sperry Corp., Blue Bell, accepts a plaque from Dr. Frank Fair, executive director of the Montgomery County Opportunities Industrialization Center, for providing the funds and equipment over several years. Culbreath, a Norristown native, is a former Olympic bronze medalist in the 400-meter hurdles.

News of Area Companies, People

Black Olympian Hall of Fame

Following is a partial list of black American Olympic medalists grouped by year and sport (Track and Field unless otherwise indicated).

1904: George C. Poag. **1908:** J.B. Taylor. **1924:** Dehart Hubbard, Edward Gordon. **1932:** Eddie Tolan; Ralph Metcalfe; Edward Gordon.

1936: Jesse Owens; Ralph Metcalfe; David Albritton; Matthew Robinson; Archie Williams; James DuValle; John Woodruff; Fritz Pollard Jr.; Cornelius Johnson.

1948: Harrison Dillard; Norwood Ewell; Mal Whitfield; Willie Steele; Herbert Douglas; Lorenzo Wright; Audrey Patterson; Alice Coachman.

1952: Andrew Stanfield; James Gathers; Ollie Matson; Mal Whitfield; Reginald Pearman; Harrison Dillard; Jerome Biffle; Meredith Gourdine; Bill Miller; Milton Campbell; Mae Faggs; Catherine Hardy; Barbara Jones; Floyd Patterson (boxing).

1956: Andrew Stanfield; Charles Jenkins; Lou Jones; Arnold Sowell; Lee Calhoun; Josh Culbreath; Charles Dumas; Gregory Bell; Ira Murchison; Milton Campbell; Rafer Johnson; Mildred McDaniel; Willye White; Mae Faggs; Margaret Matthews; Isabelle Daniels; Wilma Rudolph; Leamon King; Bill Russell (basketball); K.C. Jones (basketball).

1960: Les Carney; Lee Calhoun; Willie May; Hayes Jones; John Thomas; Ralph Boston; Irv Roberson; Ira Davis; Otis Davis; Rafer Johnson; Wilma Rudolph; Earlene Brown; Martha Judson; Barbara Jones; Lucinda Williams; Cassius Clay (boxing).

1964: Bob Hayes; Mel Pender; Henry Carr; Paul Drayton; Ulis Williams; Hayes Jones; John Thomas; John Rambo; Ralph Boston; Ira Davis; Wyomia Tyus; Edith McGuire; Marilyn White; Rosie Bonds; Willye White; Eleanor Montgomery; Earlene Brown.

1968: Jim Hines; Tommie Smith; John Carlos; Charlie Greene; Lee Evans; Larry James; Ron Freeman; Willie Davenport; Erv Hall; Ed Caruthers; Bob Beamon; Ralph Boston; Ronnie Ray Smith; Mel Pender; Vince Matthews; Wyomia Tyus; Barbara Ferrell; Madeline Manning; Mildred Netter.

1972: Vincent Matthews; Rod Milburn; Randy Williams; Larry Black; Wayne Collett; Tom Hill; Eddie Hart; Jeff Bennett; Mable Ferguson; Madeline Manning; Cheryl Toussaint; Ray Seals (boxing).

1976: Millard Hampton; Dwayne Evans; Arnie Robinson; Randy Williams; Fred Newhouse; Herman Frazier; Steve Reddick; Willie Davenport; Maxie Parks; Edwin Moses; James Butts; Sugar Ray Leonard, (boxing); Leon Spinks, (boxing); Michael Spinks (boxing); Howard Davis, (boxing); Leo Randolph, (boxing), Anita DeFrantz, (rowing).

A complete, updated list is currently being compiled by the California Museum of Afro-American History and Culture. Games were canceled in 1918, 1940, 1944. The United States boycotted the 1980 Games.

Morgan State University Athletic Hall of Fame 1985
FLYING FOUR TRACK TEAM
Flying Four Track Team

In 1951, Coach Hurt recruited James Rogers, Otis "Jet" Johnson, Herman Wade and Joshua Culbreath. Sam Lacy dubbed the team "The Flying Four" and "The Speed Merchants." In 1953, the Flying Four went on to break the Central Intercollegiate Athletic Association (CIAA) Mile Relay mark set by their 1950 predecessors, Morgan's Historic Four, with a new time 3:11:3. During their 4 seasons, this foursome won 13 national championships, 26 major titles and 3 records. The Flying Four is the only team that ever won the national AAU Championship three years in a row with the same team members. This team set a new record each year in New York and won five relay titles at Penn Relays Championship of America. They won meets at Boston Garden, Madison Square Garden, Boston Athletic Association, Knights of Columbus, Millrose Games, New York Athletic Club Championship, the Baltimore Amateur Athletic games, the Philadelphia Inquirer Games and the Washington Evening Star Games.

They were inducted into the Morgan State University Athletic Hall of Fame in 1985[3] and the CIAA Athletic Hall of Fame in 2013

Central State University Honors

Central State University in Wilberforce, Ohio named a new track, The Josh Culbreath Track in McPherson Stadium, in his honor. The dedication monument was made on August 30, 1992.

Central State's women have captured the last two NAIA championships, the men have twice been runners-up and Culbreath was acclaimed 1992 NAIA co-Coach of the Year.

Joshua "Josh" Culbreath And Central State University Track Team Honored By President Bill Clinton At The White House Rose Garden

William J. Clinton
Forty-Second President of the United States: 1993–2001

Remarks to Central State University NAIA Champion Athletic Teams

June 03, 1993

Thank you. Please sit down, ladies and gentlemen. I want to welcome all of you here and especially say a word of welcome and thanks to Senator Glenn and Mrs. Glenn and their daughter. Senator Glenn made this occasion possible today.

I want to welcome a group of extraordinary student athletes, the Marauders and Lady Marauders of Central State University, winners of the NAIA championships in football as well as men and women's indoor and outdoor track and field. I want to welcome the Central State president, Dr. Arthur Thomas.

These teams have been remarkably successful. First of all, Central State's football team captured the 1992 NAIA Division One national championship with a come-from-behind victory over what school? *[Laughter]* This was no fluke. For Coach Billy Joe, named Division One Coach of the Year, it was the second time that he's won a national title in 3 years. Coach Joe has guided Central State to the playoffs for the past six seasons and to the finals for the past three. His winning formula: the three D's he preaches to his players, drive, desire, and determination. These are good words to live by not only on the playing field but here in Washington as well. That is surely what drove the senior quarterback, Henderson Moseley, to lead his team to two touchdowns in the second half of the championship, after being carried off in the first half with a severe ankle injury. I've been through that sort of campaign myself. *[Laughter]*

Coach Joe, you've earned a fourth D for the Marauders, dynasty. That's what you've put together. And I must say, I've carried a special interest in this team because you had to run over the University of Central Arkansas a couple of times in playing for these championships. So we followed it very interestingly.

Now, let me move on to track. The Marauders and the Lady Marauders this year swept the Division One national indoor and outdoor track and field championships, making history. I'm told that this is the first time any college in any league has won four outright team championships in track and field in one year. What a sweet victory, especially for Coach Josh Culbreath, a former Olympian who was also named Coach of the Year. Where is he? You come on down here.

Now, I'm told that Coach Culbreath is known as Pop, although he doesn't look old enough to be my pop. *[Laughter]* He came out of retirement 4 years ago to revitalize track and field at Central State. It's amazing what somebody can accomplish in just 4 years.

This was the first national title in both indoor and outdoor track. At the indoor championship, they captured the title by winning the mile relay in the final event. They also swept the 600-yard run behind the winning pace of team member Neil DeSilva. This young man went on to clock winning times in both the 200- and 400-meter dash, to help them win the outdoor championship.

The Lady Marauders took their indoor title and also their first, winning 6 out of 16 events with record-setting performance and double wins by both Carolyn Sterling and Sherdon Smith. Outdoors, the Lady Marauders claimed their third consecutive NAIA championship, a "threepeat." Dionne Hemming set a world record for the 400-meter hurdles on her way to earning the title of Most Outstanding Female Performer. Jumping hurdles can also be a useful skill in this city. But I understand Dionne could not be with us here today because she's in Spain.

On behalf of our Nation, let me salute all of you for your fine performances. You are teams with truly a proven track record. As student athletes at an historically African-American institution, you can be proud of your many achievements. Your drive and your desire and your determination are an example for all Americans.

I want to congratulate both the coaches, give them a chance to say something. And thank you again, Senator Glenn, for bringing them here today to the Rose Garden.

NOTE: The President spoke at 5 p.m. in the Rose Garden at the White House.

William J. Clinton, Remarks to Central State University NAIA Champion Athletic Teams Online by Gerhard Peters and John T. Woolley, The American Presidency Project

Josh Culbreath (1994)—Wall of Fame—Penn Relays

Hall of Fame

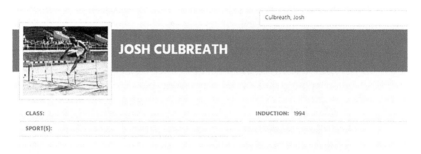

Culbreath, Josh

JOSH CULBREATH

CLASS: INDUCTION: 1994

SPORT(S):

Norristown (Pa.) High School '51, Morgan State '55, Quantico Marines '57, Philadelphia Pioneers '60

A three-time winner in the 400m Hurdles, Culbreath was an important cog in the Morgan State relay teams which came to prominence in the 1950s.

Penn Relays Wall of Fame

Josh Culbreath   **1994**

Norristown (Pa.) HS '51; Morgan State '55; Quantico
Marines '57; Philadelphia Pioneers '60

| Joshua "Josh" Culbreath Induction—March-2002 | A 1956 Olympics Bronze medalist for the 400 meter hurdles in Melbourne, Australia, Joshua "Josh" Culbreath has had an amazing career both on and off the track. Culbreath's Athletic accomplishments include. |

A 1956 Olympics Bronze medalist for the 400 meter hurdles in Melbourne, Australia, Joshua "Josh" Culbreath has had an amazing career both on and off the track. Culbreath's Athletic accomplishments include.

*Pennsylvania State High Champion in the 200 Yard Low Hurdles and ranked number two (2) in the USA, 1951.

*Three-time national AAU (USA) Champion and Records Holder 440 yard hurdles, 1953–55.

*Three-time Penn Relays Champion in the 400 Meter Hurdles.

*Penn Relays—University of Pennsylvania's Wall of Fame, 1994

*Held the ALL COMER'S record for fastest time in the following countries:

*Belgium *Greece *Lebanon

*Ceylon *India *Mexico

*Congo *Iraq *Nigeria

*Germany *Ireland *Scotland

*Ghana *Italy

*World record in the 440 Yard Hurdles, 1957 Oslo, Norway

*World Record in the 300-yard Oval Grass Track, Bendigo, Australia, 1956

*Black Athletes Hall of Fame, 1978

*Track and Field News, No 2 All Time World listing in the 400 Meter Hurdles

*Acknowledgment in Arthur Ashe's book, <u>A Hard Road to Glory,</u> 1988 as First Black Olympic Medalist—400 meter hurdles

Culbreath's career highlights include serving as:

*Management consultant on Minority Public Affairs for Reebok International

*American Specialist/Instructor/ Coach Track & field, for the U.S. Department of State, Baghdad, Iraq

*Head Track Coach—Men & Women, Central State University where he is celebrated with 250 NAIA All-American honors received by 75 athletes during his tenure and;

*Associate Professor, Department of Health and Physical Education, Morehouse College.

He is currently serving as a consultant to institutions of higher education.

Culbreath has a Master of Arts and Education from Temple University, and a Bachelor of Arts, majoring in Political Science from Morgan State University.

From the Congressional Record Online through the Government Publishing Office [www.gpo.gov]

DR. JOSHUA CULBREATH

HON. JOE SESTAK
of Pennsylvania
in the House of Representatives
Monday, July 14, 2008

Mr. SESTAK. Madam Speaker, I rise today to honor the career of a remarkable individual on the occasion of his induction into the United States Marine Corps Hall of Fame: Dr. Joshua "Josh" Culbreath, a native of Norristown, PA and an Olympic athlete, who distinguished himself as a community leader.

Dr. Culbreath was a bronze medalist as a member of the United States' 400-meter hurdling team in the 1956 Melbourne Olympics, part of an American clean sweep of the medals in that race. As a star track and field athlete, he was a state high school champion and was a three-time national 440 yard hurdles champion, setting a world record in that event.

Dr. Culbreath recognized that "sport determined his destiny." A confident and self-motivated individual, he set seemingly insurmountable goals for himself. In addition to his brilliant racing career, Dr. Culbreath dedicated more than 60 years of his life as an educator and high school, college, and university track and field coach, sharing his knowledge, expertise, and love for track and field with aspiring athletes. The athletic accomplishments of his students are astonishing, as they won ten collegiate national titles. As the Director of Athletics at Morehouse College, Dr. Culbreath developed an athletic program that received national acclaim and Central State University named a new track, the Josh Culbreath Track, in his honor. Dr. Culbreath also took pride in tutoring his athletes, with more than 90 percent of them graduating from college.

The Honorary Doctor of Humane Letters awarded to Dr. Culbreath by Edward Waters College is clearly deserved. On the international stage, he represented the United States as a lecturer, coach and sports ambassador in Iraq and India. In particular, he must be commended for his humanitarian work with the International Cultural Exchange Program, which resulted in a groundbreaking integrated competition in Africa between Black and White athletes, who raced in Northern and Southern Rhodesia and Nysaland. In the United States he led integration efforts in Hollywood, Florida, using his stature as a record-setting athlete and talent as a communicator to unite people in that community. His work produced integration in housing complexes and at sporting events.

Dr. Culbreath also served as a community leader by helping in the development and implementation of Plans for Progress in Philadelphia, a forerunner of the national Affirmative Action Program. He also assisted in the development of an affirmative action and equal employment opportunity program for the Sperry/Unisys Corporation. Through his work as a motivational speaker and lecturer, Dr. Culbreath has touched the lives of a diverse audience, appearing before corporate, governmental, and collegiate groups to discuss motivation and education, Olympic sports, and international athletics issues.

Madam Speaker, I ask that we pause and salute Dr. Culbreath, father of Sandra Allen Penn, Khaliq T. Culbreath (deceased), Maliq R. Culbreath, Jahan L. Culbreath, and Camille A.M. Culbreath, for his amazing athletics achievements, his extraordinary accomplishments as a community leader and his commitment to improving the lives of others.

Culbreath was inducted into the United States Marine Corps Sports Hall of Fame in 2008.

Culbreath (center) with Gen. James T. Conway (left) and Sgt. Maj. Carlton Kent (left) accepts his induction into the Marine Corps Sports Hall of Fame.

Marine veteran Joshua "Josh" Culbreath, US Outdoor National Champion in the 400-meter hurdles for three years in a row, 1953–55, and winner of a bronze medal in the 1956 Olympic Games, is inducted into the Marine Corps Sports Hall of Fame in July 2008 by Gen. James T. Conway, Commandant of the Marine Corps, and Sgt. Maj. Carlton Kent, Sergeant Major of the Marine Corps.

B-2 • NOVEMBER 21, 2008   HAWAII MARINE

Four Inducted into Marine Corps Sports Hall of Fame

Bryan Mitchell
Marine Corps Community Services Sports Staff

QUANTICO, Va. — Two former All-Pro football players, a New York Yankee All-Star and an Olympic track and field medalist have been inducted into the Marine Corps Sports Hall of Fame.

Edward W. LeBaron Jr., Henry A. Bauer, Joshua Culbreath and Ernest A. Stautner joined former Marines and sporting greats Ted Williams, Roberto Clemente and Lee Trevino as members of the seven-year-old shrine.

Commandant Gen. James Conway and Sgt. Maj. Carlton Kent, sergeant major of the Marine Corps, were on hand here for an induction ceremony in August, and issued plaques, statues and hearty congratulations to the four inductees.

"A Marine makes a great athlete, but a great athlete makes a superb Marine, and I think we have some brilliant examples of that here," Conway said during the ceremony.

Conway also announced that a permanent Hall of Fame would be built as a wing to the National Museum of the Marine Corps in nearby Triangle, Va.

LeBaron was a standout football player at California's University of the Pacific and led the team to an undefeated season in 1949 as a quarterback, safety and punter before he was commissioned as a Marine officer in 1950.

At 5-foot-9 and 168 pounds, LeBaron was known for his shifty play and elusive running style.

Drafted by the Washington Redskins, he postponed his pro career to serve in the Korean War, where his actions earned him a Bronze Star. He returned to football in 1952 and was named the NFL Rookie of the Year after scoring 14 touchdowns for the Redskins during his first season.

He was named to the All-Pro team four times before he retired, and went on to serve as the general manager of the Atlanta Falcons. LeBaron now lives in California and is still involved in regional athletics.

Bauer enlisted in the Marine Corps shortly after the Japanese attack on Pearl Harbor and served in the South Pacific. During 32 months of combat, he earned two Bronze Stars and two Purple Hearts, and was sent home after receiving shrapnel wounds to his leg and back.

At 26, Bauer was called up from the minor leagues to play for the Bronx Bombers. He went on to hit 164 home runs while compiling a lifetime batting average of .277 and being named to three All-Star teams. Bauer died Feb. 9, 2007 at 84.

Culbreath served in the Corps for about two years from 1956 through 1958. During that period, he was one of the top hurdlers on the planet.

He captured several military and NATO track and field medals and took home a bronze medal in the 400-meter hurdles at the 1956 Olympics in Sydney, Australia.

Culbreath went on to coach track and field worldwide and won 10 National Association of Intercollegiate Athletics championships as the coach at Central State University in Wilberforce, Ohio. He now resides in Las Vegas.

Stautner served in the Corps for three years during World War II with combat action in Formosa and the Philippines. He went on to have a standout career at Boston College and became a perennial Pro Bowl lineman with the Pittsburgh Steelers, eventually making the Pro Football Hall of Fame.

After his induction in 1969, Stautner joined the Dallas Cowboys as an assistant coach, winning two Super bowls. He died on Feb. 16, 2006, at 80.

The Corps also named the athletes of the year for 2007 at the ceremony. Gunnery Sgt. Kenneth Young, who participates on the Armed Forces Cycling Team, and 2nd Lt. Justine Whipple, who is an Armed Force Triathlon team member, were honored for their accomplishments.

Another special dear friend who admires Marine Josh Culbreath, Brigadier General Ronald Coleman:

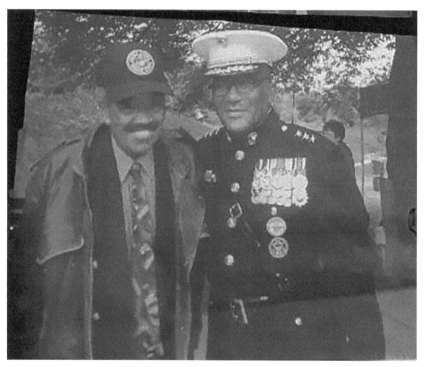

Photo courtesy: Brigadier General Ronald Coleman

The Morgan Legacy Honorees

Ammon "Bob" Barksdale
Robert Berry
Bernie Boasman*
Arthur Bragg
James Roland Brown
Carl Cager
McKinley Crew*
Josh Culbreath
Chico Davis*
George Dennis
Louis Gooden*
Bobby Gordon
Lawrence Griffin
Gerald Harrison
Donald Johnson*
Otis "Jet" Johnson
Ken Kave
Byron T. LaBeach
Samuel A. LaBeach
Robert McMurray
Charlie Mills

Howard Morgan
Linwood Morton*
Carl Pender
V. George Rhoden
Robert "Bobby" Robinson*
Jimmy Rogers
Wardell Stansberry
Clover Street
Eugene "Peaches" Thomas
Lancelott C. Thompson
John Tripplett*
Herman Wade
Herbert Washington*
Edward "Dickie" Waters*
Lonnie Wilson

* = Deceased

ACKNOWLEDGING: MSU TRACK AND FIELD
GREATS FROM THE 1951 TO 1955

APRIL 16 AND 17, 2010 HUGHES STADIUM

"The Flying Four"

Morgan State College
1951 - 1955

Joshua Culbreath, James Rogers,
Otis Johnson and Herman Wade

CIAA Hall of Fame Inductees
Charlotte Convention Center
Charlotte, North Carolina

March 1, 2013
Induction Ceremony
11:00 A.M.

CIAA Athletic Hall of Fame 2013
FLYING FOUR TRACK TEAM

Flying Four Track Team

In 1951, Coach Hurt recruited James Rogers, Otis "Jet" Johnson, Herman Wade and Joshua Culbreath. Sam Lacy dubbed the team "The Flying Four" and "The Speed Merchants." In 1953, the Flying Four went on to break the Central Intercollegiate Athletic Association (CIAA) Mile Relay mark set by their 1950 predecessors, Morgan's Historic Four, with a new time 3:11:3. During their 4 seasons, this foursome won 13 national championships, 26 major titles and 3 records. The Flying Four is the only team that ever won the national AAU Championship three years in a row with the same team members. This team set a new record each year in New York and won five relay titles at Penn Relays Championship of America. They won meets at Boston Garden, Madison Square Garden, Boston Athletic Association, Knights of Columbus, Millrose Games, New York Athletic Club Championship, the Baltimore Amateur Athletic games, the Philadelphia Inquirer Games and the Washington Evening Star Games.

They were inducted into the Morgan State University Athletic Hall of Fame in 1985 and the CIAA Athletic Hall of Fame in 2013.

The Flying Four

The achievements of the "Flying Foursome" also known as the Speed Merchants of Morgan State's Track Rela Team have not been matched in the CIAA. This foursome had 26 major titles and is credited with three records They were coached by the legendary Eddie Hurt.

Athletic Achievements of the Group

Three time 4 x 440 CIAA Relay Champions 1952, 1953 and 1955

Two time 440 yard CIAA Champions 1953 - 1955

National 4 x 440 AAU Relay Champions 1955

National AAU Indoor Mile Relay in 1954

Two time Mid-Atlantic 4 x 440 AAU Champions 1954 and 1955

USA Team - European Tour 1953

Dominated AAU National Indoor Championships for three consecutive years 1953, 1954 and 1955

Dominated the Indoor One Mile Relay

Went undefeated in winning seven (7) indoor meets a year for three years

Averaged 3:18.0-2 for the mile relay - one of the fastest running times and ranked as one of the top five in the country

Broke CIAA Indoor Record at 3:18.0 of the great Morgan team who previously held the record at 3:19.0

Conquered meets at Boston Garden, Madison Square Garden, Boston Athletic Association, Knights of Columbus, Milrose Games, New York Athletic Club Championship, the Baltimore Amateur Athletic games, the Philadelphia Inquirer Games and the Washington Evening Star Games

Credited with 26 major titles

CIAA Hall of Fame celebrates Morgan State's Flying Four: Herman Wade (1), Otis "Jet" Johnson (2), Dr. James Rodgers (3), and Dr. Joshua "Josh" Culbreath (4). Photos courtesy by Cynthia Culbreath

Trailblazer Marks 60th Anniversary of Wins

Donald Hunt
Apr. 26, 2013

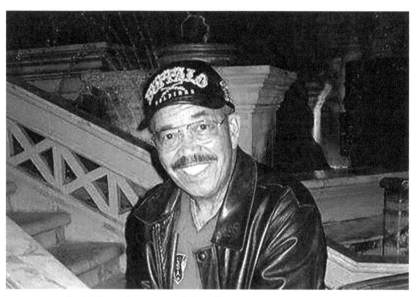

Josh Culbreath is one of the all-time great track and field
athletes in Penn Relays history.—SUBMITTED PHOTO

Josh Culbreath is one of the all-time great
track and field athletes in Penn Relays history.
This is a big week for Culbreath at the Penn
Relays. He will serve as the honorary carnival referee at Franklin Field. Moreover, this is the 60th
anniversary of the first of his three straight victories in the college men's 400-meter hurdles when
he ran for Morgan State.

Culbreath is a tremendous track and field
legend and pioneer for many African American
athletes that participated at the Penn Relays.
He ran for the Bears from 1952–55. Morgan
State was a huge attraction for many fans when

the track team made its annual trip to the Penn Relays.

"I'm looking forward to the Penn Relays," said Culbreath. "I had some great races there. We had some good teams at Morgan State. Edward Hurt was our coach. He was a great coach. He won a lot of championships. He meant a lot to me. You know Edward Hurt and Dr. LeRoy Walker were two of the greatest track and field coaches. Coach Hurt was the first Black coach in the USA Track and Field Hall of Fame.

"He coached a great 4x100 meter relay team that I had a chance to run on. I ran the hurdles, but I was a member of what Sam Lacy (late Hall of Fame sportswriter from the Baltimore Afro-American newspaper) called 'The Flying Foursome.' That included me, Otis Johnson from Ben Franklin High in Philadelphia, Dr. James Rogers and Herman Wade. We were inducted into the CIAA Hall of Fame this year."

Culbreath was a track and field star at Norristown High School. He was a tremendous 100-meter hurdler for the Eagles. He was one of the top athletes nationally in that event. Culbreath had an opportunity to run at the Penn Relays during his scholastic career.

"I ran my junior and senior years at the Penn Relays," Culbreath said. "We had some good athletes in Norristown. You know, Charles Blockson, the historian, was a great track and field star. He could really run. He went to Penn State."

In 1956, he won a bronze medal in the 400 hurdles. In addition, he held the world record for the 440-yard hurdles. He also ran for the Quantico Marines, the Philadelphia Pioneers and the Philadelphia Masters. Culbreath was one of the inaugural members of the Penn Relays Wall of Fame in 1994.

After his collegiate and Olympic career, he was a track and field coach at Central State. He was also the director of athletics at Morehouse College in Atlanta, Ga. Today, Culbreath, 81, lives in Gwynedd and still has some great memories of running in the Penn Relays.

"You know there were some good runners before me like Eugene Beatty (Eastern Michigan) and Charlie Moore (Cornell)," he said. "Eugene Beatty won the 400 meter hurdles in the 1930s (1931, 32, 33). Then, Charlie Moore won the 400 meter hurdles in the 1950s (1949, 50,51). After that, I came along and won it three consecutive years (1953, 54, 55). We're the only ones to do that in the 119 years of the Penn Relays."

That's quite an accomplishment.

The Times Herald

Nov. 24, 2013

Olympic Medalist and Norristown Native Joshua Culbreath Reflects on Life on Eve of Montco Hall of Fame Induction

NORRISTOWN—When Joshua Culbreath learned he would be inducted into the Montgomery Hall of Fame, the memories of people who affected him along the way resounded in unwavering fashion. For Culbreath, 81, whose tireless life is full of acclaim and achievement, it all would be for naught without the love and support of those closest to him.

Never once did the Marine Corps veteran, Olympic medalist, Pan-American champion, world record holder claim to deserve this award;

instead he merely attempted to scrape the surface of those who helped him along the way.

'I remember students I started with in first grade, something about their smile or the sound of their voice,' said Culbreath, who was the first Marine in active duty to make the United States Olympic team. '(Norristown) is where I was born and raised, I couldn't ask for a better occasion than to celebrate with the people I grew up with.'

Culbreath was always undersized, acknowledging that he was not bestowed with the height of his six-foot father. But, under the tutelage of Vince Farina, history teacher and track coach at the Rittenhouse Junior High School, the five-foot-seven Culbreath learned of his talent in track and field.

'I learned an awful lot from him, and it stuck with me,' Culbreath said.

At Norristown Area High School, Culbreath won the PIAA state championship in the 400-meter hurdles and dominated in the Penn Relays where he was a three-time champion. He was able to earn a scholarship to attend Morgan State University wherein he studied Political Science. He was the United States Outdoor champion for three consecutive years in 1953, 1954 and 1955.

Joining the Marine Corps in 1956, Culbreath became the first member of that military branch to qualify for the U.S. Olympic team and shocked everyone but himself when, at the Melbourne Summer Olympics in 1956, he took bronze in the 400 hurdles.

The following two years were equally successful as he set world records at the Oval Grass Track in Bendigo, Australia and in Oslo, Norway.

Twice at the Pan-American Games, in 1955 and 1959, he took home gold.

'Going to Europe where the exposure to international competition was fantastic,' Culbreath said. 'As I pursued things, I had good people, good teachers with me.'

Once out of the Corps, Culbreath returned to Rittenhouse Middle School under the behest of Farina to teach and coach alongside the same people who had instructed him as a young man.

Later, Culbreath earned his Master of Arts degree from Temple University and in 1988, he became the track and field coach at Central State University in Ohio, where he coached his team to 10 National Association of Intercollegiate Athletics championships. Four of his athletes competed in the 1996 Summer Olympics in Atlanta—Deon Hemmings won gold in the 400 hurdles.

Montgomery County Coaches Hall of Fame Honors Inductees

Nov. 26, 2013

Sandy Nadwodny was inducted into the Montgomery Coaches County Hall of Fame in 2013. She's pictured here, front row, middle, with, from left: Joe Shumock; Bill Racich; Sandy Nadwodny; Josh Culbreath; and Sherri Retif. Back row are Jim Davis, John Pergine, and Tony Leodora of the hall of fame committee.
MNG File Photo

WEST NORRITON—'We used to beat a baseball until it turned into a golf ball and then we'd wrap it up with compression tape and beat it again,' reminisced Olympian hurdler Joshua Culbreath, harking back to his early life of playing ball in the street with legendary baseball manager, player and Norristown native, Tommy Lasorda.

The two grew up just six houses apart in Norristown and years later—careers and a lifetime later—they found they were neighbors again.

'But we never forgot where we came from.'

Tuesday night marked the twelfth annual Montgomery County Coaches Hall of Fame Induction Dinner at Westover Country Club, where Culbreath joined with esteemed colleagues Sherri Retif, Germantown Academy girls' basketball coach; Sandy Nadwodny, former Bishop Kenrick High School field hockey and softball coach; Bill Racich, the Ursinus wrestling coach and Joe Shumock, former Abington High School football coach.

The honor was for all of the five new inductees, but they each took their moment in the spotlight to recognize those who have supported them along the way.

'This award is a celebration of women's basketball, it isn't just a personal validation,' Retif said. Her lifetime record as a coach stands at 565 wins and 153 losses with 14 consecutive Inter-Academic League championships.

'(As a coach) it's not a top-down structure; we have had opportunities together to become better players and a better overall team.'

Retif and fellow female inductee, Nadwodny, who made Bishop Kenrick synonymous with field hockey during her tenure, expressed their sheer gratitude in being recognized by the Montco Hall of Fame Committee. And like Retif, Nadwodny gave all the credit to her players for the honor.

'The girls under my tutelage, they were the winners; they had to come out there and do it,'

Nadwodny said. 'I'm humbled and happy for everyone involved, because all I did was something I truly enjoyed.'

More than just on-court and on-field teachings, these coaches passed on the intangibles to their players. Nadwodny touted more than 40 players named to the All-Catholic team, while one of Culbreath's athletes, Deon Hemmings, won gold at the 1996 Summer Olympics in Atlanta. Teaching young people had been the inductees' greatest joy and the honor of entering the Montco Hall of Fame is merely a cherry on top of brilliant careers.

'You don't earn recognition by stepping on people,' Culbreath said.

Culbreath lost his son along the way. The 81-year-old lost his boy, Khaliq Culbreath, his self-affirmed 'prodigal son' who had rode cross-country on bicycle and bragged about biking more than 35,000-miles on the two-wheeled saddle before being struck and killed. The pain Culbreath dealt with was more than most could handle, yet he continued to coach and mentor other young people and still does to this day.

'I went through some trauma; it really, really affected me about life and everything else,' Culbreath said. 'But, those were some of those things that kept me going, when somebody asks me to work with the young kids, I got to do it.'

A representative from a national team asked him to coach young children in Africa, and Culbreath is considering it.

'I've developed a camaraderie with children—I'm a strong disciplinarian—and they have to show me that they want to do what they were doing,' Culbreath said. 'I can see it in (their) eyes.'

Jim Donofrio, coach of the Plymouth Whitemarsh basketball team, accepted a lifetime achievement award in honor of his father, Al Donofrio, for his contribution to the game of basketball in Montgomery Country through the Donofrio Tournament held at the Friendship House in Conshohocken.

Tony Leodora was the master of ceremonies and made sure to highlight all the great memories and people of Montgomery Country past and present.

To cap off the evening, Steve Javie, 25-year NBA veteran referee, gave thanks to all the coaches who were a positive influence and fostered growth to young ones in all facets of life.

Josh Culbreath and Stan Cottrell

realstancottrell / March 29, 2014

Dr. Joshua "Josh" Culbreath knows the true Stan Cottrell, as a man and ultra-distance runner, up close and personal.

Olympic Medalist Josh Culbreath

In 1990, for 400 miles he followed Stan's "Historical Freedom Run" from Berlin to Moscow via Warsaw celebrating the tearing down of the Berlin Wall, the "Wall of Terror" between East and West Berlin. He reports he *saw Stan do what no one else has ever* done." He has known Stan for decades now.

An overcomer in his own right, at age 55, ten years *after* being paralyzed with a broken neck, Josh Culbreath was one of only two men in his age group ever to come in under 60 seconds in the 400 meter hurdles. He says his credo is akin to Cottrell's *"mindstyle of the achiever:"*

1. "If you want something, you have to train for it."
2. "Know your limitations ... but know your goals!"

Who is Josh Culbreath? What are his qualifications?

The "short list"—Olympic Medalist, two-time World Record Holder, the first great Black intermediate hurdler, inductee into five Track and Field Halls of Fame and the Marine Corps Hall of Fame, celebrated Track and Field Coach for many U.S. and international teams, Honorary Co-Chairman of Friendship Sports Association.

To date, I have never witnessed such a powerful impact on a nation as the event Stan calls a "Friendship Run."

Josh Culbreath Testifies to Stan Cottrell's True Friendship Run Impact

Track and Field, human performance, and achievement are what my 80 plus years have been about. I have been blessed to have been a two-time medalist on the 1956 Olympic Team and now a member of 5 Track & Field Halls of Fame.

Years ago, a close personal friend, Mal Whitfield, called me and asked me to drive a van for Stan Cottrell from Berlin to Moscow. I am not going to get into all the details because what I witnessed is the important part of this narrative.

[Ed. note: "The Sports Ambassador," Mal Whitfield, was inducted into 5 Track & Field Halls of Fame, founded in 1990 the Whitfield Foundation, and was personally instrumental in raising millions of dollars to fund and operate training camps and programs for Olympic teams in Africa.]

Stan Cottrell at run start in Berlin with Josh Culbreath (L) and 1988 Olympic Marathon winner (R)

Day after day, I drove a van behind Stan as he ran 50 miles over and over again. I never knew a human could do this.

I was witness to a dimension I never knew was possible.

We started from the Brandenburg Gate in Berlin on the day of the official opening between East and West Berlin. There were more than 100,000 people who cheered us as we began this great initiative. Stan was joined by many athletes and even the previous Olympic Gold Medalist in the Marathon. It was a phenomenal sendoff.

All along the way, thousands of people were along the road with smiles. We were running through Poland where we felt time had virtually stood still since Hitler had invaded in 1938.

When Stan runs, anyone can join in and run as much as they want. People of all ages would join in. Some went only a few feet...the distance did not matter. We all knew we were part of something far bigger than ourselves. For a moment in time, the magic of people laughing and playing together...not bound by ideologies or politics...we were recapturing those moments we all knew as children... we played together, and the world was a better place.

I have never experienced anything as powerful in my sports career as what Stan does. In today's world, we go to an event and security measures are rigid. A wall exists between the spectator and participant. Stan's world is just the opposite... Stan welcomes all to run. The people shake his hand, they get their picture made, and for their moment in time...the event brings significance and their world becomes significant.

Stan runs and runs...he brings a message of hope. The people seem to identify with him as he brings his message of friendship, and every person has a victory to give regardless of where we live our lives.

I was witness to sports in a whole new way. What Stan does is "Sports in Diplomacy:" not the kind our politicians bring to the table. This is about people to people communications, and that is contagious. Everyone he meets is inspired to want to be better... He is an igniter!

Stan runs and runs...he stops and listens... he is a life changing experience. I witnessed first-hand the uniqueness of what Stan does. The world is a better place because of what he does. He is making a difference.

 Marg
April 27, 2014 at 2:03 p.m.

Wish I could share all the wonderful, true stories the outstanding Olympian and "Hall of Famer," Josh Culbreath, has shared personally with me about the way it was in track and field in the "early days," about his relationship with Stan Cottrell, about running with Stan when the Berlin Wall fell and more... Josh is a remarkable man, and there's a very good reason he admires another remarkable man, ultra-distance runner Stan Cottrell... who amazingly shows that he can keep running and running long distances, day after day, for days on end.

*****

Goodwill Ambassador, Stan Cottrell, with Chairman of
ICBC, Mr. Ni, and General Bernard Loeffke.

Friendship Sports Association is honored
and privileged to have Joshua Culbreath as our
friend, partner, and Honorary Co-Chairman...
and waiting to run the last mile with Stan
(Cottrell) as he completes The Great Global
Friendship Run in Washington, DC! It will be
a grand finale and "retirement celebration" for
two great American track and field athletes, great
friends, and legends.

The Philadelphia Association of Black Sports and Culture, Inc.

9th Annual Recognition Banquet
HONORING
DELAWARE VALLEY LEGENDS

Mike Bantom

Kenny Gamble

Rev. Marshall Mitchell

Tony Williams

Leon Barnett

Josh Culbreath

Sunday September 27, 2015
The Oaks Ballroom 511 W. Oak Lane, Glenolden, PA 19036

www.phila-black-sports.org

a 501(c) 3 non profit corporation

283

The Philadelphia Association Of Black Sports And Culture, Inc

LEGEND HONOREES

Class of 2015

Mike Bantom
Leon Barnett
Josh Culbreath
Kenny Gamble
Rev. Marshall Mitchell
Tony Williams

The Municipality of Norristown Twentieth Black History Celebration (1995–2015) 2015 Keynote Speaker Mr. Joshua (Josh) Culbreath

Mr. Josh Culbreath is known for his athletics achievements. He taught in the Norristown Area School District for five years between 1958 and 1964. Previously worked in Human Resources for the former Alan Wood Steel Company in Conshohocken, Pennsylvania and Sperry UNIVAC in Blue Bell, Pennsylvania. Served as a Track and Field Official at the Olympic Games in Atlanta, Georgia (1966). Head Track Coach at Central State University in Ohio (1986–1996). He had resided in Atlanta, Georgia; and was currently the Athletic Director of Morris Brown College.

Post High School Achievements and Distinctions

He captained the Morgan State track team in 1954–1955 and upon graduation in 1955 was presented "The Most Scholarly Athlete Aware" by his Excellency V.S. Tubman, President of the Liberian Republic, a guest at commencement. Was a bronze medalist in the 400-meter hurdles at the 1956 Olympic Games in Melbourne, Australia. He set a New World's Record in the 440-yard hurdles of 50.5 seconds in a meet in Oslo, Norway, 1957. He set a World's Record for the 300-yard dash (on an oval grass track) while in Australia in 1956.

In 1958 he placed second in the 400-meter hurdles during a US vs. USSR competition on Moscow. A year later he won the same event in a meet held in Franklin Field, Philadelphia between the same two teams. He was three-time Amateur Athletic Union (AAC) 440-yard hurdles champion and record holder, a member of the one-mile relay championship team at Philadelphia's Pioneer Athletic Club.

He raced to victory in the 400-meter hurdles at the PAN-American Games in Mexico in 1955 and in Chicago in 1959. He was one of the only two men to the Penn Relays 440-yard hurdles championship. He spent several years with the U.S. Department of State and with the "Peace Corps" in "Good Will Tours" to India, Iraq, West and East Africa organizing and coaching track teams.

High School Activities

Member of Basketball, Baseball, Football and Track Teams, Sports Club, Ranked #2 scholastic hurdler in the United States, Christmas Pageant.

Post High School Education and Activities

Graduated Morgan State College with A.B. Degree in Political Science 1955.

Attended University of Colorado Law School, 1955–1956. Received MA Degree in Education, Temple University, Philadelphia, PA, 1963.

The Municipality of Norristown Twentieth Black History Celebration (1995–2015) 2015 Keynote Speaker Mr. Joshua (Josh) Culbreath

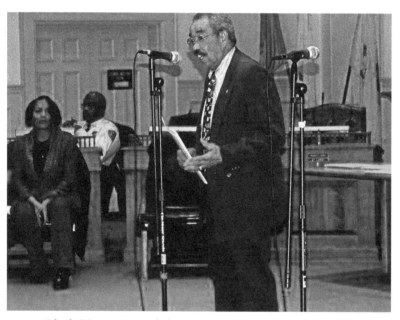

Black History Month keynote speaker Joshua Culbreath addresses the crowd at Norristown Municipal Hall Feb. 4. Oscar Gamble—21st Century Media

February 4, 2015 Norristown celebrates 20 years of Black History Month. The ceremony commenced with Opening Remarks made by municipal council President Linda Christian. Christian went on to espouse the significance of Black History Month.

"To me, it's important because lots of people who came before us impacted our lives in many major ways ... And the thing that makes it unique is that they did these things in the most challenging of circumstances and conditions in the United States of America. I think it's important to share because those individuals set out to do things to benefit us, and I believe we have an obligation to honor what they did for us by doing our best in whatever field we're in, in our communities, our homes, our state and our nation."

Norristown native and Big 5 and Montgomery County Sports Hall of Famer James Williams then introduced this year's keynote speaker, Josh Culbreath.

Culbreath took his Norristown-nurtured athletic talent across the country and around the world as a track star, and later became an educator and coach. He held several world records and won the bronze medal in the 400 meter hurdles at the 1956 Olympics in Melbourne, Australia, and first place in the same event at the PAN AM games in Mexico in 1955 and Chicago in 1959. A graduate of Morgan State and Temple Universities, Culbreath returned to Norristown as one of the school district's first black teachers, and went on to coach track at Central State University in Ohio. He is currently the athletic director at Morris Brown College in Atlanta.

Culbreath regaled young and old in attendance with tales of growing up in Norristown in the 1930s and '40s. His boyhood mates and neighborhood cronies were a veritable Who's Who of the municipality's luminaries—baseball great Tommy Lasorda, mogul Vincent Piazza, and jazz great Jimmy Smith, just to name a few.

Culbreath spoke largely about the sense of community he felt as a youngster growing up in Norristown, knowing that friends, neighbors and teachers were looking out for him and took pride in being stakeholders of a bright future. Culbreath said that at times, those values have waned, but expressed optimism that things are now changing for the better. He also stressed the value of education to the young people in the audience.

"It made me feel good to do the things and pay back to the system I came from," said Culbreath. "You want to go to school. You want to stay in school … You all have a place in this world, but you have to take advantage of it. Listen to your parents, your teachers, everyone you come in contact with is going to play a role in your young life and there are a lot people who are interested in you, what you do and where you're going."

Central State University Salutes the Sixtieth Anniversary of Olympic
Medalist Joshua Culbreath's Bronze Medal at the 1956 Summer Olympics

WILBERFORCE, OH.—While the world
watches the 2016 Rio Olympics, Central State
University remembers and honors the accomplishments of former CSU Track Coach Joshua
Culbreath.

Mr. Culbreath won a bronze medal in the
1956 Summer Olympics while competing in the
400 Meter Hurdles. He competed while he was
in the United States Marine Corps, and he went
to Melbourne, Australia as the USA Outdoor
Champion in the 400m hurdles. He held that
title for three consecutive years—1953, 1954,
and 1955. Mr. Culbreath also set the world
records in the hurdles in 1956 and 1957.

Mr. Culbreath went on to become Central
State's Track Coach in 1988. While at the
University, he coached his teams to 10 NAIA

Championships. In the 1996 Summer Olympics in Atlanta, Ga., four of his athletes competed including Deon Hemmings, who won Olympic gold in the 400 Meter Hurdles.

We salute Mr. Culbreath's great athletic ability and his contributions to the University.

Hall of Fame

1991 WOMEN'S TRACK & FIELD TEAM
CLASS:	INDUCTION: 2016
SPORT(S): Track

1991 Women's Outdoor Track and Field Team

The 1991 women's track & field team was the first group to win the track & field program's first NAIA national title.

Coached by CSU Hall of Famer Joshua Culbreath, the team claimed the '91 title with a total of 105 points, winning the event by a 28-point margin.

On their way to the title, the 400-meter relay team set a NAIA record with a pace of 44.81. Deon Hemmings won the 400 meter hurdles with a time of 58.14. Audrea Sterling took first place in the 400 meter run with a time of 52.87 while teammate Alwren Wallace placed third with a time of 54.67. Sherdon Smith finished second in the 800 meter run and Sandra Boothe earned points for the team with a fifth place finish. The Lady Marauders earned crucial points in the 200 meter thanks to a second place finish from Wallace, a fourth place finish from Carolin Sterling and fifth place run sprint from Audrea Sterling. Carolin Sterling earned the top mark in the long jump with a leap of 20.8 meters. Antoinette Jones, Carolin Sterling, Wallace and Smith teamed up to take first in the spring medley relay with a pace of 40.02. Carolin Sterling took another top place finish in the 100 meter hurdles with a time of 13.91. The Lady Marauders also won the mile relay with a time of 3:38.55 on the legs of Wallace, Hemmings, Smith and Audrea Sterling.

Carolin Sterling was named the NAIA Women's Outdoor Track and Field Most Valuable Athlete at the conclusion of the event.

The title was the first of seven national crowns earned by the women's program between 1991 through 1997.

Many members of the team went on to compete at the international level with Hemmings capturing the gold medal in the 400 meter hurdles at the 1996 Summer Olympics in Atlanta, Georgia.

Central State celebrates the 2017 Athletic Hall of Fame Induction

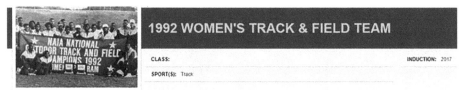

1992 WOMEN'S TRACK & FIELD TEAM

CLASS:

INDUCTION: 2017

SPORT(S): Track

1992 Women's Outdoor Track and Field Team | NAIA National Champions | Head Coach: Joshua Culbreath

Competing in Abbotford, British Columbia, the Central State University women's track & field team claimed their second consecutive NAIA Outdoor National Championship in 1992.

Coached by Olympian and CSU Hall of Famer Joshua Culbreath, the 1992 team set a record with nine individuals winning national titles—a mark that still stands twenty-five years later.

Carolin Sterling, who would end up becoming one of the most decorated female athletes in NAIA history, won the 100 meter hurdles (13.58), 200-meter dash (23.62) and long jump (20-7 ¾). At the conclusion of the championships, Sterling was named the Herbert B. Marett Outstanding Performer.

Deon Hemmings, who later went on to win the Olympic Gold Medal at the 1996 Olympics, won the 400-meter hurdles with a time of 56.56. Audrea Sterling claimed the top spot in the 400-

meter dash crossing the line at 53.37. Layphane Carnagie won the 100 meter dash with a pace of 11.54.

The Lady Marauders sealed the championship thanks to dominant performances in the relay events.

The Sterling sisters, Carnagie and Alwen Wallace finished with a top time of 45.52 in the 4 x 100 meter relays. The same group teamed up to win the spring medley with a pace of 1:40.35. CSU's 4 x 400 relay team consisting of Hemmings, Audrea Sterling, Ingrid Gordon and Sherdon Smith claimed first place with a final time of 3:38.39.

With a total team point total of 140, the Lady Marauders won the event by 14.5 points over championship host Simon Fraser University. CSU's 140 points would end up being the most accumulated by the team during their run of five NAIA outdoor titles throughout the 1990s.

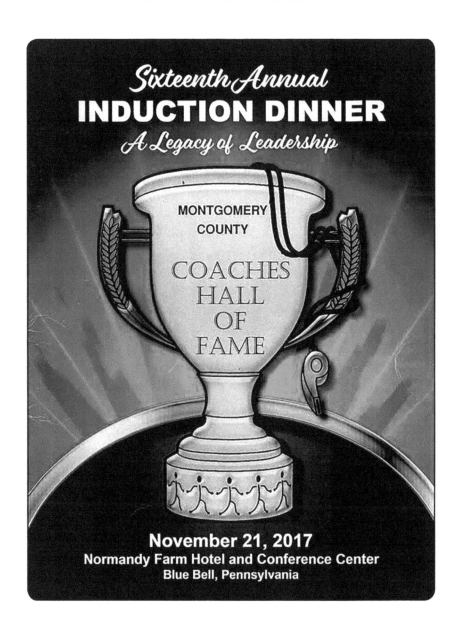

Montgomery County Coaches Hall of Fame
"A Legacy of Leadership"

Founding Fathers

John Pergine,
President Emeritus

Jim Davis

Dale Hood,
President

Tony Leodora,
Secretary/ Treasurer

Advisory Board

Jim Serratore, 1st VP

Tom Brady, 2nd VP

Val Arkoosh,
Montgomery County
Commissioner

Joseph Gale,
Montgomery County
Commissioner

Ken Lawrence,
Montgomery County
Commissioner

Kevin Steele,
District Attorney

Geoff Brandon
Kevin Burke
Dave Coupe
Bob Davis
Gordon Glantz
Emmett Harkins
Steve Harner
Joe Manzo
Tom McGee
Dave Ritting
Joe Rowan
Bob Schaefer
Bob Shoudt
Mary Jane Souder
John Strauss
Mike Toth
Rick Troncelliti
Rod Vaughan
Mark Werkiser

Message from the President

Good evening and welcome,

As President of the Montgomery County Coaches Hall of Fame, I am honored to welcome you to the 16th Annual Awards Dinner.

As I was putting my thoughts on paper for this year's President's Message, my second as President, I reflected on the theme of last year's message -- "A Legacy of Leadership -- and how humbling it is for me to be associated with the individuals we have honored in the past … and honor again this year.

These are very special people. As we shine the spotlight on the 2017 honorees, we are again adding to that continuing legacy of outstanding recipients who personify the word "leadership". Tonight we honor men and women who have not only exhibited personal leadership, but contributed greatly to the development of our leaders of tomorrow.

We recognize the many hours, days, and years, that each of our honorees has given to coaching, mentoring, teaching, helping, worrying, disciplining, rejoicing, despairing, and thoroughly engaging themselves in the lessons of character-building. We have been witness to great examples of dedication, perseverance, responsibility, and grace in the face of winning or losing. It is the essence of the value sports brings to all of our lives.

I am thrilled that we have this vehicle, the Montgomery County Coaches Hall of Fame, to be able to publically applaud their efforts and thank them for these inspiring examples of fortitude and persistence.

That brings me to the second part of my message, and it is identical to the second part of every year's message. It is about the circle that all of you have completed by your continuing support of this worthy event. Without your interest and involvement, there would be no evening such as this to publically tell our dedicated inductees and honorees how much we appreciate them and the good they have accomplished throughout our athletic community. A very large and heartfelt "thank you" to all of you here for making that possible.

Best regards,

Dale C. Hood
President
Montgomery County Coaches Hall of Fame

Montgomery County Coaches Hall of Fame
"A Legacy of Leadership"

Class of 2002
Beth Anders
Tom Lasorda
Hank Stofko

Class of 2003
Jim Crawford
Mike Pettine
Dick Shoulberg

Class of 2004
Fritz Brennan
Hank DeMito
Art Kehoe
Bob Schaefer
Bobby Wine

Class of 2005
Jim Algeo
Geno Auriemma
Al Cantello
Marge Watson
Bill Werkiser

Class of 2006
Dan Dougherty
Jim Mich
Vince Panzano
Bob Shoudt

Class of 2007
Steve Harner
Phil Martelli
Brian Thomas

Class of 2008
Fran Murphy
Libby Williams
James "Skip" Wilson
Larry Wilson

Class of 2009
Ken Davis
Larry Glueck
Vonnie Gros

Class of 2010
Roger Grove
Joe Iacovitti
Bill Leahy
George Marinkov
Tom McGee

Class of 2011
Jack Bauerle
Chris Bockrath
Barb Clipsham
Tom Shirley

Class of 2012
Bill Anderson
Rick Carroll
Gregg Downer
Ernie Hadrick
Joan Moser

Class of 2013
Josh Culbreath
Sandy Nadwodny
Bill Racich
Sherri Retif
Joe Shumock

Class of 2014
Jim Fenerty
Dominick "Mick" Lorusso
Rick Pennypacker

Class of 2015
Al Angelos
Bob Beale
Virginia Hofmann
Pat Nugent

Class of 2016
Maggie deMarteleire
Pete Lewis
Rick Mellor
Keith Mondillo
Christy Morgan

August 12, 2018—**Introducing Joshua Culbreath—Marine Veteran, Olympian, Warrior Heartbeat**

Meet our newest Warrior Heartbeat, Dr. Joshua Culbreath. Now living near Montgomeryville, PA, Josh grew up in Norristown, PA, is a United States Marine Corps Veteran, a father, a coach and a teacher. He won a Bronze medal in the 400 meter hurdles during the 1956 Olympics that took place in Melbourne, Australia. He won a Gold medal for that same event, twice at the Pan Am Games in 1955 and 1959. Dr. Culbreath did all of this after being told that he was too short to run the hurdles. In 2008, Joshua was inducted into the US Marine Corps Sports Hall of Fame. He taught special needs children when he had been told they were unteachable. Under his care and instruction, they not only learned to read and write, but also to sing the Christmas carol, Silent Night, in German, which was the language it had originally been written in. Josh grew up with baseball legend, Tommy Lasorda and was friends with many other famous people, including jazz great, Jimmy Smith. Josh suffered a stroke a short while back, has had 5 surgeries on his feet, a broken neck and is in the early stages of Parkinson's, yet he still does 200 (Yes, two hundred) pushups every night before bed. This man is a true Warrior! Dr. Joshua Culbreath, we love you and your Warrior Heart!

Josh had a special visit by Marine Veteran and Warrior Heartbeat John Notte. John visited at Cousin Josh's home in person to induct him as his newest Warrior Heartbeat, presented him with a Warrior Heartbeat patch and confirmed him as a Semper Fi Brother.

Here are John Notte's own words during his interview with Josh at his home in Montgomeryville, PA:

Today I am humbled and honored to present our newest Warrior Heartbeat Dr. Joshua Culbreath. Now, Dr. Joshua Culbreath is a Marine Corp veteran. He won the bronze medal in the 1956 Melbourne, Australia Olympic Games in the 400-meter hurdles and he gold-medaled in that same event in 1955 and 1959 in the Pan Am Games; and hurdles was something that he was told you will never be able to do because you were too short! But you did it anyway. He was a coach, he is a father, and he was a teacher. He's touched a tremendous amount of lives and had a positive impact on so many people. So, for that reason, Dr. Culbreath I would like to present you with a small token of our appreciation and welcome you as our newest Warrior Heartbeat, a warrior heart patch, and Semper Fi Brother. Josh repeats, "Semper Fi!"

John Notte said he heard Cousin Josh enjoys speaking with young people. John said there is a 15-year-old young man by the name of Tyreke who was being bullied in school. Tyreke is also a Warrior Heartbeat. John told Josh he and The Warrior Heartbeats they went and escorted him and took him out for a day of fishing. Tyreke loves veterans. John was kind enough to invite Tyreke to Josh's house to meet him. One nice thing about Tyreke is whenever he sees a veteran wherever he's at, he stops what he's doing, he goes up to them and looks them in the eye, shakes their hand, and thanks them for their service. John knew Tyreke would enjoy speaking with Cousin Josh and Josh would enjoy speaking with Tyreke. Josh has accomplished so much more in his lifetime and they both enjoyed meeting each other and chatting. Tyreke, it's your show! You get to talk with Dr. Culbreath and you guys chat about whatever you like.

Here are the exact words spoken by Josh Culbreath's conversation with Tyreke:

Aug 2018—Warrior Heartbeats Tyreke and Josh Culbreath chat

Tyreke—So, what was it like joining the Marine Corp?

Josh—It was a dream and a wish and a desire for a long, long time.

Tyreke—Were you scared to join the Marine Corp?

Josh—Of course not. What I saw in the
Marine Corp was not fear but hope, love, strength
of character and development of a man. They
developed men. You are a young person when
you go in, but you are a man when you come out.
Those are the standards. They're very high. But
they're worth it. You had to be inspired by them
because of the things they have done. Strong with
character. Wanting to help people who are less
fortunate than others, and that's what happens
that I grew up in an area with a lot of people. I
shared things with them, but it took people in
my neighborhood who taught me things. One of
them is a man that went on to become a great
baseball player and also he became a great manager, and boy I tell ya his name will live forever in
baseball and that was Tommy LaSorda in a little
place in Norristown, Pennsylvania; and my little
town by the way is the largest Borough in the
world, Norristown. It could have been a city but
it would have cost us too many taxes. So, it is the
largest Borough in the world, so that gives me
an opportunity to boast a little more about how
proud I am to be a part of where I was born; and
yet like Manhattan is a Borough in New York,
and people didn't know that. But it's a proud
place that I came from and the people I grew up
with were just wonderful. They were the ones
that encouraged me as I got older, and the thing
is I had tried to reach back and do the things that
I never had done before me when I was growing
up. But, I had a lot of good people who led me
the way. They showed me the way.

I can box, fight. So, I boxed at an Italian
club called The LAM, and there they taught me
so much. The men they are self-defense, which

is wonderful. So, I knew how it made me stronger in character, and the thing that I learned is that you had to crack books. That is, crack mean you had to study a little harder and make yourself wonderful and known. From the time I was a young boy until I graduated from high school I went off to college and I received several degrees as I toured. But I never forgotten where I started. I wanted to run and I ran throughout the world and became the best and got to run in the largest and oldest relay carnival like in the world called the Penn Relays right here in Philadelphia; and I won that two years in a row and only three men in the history of the Penn Relays that won the 400-meters hurdles three times in the world I'm one of them. So, that is like well-known because you have run in the relays you had made it to the epitome of track and field in the United States.

I went on to win at the Pan-American Games which is like the Olympic Games that is held every four years. I won the Pan-American Games in Mexico City in high altitude, and when you have not been acclimated to weather and train in it you find out it is difficult to run in it because it is a short of breath, you are in high altitude and the air is thinner. But we don't have time to train to go for how you become acclimated to that climate. We had to run in it knowing that it was hard and knowing that the air was thin meaning that you had to (Josh mimicking gasping for air) take your breath and get it the best way you could and imagine you are running against the best in the world, and I won that Pan-American Games two times, Mexico City and in Chicago. Four years later I came back and won it again. Didn't have the high altitude (didn't have that one) and I still won, and I broke my record. So, I had done many things. But I climaxed it with two things, I made the United States Olympic Teams, and we sent three men in each event and that was in Melbourne, Australia Down Under. Here, we made a promise to each other the three Americans. We said we're going to win this we only have three that win. We are going to be 1-2-3, and we did. We came in 1-2-3. I was third. That was the first clean sweep of the Olympic Games in 1956 in Melbourne, Australia 400-meter hurdles, and I had the world record as well. I couldn't go any higher than what I could have done.

But I learned when I came back I promised myself I will be a teacher. I became a Specialist of the mentally retarded. I taught them how to read, write, that people would not even think about them because they were slow learners. I taught them how to read, I taught them how to sing the greatest Christmas Carol song in the world, and you know what that is? Silent Night; and it was written in German, and I took those children and had them to sing it for all of the schools at Rittenhouse Jr. High School in Norristown. They never learned the language unless they spoke it from their home. I taught them how to sing it in the language which it was written, in German. I taught them how to sing it, "Stille Nacht." I had a very beautiful career. I loved the young people. I helped them each and every time I had an opportunity, and you are a great individual to start with, because I talked to a lot of young people, loved everyone I talked to. I hope by us being friends and having a conversation that you too going to reach out and help other people. God Bless You.

Tyreke—Thank you.

Josh to Tyreke with a smile and with a handshake—"Warriors, that's what you are."

John said he appreciates Josh and honored to meet Josh. You are in your life is living proof that the only person that can put any limits on you is yourself. You didn't let anyone tell you couldn't do it. Whether it was hurdles, whether it was the Marine Corp, whether it was teaching mentally disabled children back in the day and I think you told me the story that you actually taught them not only how to read and write but how to sing Silent Night in the language it was originally written which was German.

Tonight, Warrior Heartbeat Tyreke and I had the honor of meeting an amazing man!

Pennsylvania Track and Field Coaches Association

Cousin Josh was honored and inducted into the Pennsylvania Track and Field Coaches Association (PTFCA) Hall of Fame Class of 2020 during the meet festivities at Penn State University's State College, Pennsylvania in March 2020. Gerry Stemplewicz is chairman of Hall of Fame.

Hall of Fame
Pennsylvania High School Track & Field
Hall of Fame—Class of 2020

Chris Sydnor—Radnor (Wayne, 1981). A
three-time boys PIAA 3A sprint champion, and

twice a PTFCA indoor state champ, Chris Sydnor was one of the state's outstanding sprinters in the early 1980s. He won a PIAA sprint double as a senior in 1981 with season best times of 10.68 and 21.74. But his best outdoor marks came as a junior, when times of 9.6 for 100 yards and 21.4 for the 220 placed him equal-6th on both all-time state lists. Indoors as a junior, he won state titles in the 60- and 300-yard dashes. His best 60-yard time of 6.40 from his senior year placed him equal-2nd on the all-time state list, and his 31.6 as a junior in the 300 placed him equal-5th all time.

Chris Williams—Strath Haven (Wallingford, 2012). An outstanding double threat in the hurdles and pole vault, it's difficult to know which event was his best. A PIAA champion in the vault, he twice finished 2nd at outdoor states, and his best placing at the PTFCA indoor states was another 2nd. His outdoor best of 16-6 put him behind only one Pennsylvanian on the outdoor all-time list. As a hurdler, he won two outdoor PIAA titles at 110 meters and added a PTFCA 60-meter hurdles indoor title as a junior. His best marks of 13.82 and 7.77 placed him equal-7th and 2nd on the state all-time lists. His efforts at the two state meets as a senior helped Strath Haven to a pair of state titles.

Kyle Long—Hempfield (Landisville, 2012). A Track & Field News 4th-team All-American discus thrower as a junior, Kyle Long was a three-time PIAA 3A champion, twice in the discus and once in the shot put. His best discus throw of 202-10 came while setting a state meet record which lasted for six years. The mark placed him second on the all-time state list and made him the fifth-farthest thrower in the nation that year as he placed 3rd in both the Penn Relays and the National Scholastic Championships. As a senior Long finished 2nd at Penn Relays on his was to successfully defending his state championship. A solid shot putter, he finished with a win and 2nd place in his junior and senior years.

Tessa Barrett—Abington Heights (2014, Scranton Prep 2011). Home-schooled for the peak of her high school career, Tessa Barrett competed for Abington Heights High School and put together one of the state's greatest distance running seasons ever as a senior. After going undefeated in cross county, including wins in the PIAA states and FootLocker Nationals, she repeated her PTFCA state win of 2013 over 3000 meters, and then won a National Scholastic double at 3000 and 5000, winning with a Pennsylvania record of 9:31.09 and a national record of 16:11.85. Her 3000 mark was her fourth improvement of the state record that year, after first setting it at 9:47.73 as a junior.

Abby Schaffer—Easton Area (2008). A two-time PIAA 3A pole vault champion, Abby Schaffer added a PTFCA indoor titles as a senior in 2008. Runner-up at indoor states as a junior, Schaffer went on a tear outdoors, winning the Penn Relays, her District meet and states, and clearing a season best of 12-6 in each of the latter two meets. As a senior, she won the PTFCA indoor title with a state record 13-0¼, then took 2nd in both the National Scholastic indoor meet and the Nike Indoor Nationals, the latter with another state record, this one at 13-2½. Outdoors, she again won all her major meets through the end of May, before tying for 2nd at the National Scholastic outdoor meet.

Chris Robertson—Reading (1992). A four-time PIAA 3A sprint champion in the 100- and 200-meter dashes, Chris Robertson also won a pair of PTFCA indoor titles at 60 yards. An accomplished long jumper, she was PIAA runner-up as a junior in 1991, when she also ran on her team's 3rd-place 4×100-meter relay, giving her an impressive two gold medals, a silver and a 3rd-place bronze that day. Robertson was a finalist in the National Scholastic Indoor championship meet, both as a junior and again as a senior. Her best indoor 60-yard time of 7.01 put her 3rd among Pennsylvanians to that point, and her 100-meter time of 11.72 from her junior year put her 4th on the all-time state list.

Mary Rawe—Camp Hill (1976). The first great distance runner of the PIAA era for girls, Mary Rawe was a three-time state champion in the 880-yard run and won both PIAA mile titles contested at the time. She also won the state cross country title as a junior, having suffered her only PIAA loss the year before in the cross country states. All of this happened before her senior year, by which time she had moved away to Georgia. Her only PIAA loss occurred as a sophomore in cross country when she finished 2nd. The state record holder for the mile at 4:55.9 *and for the 1500-meters at 4:37.5, she may have been equally good in the 880, but always ran the event doubling back from the mile.*

Art Pollard—Horace Scott (Coatesville, 1952). One of the great sprinters of his generation, Art Pollard was a three-time PIAA champion, winning the 100-yard dash in 1951 and '52 and the 220 in '51. A pulled muscle forced him out of the 1952 220 on a day when most of the track was under more than an inch of water. Pollard's confirmed bests of 9.7 for the 100 was faster than all but five Pennsylvanians to that point, and his 21.3 for the straightaway 220 had been better by only two Pennsylvanians. In lesser meets under unknown wind conditions, Pollard had run as fast as 9.6 for the 100 and 21.0 in the 220, the better of his two events.

Erv Hall—Overbrook (Philadelphia, 1965). An exceptional hurdler and sprinter, Erv Hall began to shine as a senior when the team's lead hurdler suffered an injury. Hall became a major star, winning Philadelphia League titles in both hurdles, the 120-yard highs in 13.9 to tie the state record, and the 180-yard lows in 19.2, a time bettered by only four Pennsylvanians to that point. At the city championship meet, he won both sprints and during the summer recorded a 9.8 for 100 yards at a time when the state record was 9.6. Hall went on to Villanova and won the Olympic silver medal in the 110-meter hurdles in 1968, and tied the world record of 13.2 for the 120-yard hurdles in 1969.

Ed Ulmer—Coach, Archbishop Ryan (Philadelphia, 1967–2016). A high school coach for 50 years, Ed Ulmer took on the track program at newly created Archbishop Ryan High School in the fall of 1967. Within ten years, the Ryan boys had won Philadelphia Catholic League titles three times in cross country, two times in outdoor track, four times in indoor track, and the first two of four successive PTFCA state indoor championships. Adding the Ryan girls' teams in the fall of 1980 to his responsibilities, Ulmer's girls' teams have won five PCL indoor titles and six outdoor championships to go along with his boys' team records of six wins in cross country, eight indoors and four outdoors. He was named National High School Athletic Coaches Association, Region 2, BoysTrack Coach of the Year in 1991 PTFCA Girls Coach of the Year in 2002. His boys set a national record in the distance medley relay in 2004.

Mark Schwartz—Contributor. A graduate of Peabody High School in Pittsburgh and Washington & Jefferson University, Mark Schwartz has had a long and varied career in track and field as an official, administrator, public address announcer, and contributor to a large number of news organizations, both print and electronic. Through the years, he has coached at the high school, college, club and youth levels. A long-time member of many track & field associations including USATF, PIAA, PTFCA, and Tri-State Coaches, Schwartz has been president of his PIAA Officials Chapter and a member of the Pennsylvania High School Track & Field Hall of Fame Committee since its inception in 1995.

Josh Culbreath—Alumnus, Norristown (1951). A PIAA state champion in the 200-yard low hurdles as a senior, Josh Culbreath became internationally famous in the 400-meter hurdles, earning Track & Field News world rankings in eight successive years from 1953 through 1960. Only in 1960 was he ranked below 3rd in the world. Culbreath was the Olympic bronze medalist in 1956, and the next year broke the world record in the 440-yard hurdles. A 1955 graduate of Morgan State College, he was a three-time winner of the Penn Relays 400-meter hurdles, twice won the Pan-American Games title, and won the U.S./Soviet Union dual meet at Philadelphia's Franklin Field in 1959

Culbreath Elected to Pennsylvania High School Track and Field Hall of Fame

Josh Culbreath, Norristown Area HS class of 1951, has been elected to the *Pennsylvania High School Track and Field Hall of Fame.*

A PIAA state champion in the 200-yard low hurdles as a senior, Josh Culbreath became internationally famous in the 400-meter hurdles, earning Track & Field News world rankings in eight successive years from 1953 through 1960. Only in 1960 was he ranked below 3rd in the world. Culbreath was the Olympic bronze medalist in 1956, and the next year broke the world record in the 440-yard hurdles. A 1955 graduate of Morgan State College, he was a three-time winner of the Penn Relays 400-meter hurdles, twice won the Pan-American Games title, and won the U.S./Soviet Union dual meet at Philadelphia's Franklin Field in 1959.

The induction ceremony will take place on Sunday, March 1, 2020, during the Indoor State Championship Meet at Penn State University.

The three American Athletes who made a three place sweep in the 400 meter hurdles of the Olympics display smiles and medals here. Left to right: Silas Edward Southern, Dallas, Texas, second place; Glenn Davis, Clinton, O., first place; and **Josh Culbreath, Norristown, Pa.,** *third place.*

NORRISTOWN AREA SCHOOL DISTRICT

Culbreath Elected to Pennsylvania High School Track and Field Hall of Fame

Josh Culbreath, Norristown Area HS class of 1951, has been elected to the *Pennsylvania High School Track and Field Hall of Fame.*

A PIAA state champion in the 200-yard low hurdles as a senior, Josh Culbreath became internationally famous in the 400-meter hurdles, earning Track & Field News world rankings in eight successive years from 1953 through 1960. Only in 1960 was he ranked below 3rd in the world. Culbreath was the Olympic bronze medalist in 1956, and the next year broke the world record in the 440-yard hurdles. A 1955 graduate of Morgan State College, he was a three-time winner of the Penn Relays 400-meter hurdles, twice won the Pan-American Games title, and won the U.S./Soviet Union dual meet at Philadelphia's Franklin Field in 1959

The induction ceremony will take place on Sunday, March 1, 2020, during the Indoor State Championship Meet at Penn State University. The Hall of Fame was established in 1995 to honor the elite individuals in our state's distinguished track and field history. A selection committee consisting of more than thirty coaches, officials, and journalists collect and reviews information about individuals who have been nominated. Further research is conducted, and a new ballot is formed each summer. Voting by the selection committee takes place in the fall, and the newly elected members are inducted at the Indoor State Championship Meet.

Each year, 6-to-12 athletes, one coach, one contributor, and one distinguished alumnus are inducted. Athletes become eligible for nomination five years after their high school graduation. Once nominated, a candidate remains under consideration in perpetuity. The committee currently has information on over 400 athletes, 100 coaches, and 50 contributors—more than a century's worth of outstanding individuals— who have been nominated but not yet inducted. Those wishing to share details about deserving candidates are encouraged to submit a nomination through the PTFCA website (ptfca.org)

Fun Fact: Culbreath (left) took the Bronze medal in the 400 meter Hurdles at the 1956 Melbourne Olympics.

Josh Culbreath, Norristown High School, class of 1951
1956 Melbourne Olympics
400 meter Hurdles ~ Bronze Medal
PICTURED IN LIFE MAGAZINE ON THE VICTORY STAND (LEFT) WITH TEAMMATES
GLENN DAVIS, OHIO STATE AND EDDIE SOUTHERN, TEXAS, DURING OUR NATIONAL ANTHEM.

(Original Caption) The three American Athletes who made a three place sweep in the 400 meter hurdles of the Olympics display smiles and medals here. Left to right: Silas Edward Southern, Dallas, Texas as, second place; Glenn Davis, Clinton, O., first place; and **Josh Culbreath, Norristown, Pa.**, third place. Davis won in 50.1, a new Olympic record which is southern equaled in the semi-finals.

Famous Norristonians

Did you know that Norristown has been home to numerous people of renowned stature in U.S. history?

Prominent Norristonians

From civil war era abolitionists, generals, and scientists to modern day athletes, actors, and artists, here is a list of some prominent Norristonians (in alphabetical order):

- Geno Auriemma, Hall of Fame women's basketball coach at UConn
- Maria Bello, actress (ER, A History of Violence)
- Charles L. Blockson, Historian, Scholar, and Author
- Steve Bono, former NFL quarterback
- Peter Boyle, actor (Everybody Loves Raymond, Young Frankenstein)
- Al Cantello, Olympian Athlete (1960 Rome Summer Olympics, Javelin Thrower)
- Josh Culbreath, Olympian Athlete (1957 400 meter hurdles world record)
- David C. Dolby, Medal of Honor
- Jules Fisher, lighting designer
- Joseph Fornance, US Congressman and Norristown Borough council president
- Larry Glueck, football player for Villanova and 1963 NFL champion Chicago Bears, head coach for Fordham University
- Marques Green, basketball player

- Winfield Scott Hancock, field commander at Gettysburg, presidential candidate
- John F. Hartranft, Governor of Pennsylvania 1873 to 1879
- Si Jenks, actor who worked in vaudeville, television and movies from 1920s to the 1950s.
- Tommy Lasorda, manager of Los Angeles Dodgers, Baseball Hall of Famer
- Drew Lewis, CEO Union Pacific, US Secretary of Transportation
- Thaddeus Lowe, Civil War-era aeronaut, scientist, and inventor
- William Moore, US Congressman representing New Jersey 1869–1871
- Timothy L. O'Brien, journalist
- Jaco Pastorius, musician
- Mike Piazza, professional baseball player, Baseball Hall of Famer
- David Rittenhouse Porter, Governor of Pennsylvania 1839 to 1845
- Martha Settle Putney, educator and historian
- Lisa Raymond, WTA tennis player
- Bill Schonely, broadcaster
- Richard Schweiker, US Senator from Pennsylvania 1969 to 1981 and Secretary of Health and Human Services under President Ronald Reagan from 1981 to 1983
- Jimmy Smith, jazz musician
- Art Spiegelman, cartoonist, Maus
- Jerry Spinelli, author
- Kellee Stewart, actress

- Ralph B. Strassburger, newspaper publisher, thoroughbred racehorse owner
- John F. Street, Mayor of Philadelphia 2000 to 2008
- Roy Thomas, Philadelphia Phillies outfielder 1899 to 1908 and University of Pennsylvania head baseball coach
- Henry "Hank" Williams is an American former professional basketball player. He played in 39 games for the Utah Stars in the American Basketball Association.
- Bobby Wine, professional baseball player, coach, manager and scout

17

Conclusion

His name may forever be muted and not recognized in the town he grew up and always love, he may not have his name honored on a street sign where he grew up in the streets of Norristown, he may not have his name placard where he graduated from and not honored at AD Eisenhower Jr. High School and Norristown Sr. High School gyms and track fields, he may not have a downtown Main Street Sports Memorial statue named in his honor, he may not have park track trails named after him, or not named after him on Norristown Sr. High School's new Sports Complex because HIS NAME was voted by rejections. Those latter listed are the not deserving ending finale of Josh's trials and tribulations of his incredible and remarkable steadfast life. I must say it is very spectacular and truly a glorious homage for Norristown to have a representation of an Olympian icon. His name is a legacy at these schools, and he ignited to become a celebrated athlete. *Mr. Joshua Culbreath*, one of Norristown's *first Olympians and Olympic medal winners*, is a former world-record holder and local sports legend. He was a noted high school track star at Norristown High and went on to a great collegiate career. He was a renowned international track star who represented his country and his hometown in a great fashion. It is time to pay tribute to someone who was a great athletic talent, but more importantly who put Norristown "on the map" around the world. *Times Herald* Editor, Mr. Stan Huskey, published a book describing Norristown's history, in which he vividly cites Mr. Culbreath's accomplishments and experiences. Josh's name will always be lit in lights as a local pioneer, a legend, an aspiring Track and Field Olympic Champion, and a permanent historic fixture of Norristown, Pennsylvania, in the school district and our community—one we can all be proud of for years to come. His story is an inspiration to encourage youths to dream big, be positive, believe, and stay encouraged. It does not matter what neighborhood you come from. If you have a vision and foresee what you want to be in life successfully, you have the power to channel that energy into the atmosphere and it will come to pass. Josh didn't let anything stop him. Like Josh, you may encounter rejections, challenges, trials, and tribulations along the way. He did not worry about it. It is a learning and growing experience. Level up! And keep it moving like he did. His winning spirit continues to soar through the decades and on to this day.

Olympian Josh Culbreath—his name—is the Who's Who rooted with accolades constantly penned about him headlined on the front pages and Sports headlined in local newspaper *The Times Herald* commentated by sports editor Red McCarthy, *Time* Magazine, *The New York Times*, *The Philadelphia Tribune*, international Indian magazine *The Span*, and many others; recognized in person and highly honored by President Dwight Eisenhower, prominent Philadelphian Jim Kelly, invited to the Rose Garden at the White House by President Bill Clinton, Congressman Joe Sestak; and he was inducted in many Halls and Walls of Fame and many other awards which are highlighted in his biography. Even a local Norristown distillery in downtown Norristown on E. Main Street called Five Saints Distilling paid homage to Olympian Josh Culbreath by naming one of their beverages after him called the "Culbreath Smash." Cheers to you, Cousin Josh! Josh certainly built a name and left his mark in Norristown not only locally but around the world.

A world-traveler in his walk of life, he has met many well-known remarkable sports figures, dignitaries, music artists, TV and movie celebrities through his years, and has remained friends with them such as Jesse Owens, Wilma Rudolph, Willye B. White, and Tommy LaSorda (all deceased). From the beginning of it all, he had first dibs growing up in the same neighborhood with well-renowned sports legend Tommy LaSorda, music extraordinaire Jimmy Smith, historian and author Charles L. "Charlie" Blockson, and Olympian javelin thrower Al Cantello. Encounters of other celebrities are highlighted in his biography.

The power of *kismet*—Early in his childhood life Josh tells his story his running days all started at the Field Day which was the only time he was exposed to running that one day at Roosevelt Field, where everything had begun because it was organized sports. Later in life, Josh strongly believes in the power of kismet, a meaning that leads to control what happens in the future. Josh believes kismet explains his achievements throughout his life. He recognized that "sport determined his destiny." A confident and self-motivated individual, he set seemingly insurmountable goals for himself. Full circle later in his life, he returns to Roosevelt Field to be honored as a world champion Olympian athlete by the one and only President Dwight D. Eisenhower. Now, that is the power of kismet.

The Story of Lane 1 at the Melbourne, Australia, Olympics 1956— When Josh tells his story about Lane 1 and how he was displeased with his placement in a lane dug up and cinder track all chewed up, you can tell in his tone he was disheartened. But he fought the good fight. Nothing was against him. He ignored his challenges and prevailed. He faced an obstacle and rose above it. He came out on top. He had a strong desire to persevere. He crossed the finished line and won the race. With a decorated demeanor, he earned a place on the victory stand in a gallant stature representing Norristown and the Marines. Josh's dear friend Dr. Charlie Jenkins said, "There's an equal number of factors that go into earning a place on the victory stand." Here is a direct heartwarming quote by Olympian Dr. Charlie Jenkins reflecting on the words of his and Josh's dear friend Olympian Mr. Herb Douglas who often says:

> I am as proud of my bronze medal as those that won gold and silver medals. I believe that and I have a great deal of respect for those athletes who were on the victory stand with me.
>
> I also believe that standing on top of that victory stand was a gift from God.

Josh had a pocket full of dreams, and he lived out his dreams to the fullest. From the November 1956 letter, he wrote to *Times Herald* sports editor Red McCarthy: "Time is drawing nigh. A dream in a dream, and a dream of a lifetime! Regards to all, and please say a prayer that I can do my best. Thanks—Josh." To his conversation with young Warrior Heartbeat Tyreke, who had asked Cousin Josh what it was like joining the Marine Corp, Josh's response was, "It was a dream and a wish and a desire for a long, long time." Another ending *dream* quote by Josh is, "Stay focused and believe in your dreams and your hopes and your aspirations." These are the words of a man who was an overcomer of adversity and triumphed in the end. Digging in the trenches even, Josh turned out to be an Olympian champion, broke records, won bronze and gold medals, and was the first active-duty Marine to be a bronze-medalist Olympic hero. His purpose in life was not only being a winner; he was on a mission. Determined, Josh accomplished the mission because he remained focused.

Josh is overwhelmingly loved and remembered by all community circles of family and friends. Love conquers overall. So we will continue to follow love and finish our task to honor Josh.

Like that high school junior running barefoot on a cinder track, Culbreath was willing to stay true to himself. Track and field, human performance, and achievement are what my eighty-plus years have been about.

Spoken Word by Josh:

If I could live by example,
And running was what I could do best, and hurdling was what it was. I was the shortest hurdler in the world, and I wanted to leave some type of legacy. I think it was my love of people, I left along the way. I made a difference representing my country, and I think I represented it well.

Well done, Dr. Joshua "Josh" Culbreath. Thank you for your service. We Salute You. Your legacy will live on…

MISSION ACCOMPLISHED

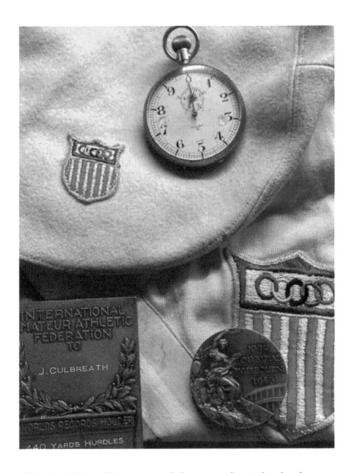

Some of Josh Culbreath's memorabilia—on the right, his bronze medal from 1956 Olympics; on the left, his medal from breaking a world record in Oslo in 1957, his Olympics beret, and his coaching stopwatch.

*****

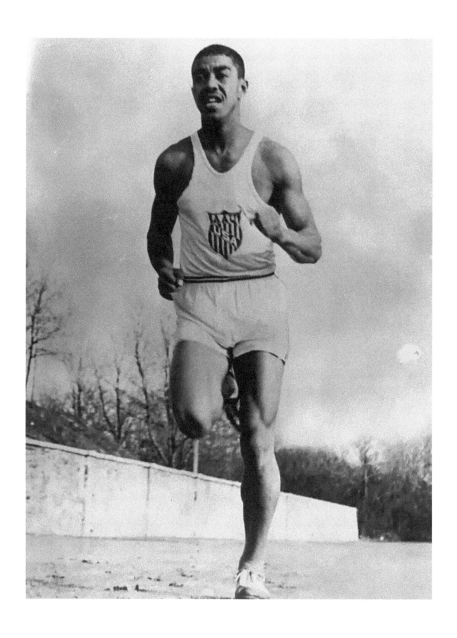

18

Friends of Josh in His Past

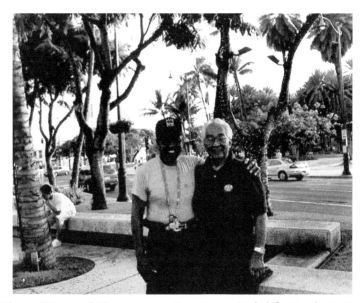

Tamio "Tommy" Kono was an American weightlifter in the 1950s and 1960s. Kono set world records in four different weight classes: lightweight, middleweight, light-heavyweight, and middle-heavyweight. Kono was a gold medalist at both the 1952 Summer Olympics and 1956 Summer Olympics, and a silver medalist at the 1960 Summer Olympics under coach Bob Hoffman. Kono won the World Weightlifting Championships six consecutive times from 1953 to 1959 and was a three-time Pan American Games champion; in 1955, 1959, and 1963.

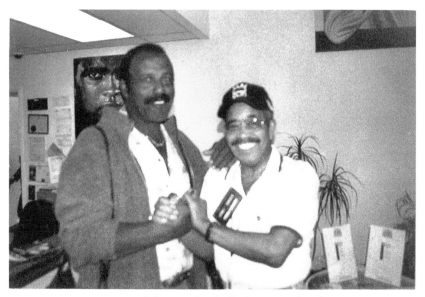

Actor and former football player Fred "The
Hammer" Williamson and Josh

Actor Anthony Quinn and Josh

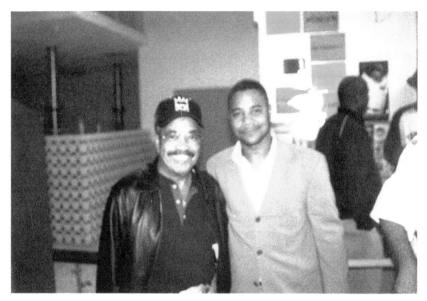

Actor Cuba Gooding, Jr. and Josh

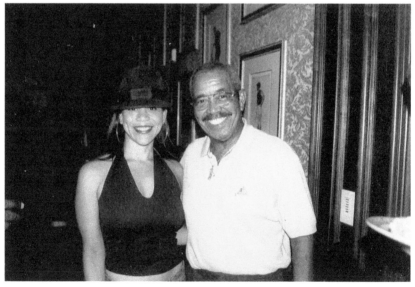

Actress Rosie Perez and Josh

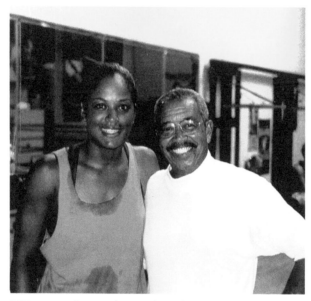

American TV personality and retired professional boxer Laila Ali and Josh

Clyde Drexler and Josh

Comedian Eddie Griffin and Josh

Comedian Chris Rock, Josh, and Comedian Adam Sandler

Actor Emmanuel Lewis and Josh – Caesars Palace, Las Vegas, NV

Hall of Fame, California

Jazz saxophonist Grover Washington, Jr. and two
women Morganites posing with Josh

Josh shaking hands with Joe Jackson an American talent
manager and patriarch of the Jackson family of entertainers
that includes his children Michael and Janet.

Joe "Jellybean" Bryant and Josh

Joe "Jellybean" Bryant and Josh

Former professional boxer James "Lights Out" Toney and Josh

Josh and The Mighty Great boxer Mike "Iron
Mike" Tyson, Las Vegas, NV

Josh and former professional NBA basketball player Julius "Dr. J" Erving

Julius "Dr. J" Erving

Josh and "Lets Get Ready to Rumble" Boxing Announcer Michael Buffer

Josh and singer, entertainer, and actress Suzette Charles. She
was Miss New Jersey in 1983 and served as Miss America
1984, 30th Street Railway Station, Philadelphia, PA

Josh getting the best of Mohammed Ali

Mohammed Ali Olympic Games Rome 1960
gold medal with teammates and coaches

Mohammed Ali and Josh

Actor Mr. T known for his roles as B. A. Baracus in the 1980s
television series The A-Team and Josh at Caesars Palace, Las Vegas

Josh and former NFL football wide receiver Terrell "T.O." Owens

Josh and former NFL wide receiver and potential
Olympic Athlete Willie Gault.

Actress Phylicia Rashad and Josh

Actress Phylicia Rashad

Josh and One of the Greatest former professional
boxer "Sugar" Ray Leonard

Suzette Charles

Suzette Charles

19

A Service of Thanksgiving

In Memory of my Beloved Cousin Josh

Cynthia Culbreath

SPOKEN WORD:

"He had charisma, He was box office".
Al Cantello, In 1959, he set the world
record in the javelin and won the bronze
medal at the 1959 Pan American Games,
and made the US Olympic Team in the
1960 Summer Olympic in Rome. "We
played sports in high school together".

"He is a national treasure. This is about
preservation". Dr. Geneive Brown
Metzger, Caribbean-US Advocate

"I'm glad that Josh's story will be
documented and never forgotten".
Hagar Eldeeb, Artist, Illustrator and
USC college student.

"I don't remember meeting him but
impressed with his accomplishments in
track. I also ran the 400-meter hurdles in
college but not nearly as good as him.
Smile!!". John Woolfolk

"Josh was the 1st cousin to my
brother-in-law Freddie Culbreath
(husband) of Sarah Collins Culbreath of
Aubry Ave,, Ardmore. Josh always had a
smile and never let his fame "go to his
head."" Jim Williams

"Completing your book is much like
completing an olympic experience".
Dr. Charles Jenkins, winner of two gold
medals at the 1956 Melbourne, Australia
Summer Olympic Games".

Dr. Joshua Culbreath
1932 - 2021
MOTTO: ONCE AN OLYMPIAN; ALWAYS AN OLYMPIAN
NEVER FORMER; NEVER PAST®

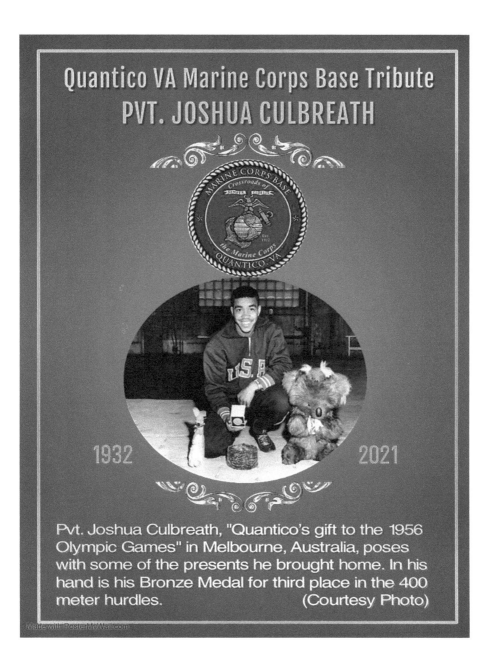

Pvt. Joshua Culbreath, "Quantico's gift to the 1956 Olympic Games" in Melbourne, Australia, poses with some of the presents he brought home. In his hand is his Bronze Medal for third place in the 400 meter hurdles. (Courtesy Photo)

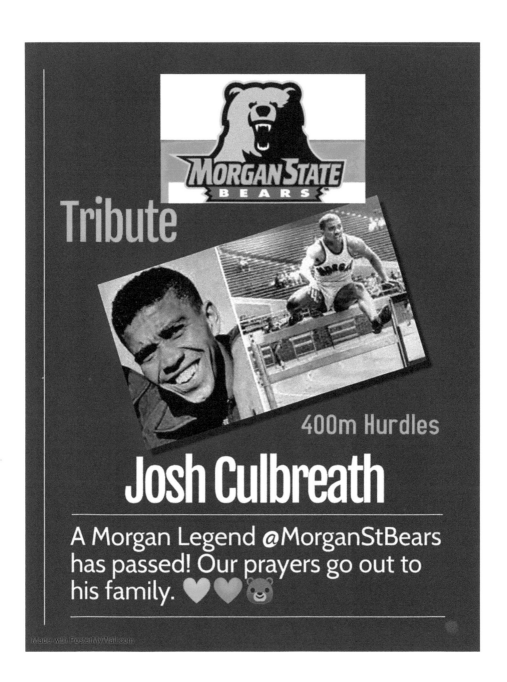

Tribute

400m Hurdles

Josh Culbreath

A Morgan Legend @MorganStBears has passed! Our prayers go out to his family. 🤍🤍🐻

Made with PosterMyWall.com

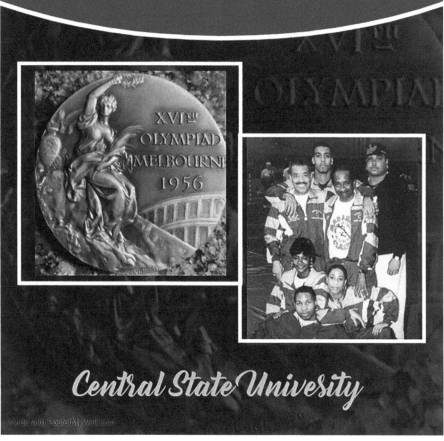

Photo courtesy: Central State University Athletics Communications

Photo courtesy: Central State University Athletics Communications

Group photo: Josh's Ohio Central State University track and field Jamaican protégés. They lovingly called him "Pop" and "Coach." Photo courtesy: Cynthia Culbreath

References/Sources/ Research

NASDtv. "NASDtv interviews Josh Culbreath 2015." YouTube, uploaded June 16, 2015. https://www.youtube.com/watch?v=ViXG4CGeHDE.

Pages 273–276
"Montgomery County Coaches Hall of Fame Honors Inductees." *The Times Herald*, November 26, 2013.

Page 273
"Olympic Medalist and Norristown Native Joshua Culbreath Reflects on Life on Eve of Montco Hall of Fame Induction." *The Time Herald*, November 24, 2013.

Page 59
"The challenges of running hurdles." https://www.encyclopedia.com/sports/sports-fitness-recreation-and-leisure-magazines/running-hurdles

Pages 46–47
Huskey, Stan. *Remembering Norristown: Stories from the Banks of the Schuylkill River,* 80. Charleston: The History Press, 2009.

Page 64
Barshad, Amos. *"Ill Communication* at 20: An Everything Guide to the Beastie Boys Masterpiece." Grantland, last modified March 27, 2014. https://grantland.com/hollywood-prospectus/ill-

communication-at-20-an-everything-guide-to-the-beastie-boys-masterpiece.

Huskey, Stan. *Remembering Norristown: Stories from the Banks of the Schuylkill River*, 78. Charleston: The History Press, 2009.

Huskey, Stan. *Remembering Norristown: Stories from the Banks of the Schuylkill River*, 78–79. Charleston: The History Press, 2009.

Page 66

Huskey, Stan. *Remembering Norristown: Stories from the Banks of the Schuylkill River*. Charleston: The History Press, 2009.

Page 69

https://www.pressreader.com/

"Josh Culbreath." *The Times Herald*, August 12, 2013.

We had imagination. East End was a bunch of proud people. Lasorda used to say, 'Our fathers never had to come to City Hall for us.'"

Page 58

Huskey, Stan. *Remembering Norristown: Stories from the Banks of the Schuylkill River*, 79. Charleston: The History Press, 2009.

Pages 65, 270

"Olympic Medalist and Norristown Native Joshua Culbreath Reflects on Life on Eve of Montco Hall of Fame Induction." *The Time Herald*, November 24, 2013.

Page 65

Huskey, Stan. *Remembering Norristown: Stories from the Banks of the Schuylkill River*, 76. Charleston: The History Press, 2009.

Page 74

Huskey, Stan. *Remembering Norristown: Stories from the Banks of the Schuylkill River*, 77–78. Charleston: The History Press, 2009.

Pages 74–76
Brown, Doug. "Last Morgan Medalist on Track, Thanks to Cosby." *The Baltimore Sun*, August 4, 1992. https://www.baltimoresun. com/news/bs-xpm-1992-08-04-1992217078-story.html.

Page 76
"Josh   Culbreath."   Olympedia.   http://www.olympedia.org/ athletes/78284.

Page 76
Marshall, Kenneth. "In Dad's Footsteps Former ACU All-American Rebuilding Central St. Track Program Father Built." TexNews. June 4, 1999. https://web.archive.org/web/20110614110417/ http://www.texnews.com/1998/1999/sports/jahan0604.html

Page 78
"The Flying Four." Wikipedia. https://en.wikipedia.org/wiki/ The_Flying_Four

Pages 78–81
"The History of the MSU Legacy Track Meet." Morgan State Athletics, last modified April 12, 2016. https://morganstate-bears.com/sports/2016/4/12/legacy-track-meet-history
"Edward Hurt." USA Track & Field Hall of Fame 1975. http://leg-acy.usatf.org/HallOfFame/TF/showBio.asp?HOFIDs=78

Page 81:
"Edward P. Hurt." https://en.wikipedia.org/wiki/Edward_P._Hurt

Pages 84–86
"Morgan's 'Mom' Leaves Rich Legacy." *Morgan Magazine*. Spring 2004. https://issuu.com/morganstateu/docs/morganmag_s04.

Pages 88 and 227
"Josh Culbreath." Penn Relays Hall of Fame 1994. https://pennre-lays.com/honors/hall-of-fame/josh-culbreath/32

Page 246

"Olympic Medalist and Norristown Native Joshua Culbreath Reflects on Life on Eve of Montco Hall of Fame Induction." *The Time Herald*, November 24, 2013.

"The Flying Four." Wikipedia. https://en.wikipedia.org/wiki/The_Flying_Four

Page 96

Presenting the 7th Annual Legacy Track Meet Morgan State University Acknowledging: MSU Track & Field Greats from the 1951 to 1955 April 16 & 17, 2010 Hughes Stadium page 15

Page 98

Marshall, Kenneth. "In Dad's Footsteps Former ACU All-American Rebuilding Central St. Track Program Father Built." TexNews. June 4, 1999. https://web.archive.org/web/20110614110417/http://www.texnews.com/1998/1999/sports/jahan0604.html

Page 103

Huskey, Stan. *Remembering Norristown: Stories from the Banks of the Schuylkill River*, 79. Charleston: The History Press, 2009.

Page 127

Brown, Doug. "Last Morgan Medalist on Track, Thanks to Cosby." *The Baltimore Sun*, August 4, 1992. https://www.baltimoresun.com/news/bs-xpm-1992-08-04-1992217078-story.html.

Page 132

"1956 Summer Olympics." Olympedia. http://www.olympedia.org/editions/14

Page 133

Man with Seven Feet (clipping)

Charles Dumas *Photo Credit* (page 8): https://www.panamsports.org/downloads/pdf/panamgames/1959-chicago-tomo-2-lq.pdf

Page 134

Emery, Curtis R. 1975. "The Historical Aspects of the Pan-American Games." Paper presented at the *Annual Meeting of the American Alliance for Health, Physical Education, and Recreation. Atlantic City, NJ, 1975*. Atlantic City. https://files.eric.ed.gov/fulltext/ED106290.pdf

"Athletes Vs. Altitude." *Sports Illustrated*. March 28, 1955. https://vault.si.com/vault/1955/03/28/athletes-vs-altitude

Glantz, Gordon. "Clearing Another Hurdle: Norristown's Culbreath to Enter MCCHOF." *Ingordonville*. October 29, 2013. https://ingordonville.com/2013/10/29/clearing-another-hurdle-norristowns-culbreath-to-enter-mcchof.

"Salute Cantello and Culbreath Tonight—Military Parade Highlights Program at Roosevelt Field." *Norristown Times Herald,* September 14, 1959. Article credits provided by the Norristown Historical Society.

Page 136

Levine, Ben. "How High-Altitude Training Can Benefit Elite Endurance Athletes Like Runners and Swimmers." UT Southwestern Medical Center. November 21, 2016. https://utswmed.org/medblog/high-altitude-training/

Emery, Curtis R. 1975. "The Historical Aspects of the Pan-American Games." Paper presented at the *Annual Meeting of the American Alliance for Health, Physical Education, and Recreation. Atlantic City, NJ, 1975*. Atlantic City. https://files.eric.ed.gov/fulltext/ED106290.pdf

Page 139

Emery, Curtis R. 1975. "The Historical Aspects of the Pan American Games." Paper presented at the *Annual Meeting of the American Alliance for Health, Physical Education, and Recreation. Atlantic City, NJ, 1975*. Atlantic City. https://files.eric.ed.gov/fulltext/ED106290.pdf

Page 144
Huskey, Stan. *Remembering Norristown: Stories from the Banks of the Schuylkill River*, 75. Charleston: The History Press, 2009.

Page 145
"Best Ever." *Time*, July 9, 1956. https://wayback.archive-it.org/1218/20081214122406/http://www.time.com/time/magazine/article/0,9171,893479,00.html?iid=digg_share
Huskey, Stan. *Remembering Norristown: Stories from the Banks of the Schuylkill River*, 75. Charleston: The History Press, 2009.

Pages 145–147
Tremoglie, Christopher. "Sixty years ago today, Philly Was the Center of US-Soviet Union Tensions." *The Philadelphia Inquirer*, July 18, 2019. https://www.inquirer.com/opinion/commentary/us-russia-relations-philadelphia-track-meet-soviet-union-20190718.html

Page 147
Fitzpatrick, Frank. "US-Soviet Track Meet in Philadelphia Came at Height of Cold War." *The Philadelphia Inquirer,* April 30, 2016. https://www.inquirer.com/philly/columnists/frank_fitzpatrick/20160501_U_S_-Soviet_track_meet_in_Philadelphia_came_at_height_of_Cold_War.html

Pages 148–162
Story write-up referencing *Norristown Times Herald* newspaper clippings provided by the Norristown Historical Society.

Pages 163–169
Span. August 1962. Uploaded May 10, 2018. https://issuu.com/spanmagazine/docs/08-1962-cr

Page 169
Span Magazine. "*Span* Covers—1960s" Pinterest. https://www.pinterest.com/pin/48976714671810012/

Pages 170–171

"Milkha Singh Wiki, Biography, Wife, Age, Family, Career, Facts and More." YourWikiBio. https://yourwikibio.com/milkha-singh.

"Milkha Singh." Wikipedia. https://en.wikipedia.org/wiki/Milkha_Singh.

Pages 173–177

National Masters News. September 1982. http://www.mastershistory.org/NMN/NMN-September-1982s.pdf

Edwin Moses.

https://ethw.org/Edwin_Moses_and_the_Engineering_of_World_Records, https://sports.jrank.org/pages/3342/Moses-Edwin-Awards-Accomplishments.html, https://www.google.com/search?q=list+all+the+awards+by+Edwin+Moses&gs_ivs=1#tts=0

Pages 175

"V World Veteran's Track & Field Games, September 23–September 30, 1983." Sri Chinmoy Marathon Team. https://us.srichinmoyraces.org/archives/1983/worldmastersgames

Pages 177–182

Chadbourne, Mary M. "Throwers break Records in Cleveland." *National Masters News*. April 1984. http://www.mastershistory.org/NMN/NMN-April-1984s.pdf.

Ceronie, Rich. "Midwest Indoor Draws 160." *National Masters News*. April 1984. http://www.mastershistory.org/NMN/NMN-April-1984s.pdf.

"300 Compete at UCLA." *National Masters News*. June 1984. http://www.mastershistory.org/NMN/NMN-June-1984s.pdf.

Hopkins, Suzanne. "51 Compete in National Decathlon." *National Masters News*. September 1984. http://www.mastershistory.org/NMN/NMN-September-1984s.pdf.

Pages 182–183

Jordan, Joe. "Beyond the Track: The Triumphs and Trials of Ira Davis." La Salle University Athletics. February 24, 2020. https://goexplorers.com/news/2020/2/24/mens-track-and-field-if-you-build-it-the-story-of-the-first-black-hall-of-athletes-inductee-ira-davis.aspx

Page 183

Glantz, Gordon. "Clearing Another Hurdle: Norristown's Culbreath to Enter MCCHOF." Ingordonville. October 29, 2013.https://ingordonville.com/2013/10/29/clearing-another-hurdle-norristowns-culbreath-to-enter-mcchof/

Pages 186

Lawrence, Allan. *Olympus and Beyond (A Story of Life, Sport, and Love on Four Continents)*. Pittsburgh: Dorrance Publishing Co., 2014.

Pages 187–193

Hardwood, Rod. "Sharing Their Journeys." *Coeur d'Alene Press*, January 17, 2008. From the *Kootenai County Task Force on Human Relations Scrapbooks 2007*. 74–77. Uploaded October 6, 2017. https://issuu.com/molsteadlibraryatnic/docs/kootenai_county_task_force_on_human_5fd4ca9183584e.

Dukes, Lucy. "Rising Above the Hate." *Coeur d'Alene Press*, January 22, 2008. From the *Kootenai County Task Force on Human Relations Scrapbooks 2007*. 83–85. Uploaded October 6, 2017. https://issuu.com/molsteadlibraryatnic/docs/kootenai_county_task_force_on_human_5fd4ca9183584e

Pages 200–201

Sayon Cooper

"Hanging with Mr. Cooper: Liberia's Track Team Coach." Go Team Liberia. August 7, 2016. Last modified June 13, 2018. https://www.goteamliberia.com/2018/06/13/mr-cooper-liberias-track-team-coach/

Page 207
Deon Hemmings
Glantz, Gordon. "Clearing Another Hurdle: Norristown's Culbreath to Enter MCCHOF." Ingordonville. October 29, 2013.https://ingordonville.com/2013/10/29/clearing-another-hurdle-norristowns-culbreath-to-enter-mcchof/

"Deon Hemmings." Wikipedia. https://en.wikipedia.org/wiki/Deon_Hemmings

Photo Credit: http://www.athleticsnacac.org/2020/10/18/jam-deon-hemmings-mccatty-receive-jamaicas-order-of-distinction-in-the-rank-of-commander/

Pages 208–224
Series of Rich Perez interviews with Josh at the M Resort Hotel in Las Vegas, Nevada
Willye B. White Reference:
Think2008. "Dr Joshua Culbreath & Rich Perez Talking Of Willye B. White." YouTube. Uploaded June 29, 2008. https://www.youtube.com/watch?v=VVUTiBtwr6U

Johnny Woodruff Reference:
Think2008. "Dr Joshua Culbreath & Rich Perez Talk Of Johnny Woodruff." YouTube. Uploaded June 29, 2008. https://www.youtube.com/watch?v=3JMXBipAf9s

Johnny Woodruff and the Nazi Olympics quote Reference:
United States Holocaust Memorial Museum. "John Woodruff and the Nazi Olympics." Facebook, August 26, 2020. https://www.facebook.com/holocaustmuseum/videos/john-woodruff-and-the-nazi-olympics/3352160974850402/

Josh discusses Triumphs in Life and Sports Reference:
Think2008. "1956 US Olympian Medalist Joshua Culbreath Discusses Triumphs in life and sports with Rich Perez." YouTube. Uploaded July 20, 2009. https://www.youtube.com/watch?v=YQRWCpa3RGE

Josh discusses the Heroes of Track and Field Reference (pages 212–213):

Think2008. "Dr. Joshua Culbreath Discusses the heros of track and fields past with Rich Perez." YouTube. Uploaded July 20, 2009. https://www.youtube.com/watch?v=t-_Lajca_Mg

Josh discusses The Civil Rights Movement in Athletics Reference (page 215):

Think2008. "Dr. Joshua Culbreath July 19, 2009, M resort, Las Vegas, NV. Discusses Greatness with Rich Perez." YouTube. Uploaded July 20, 2009. https://www.youtube.com/watch?v=x8SEZAqkJAQ
Personal possession from one of Josh's DVD about Willye B. White (page 224)
Willye B. White Quote reference:
"Willye B. White." The History Makers. https://www.thehistory-makers.org/biography/willye-b-white-39.

Page 230
Litsky, Frank. "TRACK AND FIELD; At Beginning of Penn Relays, Villanova Finishes First." *New York Times.* April 29, 1994. https://www.nytimes.com/1994/04/29/sports/track-and-field-at-beginning-of-penn-relays-villanova-finishes-first.html.
McMullen, Paul. "Penn Relays is Baton Marylanders Have Passed With Joy." *The Baltimore Sun.* April 28, 1994. https://www.bal-timoresun.com/news/bs-xpm-1994-04-28-1994118139-story.html
Denman, Elliot. "Dr. Gregory Bell & Olympians At Penn Relays." *The Olympian.* Summer 2019 https://www.teamusa.org/-/media/TeamUSA/Athlete-Services/ONLSummerIssue2019.pdf

Pages 232–233

"Edwin Moses." Wikipedia. https://en.wikipedia.org/wiki/
Edwin_Moses

Page 324 Conclusion

https://www.pressreader.com/search?query=Joshua%20
Culbreath&languages=en&groupBy=Language&hideSimilar=
0&type=1&state=1

https://www.daytondailynews.com/sports/archdeacon-a-son-says-
goodbye-to-superman/TXIVHJCCIVBFJCYIBMYGX6STEQ/

Photo Credits

Melbourne Olympics

Pages 19–20
https://apnews.com/article/sports-australia-equestrian-sports-general-melbourne-e22bc75115094929d4a35f36f497a42e
https://www.olympedia.org/editions/14

Page 25
SPOKEN WORD PHOTO CREDIT—(insert of Cousin Josh) Western Illinois Athletic Hall of Fame Track & Field Inductees Apr 10, 2009
2010 Lee Calhoun Memorial Invitational Ralph Boston / Special Guests & Olympians
https://www.nmnathletics.com/pdf8/687249.pdf

Pages 42–45
Cynthia Culbreath Family photos

Page 51
Norristown High School Class of 1951 Fiftieth Anniversary, November 17, 2001—Whitemarsh Valley Country Club, Whitemarsh, Pennsylvania.

Page 62
Josh Culbreath church scene with hat in *Boycott* movie. Photo courtesy: Cynthia Culbreath

Page 66

1949 NHS JV Basketball Photo Yearbook (Credit: Norristown Historical Society, Norristown PA)

http://hsmcpa.org/index.php/learn/found-in-collection/item/174-a-local-olympian

Page 66

1949 NHS JV Football Photo Yearbook (Credit: Norristown Historical Society, Norristown PA)

http://hsmcpa.org/index.php/learn/found-in-collection/item/174-a-local-olympian

Pages 78–79

Hall of Fame—USATF http://legacy.usatf.org/halloffame/TF/showBio.asp

Edward "Eddie" P. Hurt (PHOTO CREDIT)

Pages 78–79

PHOTO CREDIT (page 27)—Josh and Eddie Hurt

https://issuu.com/morganstateu/docs/morganmag_s04

Page 84

Mrs. Hurt photo Courtesy of Cynthia Culbreath

Page 87

Coach Edward P. Hurt and Bea Hurt on vacation during the 1950s. Photo credit:

https://issuu.com/morganstateu/docs/morganmag_s04 (page 29 in link)

Page 88

Morgan State's Flying Four 1-2-3-4 Photo courtesy: Cynthia Culbreath

Page 89
Morgan's Track Team sweeps Howard Meet Photo courtesy: Jimmy and Brenda Rogers

Page 110
Montgomery County—Norristown Public Library Melbourne Mail Call Photo credit

Page 126
https://www.gettyimages.fi/detail/news-photo/josh-culbreath-and-eddie-southern-embracing-at-the-summer-news-photo/50364059

Page 127
https://www.gettyimages.com/detail/news-photo/hurdles-winners-josh-culbreath-glenn-davis-and-eddie-news-photo/50364055

Page 128
https://www.panamsports.org/downloads/pdf/panamgames/1959-chicago-tomo-2-lq.pdf
Insert Report of US Marine Corps by Major James K. McCreight (page 101 in link)

Pages 129–132
http://www.olympedia.org/results/59341

Page 136
1955 Second Pan-American Games collapse
https://www.gettyimages.com/photos/1955-pan-american-games?-family=editorial&phrase=1955%20pan%20american%20games&sort=best

Page 138
PHOTO CREDIT (page 1)
https://www.panamsports.org/downloads/pdf/panamgames/1959-chicago-tomo-2-lq.pdf

Page 139
PHOTO CREDIT (pages 6 and 8)
https://www.panamsports.org/downloads/pdf/pana-
mgames/1959-chicago-tomo-2-lq.pdf

Pages 140–141
PHOTO CREDITS (pages 10 and 14):
https://www.panamsports.org/downloads/pdf/pana-
mgames/1959-chicago-tomo-2-lq.pdf

Page 142
PHOTO CREDITS (pages 11 and 15)
https://www.panamsports.org/downloads/pdf/pana-
mgames/1959-chicago-tomo-2-lq.pdf

Page 142
PHOTO CREDITS (page 27)
https://www.panamsports.org/downloads/pdf/pana-
mgames/1959-chicago-tomo-2-lq.pdf

Page 143
Althea Gibson (page 143)
https://www.panamsports.org/downloads/pdf/pana-
mgames/1959-chicago-tomo-2-lq.pdf
Althea Gibson was credited First U.S. Gold Medal in Women's
Tennis. Althea Gibson, the former US and Wimbledon queen,
came out of a "temporary" retirement to win the single's title—
the first ever for the USA in the Pan-American women's tournament. (page 143)

Page 145
PHOTO CREDIT Josh, "Scag" Cottman and Jesse Owens. Courtesy by
the "Scag" Cottman Family

Pages 143–149
Norristown Times Herald sport wave headlines Tuesday, July 14, 1959
by *The Sport Show* editor Red McCarthy—Courtesy Norristown
Historical Society

Page 150
March 30, 1958 *NY Times* headlines in an article "CULBREATH WINS
DASH" at a race in Ankara, Turkey.

Page 154
"Day of Tribute Starts with Service Club Luncheon," *Norristown
Times Herald.* September 1959—Courtesy Norristown
Historical Society

Page 154
"President Sends Congratulations to Cantello, Culbreath." *Norristown
Times Herald.* September 1959—Courtesy Norristown
Historical Society

Page 158
"Congressman Join in Tribute To World Champion Athletes."
Norristown Times Herald. September 15, 1959—Courtesy
Norristown Historical Society

Pages 163–169
https://issuu.com/spanmagazine/docs/08-1962-cr
Span: August 1962
Uploaded on May 10, 2018

Page 169
https://www.pinterest.com/pin/48976714671810012/

Pages 170–171
https://yourwikibio.com/milkha-singh/
https://en.wikipedia.org/wiki/Milkha_Singh

Page 175
Remember Him?
https://us.srichinmoyraces.org/archives/1983/worldmastersgames

Pages 173–179
Lake Erie Open Masters Indoor Track and Field Championships, January 8, 1984 hosted by the Over The Hill Track Club and sponsored by the Seven-Up Company.
http://www.mastershistory.org/NMN/NMN-April-1984s.pdf
http://www.mastershistory.org/NMN/NMN-June-1984s.pdf
http://www.mastershistory.org/NMN/NMN-September-1984s.pdf

Pages 187–193
Sharing Their Journeys / Rising Above The Hate (starting on pages 74–77, 83–85 from link)
https://issuu.com/molsteadlibraryatnic/docs/kootenai_county_task_force_on_human_5fd4ca9183584e

Pages 199–201
Sayon Cooper
https://www.goteamliberia.com/2018/06/13/mr-cooper-liberias-track-team-coach/

Page 206
Deon Hemmings
https://ingordonville.com/2013/10/29/clearing-another-hurdle-norristowns-culbreath-to-enter-mcchof/
https://en.wikipedia.org/wiki/Deon_Hemmings
Photo Credit: http://www.athleticsnacac.org/2020/10/18/jam-deon-hemmings-mccatty-receive-jamaicas-order-of-distinction-in-the-rank-of-commander/

Page 209
Josh interview by Rich Perez at the M Resort Hotel in Las Vegas. Courtesy photo: Cynthia Culbreath

Page 226
The Penn Relays
JOSH PHOTO INSET CREDIT: https://ehbcsports.com/the-penn-relays/

Page 230
https://www.google.com/search?q=ONLSummerIs-
sue2019&rlz=1C1CHBF_enUS777US777&oq=ONLSum-
merIssue2019&aqs=chrome..69i57.979j0j15&sourceid=-
chrome&ie=UTF-8
ONLSummerIssue2019 (page 4 in link)

Page 232
https://en.wikipedia.org/wiki/Edwin_Moses

Page 236
https://en.wikipedia.org/wiki/Josh_Culbreath

Page 230
Culbreath Family photo

Page 238
https://www.wikiwand.com/en/List_of_Morgan_
State_University_alumni#/google_vignette

Page 239
https://pennrelays.wordpress.com/timeline-at-the-penns/
https://web.archive.org/web/20080613121103/http://www.usatf.
org/statistics/champions/USAOutdoorTF/men/m400mH.asp

Page 240
https://www.pinterest.com/pin/54535845463506785/

Pages 241–242
https://morganstatebears.com/honors/hall-of-fame/
joshua-culbreath/10

Page 243
Sperry Univac News, August 1978

Page 245
https://books.google.com/books?id=3KdbR4eqgfEC&p-
g=PA151&lpg=PA151&dq=Joshua+culbreath+Jes-
se+Owens&source=bl&ots=PkBGYDOKA_&sig=AC-
fU3U3Q0MydkdadyAzIykEninGAbwH5Pw&hl=en&sa-
=X&ved=2ahUKEwim_puUydDuAhWqg-AKHftoDBY4Ch-
DoATAIegQICRAB#v=onepage&q=Joshua%20culbreath%20
Jesse%20Owens&f=false

Page 246
https://en.wikipedia.org/wiki/The_Flying_Four

Pages 248-251
https://www.presidency.ucsb.edu/node/220133
https://www.presidency.ucsb.edu/documents/remarks-
central-state-university-naia-champion-athletic-teams

Page 253
https://pennrelays.com/honors/hall-of-fame/josh-culbreath/32

Pages 254–255
Reference (photo of Cousin Josh w/medals):
"Joshua "Josh" Culbreath—Induction—March-2002". *Hall of Fame.*
Bob Hayes Invitational Track & Field Meet. Archived from the
original on January 6, 2007. Retrieved December 18, 2008.

Pages 256–258
Honorable Joe Sestak's remarks:
https://www.congress.gov/congressional-record/2008/07/14/
extensions-of-remarks-section/article/E1445-3

Pages 259–260

Josh Culbreath | Military Wiki | Fandom Mitchell, Bryan (July 23, 2008)

https://static.dvidshub.net/media/pubs/pdf_22870.pdf (page 8)

https://web.archive.org/web/20080905220346/http://www.marine-corpstimes.com/news/2008/07/marine_induction_072208w/

4 inducted into Marine sports Hall of Fame

By Bryan Mitchell—Staff writer

Posted: Wednesday Jul 23, 2008 14:10:48 EDT

Bryan Mitchell (July 23, 2008) "inducted into Marine sports Hall of Fame." *Marine Corps Time*

Find this Pin and more on USMC Sports by Marine Corps Association & Foundation

Photo by Cpl. J. J. Johnson. For more historic photos visit www.mca-marines.org.

Page 261

Photo courtesy: Brigadier General Ronald Coleman

Pages 262–265 Front cover book

Presenting the Seventh Annual Legacy Track Meet Morgan State University

Acknowledging: MSU Track and Field Greats from the 1951 to 1955

April 16 and 17, 2010, HUGHES STADIUM

Page 266

CIAA Hall of Fame celebrates Flying Four Photo courtesy: Cynthia Culbreath

Pages 267–269

Philadelphia Tribune by Sportswriter Don Hunt

Pages 270–272

The Norristown Times Herald, November 24, 2013

Olympic medalist and Norristown Native Joshua Culbreath reflects on life on eve of Montco Hall of Fame Induction

Pages 273–276
The Norristown Times Herald, Nov 26, 2013
Montgomery County Coaches Hall of Fame honors inductees

Pages 277–282
https://realstancottrell.wordpress.com/2014/03/29/
josh-culbreath-testifies-stan-cottrell-truth/
Woman in photo: Margaret Hampton

Page 283
Front book cover

Page 284
https://www.phila-black-sports.org/legend-honorees/

Pages 287
Norristown celebrates 20 years of Black History Month
https://www.montgomerynews.com/thecolonial/news/norristown-
celebrates-20-years-of-black-history-month/article_f045c2dd-
af5a-58b7-be53-79edcd3db194.html
By Oscar Gamble
ogamble@21st-centurymedia.com
@OGamble_ TH on Twitter Feb 12, 2015

Page 290
https://www.facebook.com/CentralState87/photos/cen-
tral-state-university-salutes-the-60th-anniversary-of-olym-
pic-medalist-joshua/1164326303626508/

Pages 292–293
Induction 2016
https://maraudersports.com/honors/
hall-of-fame/1991-womens-track-field-team/156

Pages 294–295
Induction 2017
https://maraudersports.com/honors/hall-of-fame/1992-
   womens-track-field-team/164/kiosk

Pages 296–298
Book

Pages 299:
https://www.google.com/search?q=getty+image+Josh+Cul-
   breath+melbourne+olympics&rlz=1C1CHBF_enU-
   S777US777&sxsrf=ALeKk03LIJOsyLGjYmxXFZ-
   toY821-tkR9A:1616686124209&tbm=isch&source=i-
   u&ictx=1&fir=OOhbTHpW6RHx4M%252CbHC4SqgRx_
   O62M%252C_&vet=1&usg=AI4_-kSZ0XUBQS78goFTl5z
   drgD9nVafZw&sa=X&ved=2ahUKEwi94JWR4cvvAhVqmu
   AKHTZaDaIQ9QF6BAgNEAE&cshid=1616686323428333

Pages 306–311
https://www.ptfca.org/hall-of-fame/

Pages 312–317
https://www.nasd.k12.pa.us/site/default.aspx?PageType=3&Do-
   mainID=4&ModuleInstanceID=1121&View-
   ID=6446EE88-D30C-497E-9316-3F8874B3E108
   &RenderLoc=0&FlexDataID=6627&PageID=1
Gerry Stemplewicz's contact info: (215) 667-7102, email: thes-
   temps@gmail.com

Pages 318–320
https://www.norristown.org/314/Famous-Norristonians

Dedication Photo Credit:

Willye B. White (amsterdamnews.com)—*New York Amsterdam News*:

https://www.google.com/search?rlz=1C1CHBF_enU-
S777US777&sxsrf=ALeKk03VjKwr2YKlOYHE2vFf9VZG-
JGJg1w:1618390165445&source=univ&tbm=isch&q=willy
e+be+white+photo&sa=X&ved=2ahUKEwiA6KyXrf3vA-
hUHOs0KHconCR8Q7Al6BAgEEDY&biw=1600&bi-
h=757#imgrc=jJ8QdrSK9E_dLM

Wilma Rudolph (Pinterest image):

https://www.google.com/search?rlz=1C-
1CHBF_enUS777US777&sxsrf=ALeKk-
03GfgDbK7Oh6g333UAcw8DFdC8tU-
w:1618389313323&source=univ&tbm=isch&q=wilma+ru
dolph+photos&sa=X&ved=2ahUKEwjeuYOBqv3vAhX-
DKs0KHbiYAEAQ7Al6BAgFEBo&biw=1600&bi-
h=757#imgrc=RBRE2TkNQHp4uM&imgdii=mk9_
B5FDnKfprM

Tommy LaSorda (baseballhall.org)—Baseball Hall of Fame:

https://www.google.com/search?q=tommy+lasorda&rlz=1C-
1CHBF_enUS777US777&sxsrf=ALeKk02jtUVm7N-
gR0TTgpBUHIRd2pQ-mLw:1618390622259&tbm=is-
ch&source=iu&ictx=1&fir=aZ4Tp6Jlvq-
Jn_M%252C9XCknH8mbzBA-M%252C_&vet=1&u-
sg=AI4_-kSSqu9R-G2uLeJR3sBBZaVVEj0P6g&sa=X-
&ved=2ahUKEwjxwZbxrv3vAhXZZc0KHSAHD1UQ_
h16BAhGEAE#imgrc=czF3N4N14cRntM

https://bible.knowing-jesus.com/topics/Fast-Runners

Artist and Illustration Credits

Hagar Eldeeb, Artist/Illustrator designed *The Olympian Leap: The Life and Legacy of Josh Culbreath* front and back Book cover.

Yvonne Livers Massie, created the Page Designs for Edwin Moses Foreword and *A Service of Thanksgiving*.

"ATTACK" MENTALITY

The Olympian Leap: The Life and Legacy of Josh Culbreath by Author Cynthia Culbreath wants you to be part of a memorable sports biography to experience Culbreath—One Name, One Legend—the *life* of her Olympian cousin Josh Culbreath. Revered as an Olympic hero and legend, he was a dominant fierce hurdler and opponent in track and field. You will discover new things about Josh you never realized. While the track and field were his battlefields, Josh knew he would win the race with every intention by that sly grin of his he's going to kick your butt. You will feel hype like a global winner as you trek through the read of The Olympian Leap. Every turning page of each chapter is like carrying the torch of the Olympic Flames, championing your running journey to every destination you visit. It's Fast, It's Furious, It's Culbreath! Get ready to cross that finish line to victory! Enjoy your reading!

The Olympian Leap: The Life and Legacy of Josh Culbreath
by Author Cynthia Culbreath

Norristown (Pa.) High School '51; Morgan State '55; Quantico Marines '57; Philadelphia Pioneers '60

A MAN WITH MANY STORIES TO TELL: AN AMERICAN OLYMPIAN WORLD RECORD HOLDER, INDUCTED IN MANY HALLS OF FAME AND THE PENN RELAY WALL OF FAME, ATHLETIC ACHIEVEMENTS AND DISTINCTIONS, AN U.S. MARINE VETERAN, A WARRIOR HEARTBEAT, TRACK, AND FIELD COACH, A DISTINGUISHED COMMUNITY LEADER, AND EDUCATOR.

Leader Motivator Speaker Teacher Dedication Devotion Loyalty Commitment Friend=COACH

TO ATHLETES—NEVER GIVE UP, STAY HUNGRY:

The most dangerous thing for an athlete is to be content. They can never sit down and think, now I have got what I want. They always have to push for new goals. If they are to win, they must stay hungry.

First place will go to the one that wants it the most. The Bible encourages us to run so we may obtain the prize. And the only way we can do that is to stay hungry.

About the Author

Cynthia Culbreath has an inquisitive, curious mind, and passion for researching her family roots. Cynthia has an intuition when she wants to find out about something, she executes it very well to prove her point. She loves sports which led her with a leap of faith to write her cousin's sports biography *The Olympian Leap: The Life and Legacy of Josh Culbreath.*

Cynthia is known to wear her high stiletto dress heels, showcasing her stride on the walkway like a runway model when she gets dressed up for an evening out on the town. Leaving a trail of dust by each strut of her fierce walk in heels, Cynthia decided to change lane and put on her winged laced track shoes to pay homage to her Olympian Cousin Josh who was known for blazing the trails of the track and field on fire, blasting his competitors in the dust. Cynthia is ready to run the race, cross that finish line, and win the race to victory by sharing the same sentiment feelings for her readers and to young aspiring athletes—you are champions too as you follow the shadow of your journey full circle like the Olympian rings.

A Norristown, Pennsylvania, native, Cynthia is a System Engineer, a foodie, loves watching the Food Network, loves vintage cars/attending car shows and motorcycles, is involved in community service, and is actively involved in her church ministries.

CPSIA information can be obtained
at www.ICGtesting.com
Printed in the USA
BVHW021955081122
651462BV00013B/64

9 781638 603405